Contents

MANAGEMENT ACCOUNTING
A Self-Teaching Guide

DONALD L. MADDEN

Don Madden & Associates, Inc.
and
Professor of Accounting, University of Kentucky

Instructional Editing by Karen M. Hess

Innovative Programming Systems, Inc.
Minneapolis, Minnesota

John Wiley & Sons, Inc.
New York · Chichester · Brisbane · Toronto

Library of Congress Cataloging in Publication Data

Madden, Donald L.
  Management accounting.
  (Wiley self-teaching guides)
  Includes index.
  1. Managerial accounting.   I. Title.
HF5635.M19   658.1'511   80-17277
ISBN 0-471-03135-6

Printed in the United States of America

81   80   10 9 8 7 6 5 4 3 2 1

CROSS-REFERENCE CHART TO SOME POPULAR MANAGEMENT ACCOUNTING TEXTS

Chapter	Anthony and Welsch	Copeland and Dascher	Decoster and Schafer	Garrison	Horngren	Louderback and Dominiak
1. C/V/P analysis	199–221	115–132	30–37, 74–88	24–38, 214–219	119–131, 161–180	16–30
2. Profit planning	490–504	31–47	38–52, 299–326	147–156, 219–225	131–139, 253–274	124–143
3. Cash budgeting	505–506	47–73	326–333	156–158	269–270	161–179
4. Job-order costing	71–90	155–174	161–174	420–444	58–78	471, 483–485
5. Process costing systems	90–98	189–208	176–184	444–445	57, 79–88	470–476, 480–482
6. Standard costing systems	540–565, 583–591	381–400	202–227	178–189	305–320	382–402, 476–480
7. Responsibility accounting systems	403–413, 591–600	319–337	311–314, 361–369	262, 280–293	390–403	312–321
8. Short-range operating decisions	267–273	447–463	473–478, 509–514	81–87, 113–128	432–445, 500–506	200–219
9. Long-range decisions: capital budgeting	311–335, 348–365	479–525	609–625, 653–674	351–374	521–545, 566–585	242–256

CHART REFERENCES

The following are some popular management accounting textbooks. The chart on the facing page shows what parts of these books correspond to *Management Accounting: A Self-Teaching Guide.*

Anthony, Robert N., and Glenn A. Welsch, *Fundamentals of Management Accounting*, revised edition (Homewood, Ill.: Richard D. Irwin, Inc., 1977).

Copeland, Ronald M., and Paul E. Dascher, *Managerial Accounting: An Introduction to Planning, Information Processing and Control*, 2nd edition (New York: John Wiley & Sons, Inc., 1978).

Decoster, Don T., and Eldon L. Schafer, *Management Accounting: A Decision Emphasis*, 2nd edition (New York: John Wiley & Sons, Inc., 1979).

Garrison, Ray H., *Managerial Accounting*, revised edition (Dallas, Tex.: Business Publications, Inc., 1979).

Horngren, Charles C., *Introduction to Management Accounting*, 4th edition (Englewood Cliffs, N.J.: Prentice-Hall, Inc., 1978).

Louderback, Joseph G., and Jeraldine F. Dominiak, *Managerial Accounting*, 2nd edition (Belmont, Calif.: Wadsworth Publishing Company, Inc., 1978).

How to Use This Book

This book is carefully designed to provide systematic practice in the techniques encompassed in management accounting. Each chapter contains the following:

- A list of objectives, cast in the form of the question "Can you...?"
- Explanations of concepts or techniques.
- Boxed statements containing important information you should learn.
- Examples of the concepts or skills.
- Exercises in which you use what you have learned.
- Answers to the exercises so that you can evaluate your performance.
- A Self-Test, with answers for self-evaluation.

For easy reference, each chapter is presented in numbered sections called *frames*. Although the answers are provided for the frames, it is important that you do *not* look at them until you have formulated your own answer. A dashed line (—————) indicates the end of an exercise and the beginning of the answers. All material following this dashed line should be covered up until you have written your answers. When you are satisfied with your answers, compare them with those provided. If you have made a mistake, reread the preceding material before continuing.

When you finish a chapter, review the material and take the Self-Test. Check your answers carefully and compare your score with the score indicating mastery. If your score is lower than the mastery level, review the specific frames given in parentheses for each item you missed. It is important to understand the material in one chapter before going to the next because this information will be needed to successfully complete succeeding chapters.

To make the book more useful for study now and reference later, some special features are included. The last chapter, "Review for Application," brings together in one place the key concepts and techniques presented in the book. The Glossary defines all the major terms introduced in the book, as well as some additional terms you may encounter in materials about or discussions of management accounting. The Index will allow you to find the discussion of major concepts for review. The Cross-Reference Chart to Some Popular Management Accounting Books shows parts of textbooks corresponding to chapters in this guide, and will be useful for teachers and students interested in further study of particular areas of management accounting. If you are using this book in business or training, you may skip the chart.

If you follow the recommended procedures throughout the book, your ability to use management accounting techniques in making decisions should improve dramatically.

A Comprehensive Exam for this Self-Teaching Guide is available on request from:

> Editor, Self-Teaching Guides
> John Wiley & Sons, Inc.
> 605 Third Avenue
> New York, New York 10158

DONALD L. MADDEN
KAREN MATISON HESS

Introduction

A large manufacturing organization initiated a plan to add a new product line. Although the original product cost estimates seemed reasonable, actual expenditures for materials are now far greater than expected. Management must take corrective action.

A local pharmacy owner is considering the financial feasibility of opening a luncheon counter and soda fountain. The total project would cost $20,000 and interest on a loan for this amount would exceed 12% per year. Is this a wise investment?

Decisions such as the preceding are critical to the success of any business. A knowledge of *management accounting* allows you to make such decisions logically and intelligently.

Management accounting goes well beyond what is traditionally thought of as "accounting." The *American Heritage Dictionary* defines accounting as "the bookkeeping methods involved in making a financial record of business transactions and in the preparation of statements concerning the assets, liabilities, and operating results of a business." The emphasis in financial accounting is directed toward external audiences—owners, creditors, and various governmental agencies, particularly the IRS.

Also important, however, are the accounting needs of decision makers within the business. The field of management accounting has developed to satisfy these internal needs.

> **Management accounting** uses financial information to plan future actions, control results, and make decisions.

The definition of management accounting given by the American Accounting Association publication, *A Statement of Basic Accounting Theory* (1966), is a good starting point for understanding this new field:

> Management accounting is the application of appropriate *techniques and concepts* in processing the *historical and projected data* of an entity to assist management in *establishing plans for reasonable economic objectives* and in the making of *rational decisions* with a view toward achieving these objectives.

A knowledge of the principles of management accounting will allow you to look at past financial statements to make valid predictions regarding future potential. It will allow you to set realistic goals and then evaluate how well these goals are being met. It will assist in every type of financial decision that arises.

Management accounting addresses your information needs as a business manager. It will equip you to:
—Determine the level of activity at which you must operate to earn a profit.
—Develop a profit plan.
—Establish financial targets through financial ratios.
—Prepare projected balance sheets and income statements.
—Prepare cash receipts and disbursements budgets.
—Compare actual performance data with expected results.
—Prepare capital budgets to assess the desirability of long-range resource commitments.
—Establish responsibility centers and communicate to managers at different levels of authority.
Skill in the preceding areas can often make the difference between the success and failure of a business.

To be effective, management accounting must provide data for decisions in a timely manner. The measures must be communicated in an understandable manner, and all data must be relevant to decisions that managers must make.

This book will introduce you to the terms, concepts, and techniques currently used in management accounting to make effective business decisions.

Management Accounting—A Working Model

Section One focuses on financial planning, Section Two on the cost accounting and control framework, and Section Three on specialized decisions faced by managers.

SECTION ONE

Financial Planning

Every business has objectives or goals, formally or informally stated. These can include profits, growth, a favorable image, and similar targets. An effective manager establishes realistic objectives and then formulates plans to meet them. Financial considerations inevitably influence planning. In fact, successful accomplishment of business objectives usually depends on sound financial planning.

Section One presents a management accounting approach to financial planning. Basic to such planning is the ability to determine the level of activity at which a business must operate to earn a profit by using cost/volume/profit analysis (Chapter 1). Profit planning (Chapter 2) and cash budgeting (Chapter 3) are two other techniques that make realistic, effective financial planning possible. Such planning can reduce financial uncertainty and increase income dollars available to meet business objectives.

CHAPTER 1

Cost/Volume/Profit Analysis

 Can you . . .

- Explain the three key variables in cost/volume/profit (C/V/P) analysis?
- State the basic concept underlying C/V/P analysis?
- Define and identify fixed, variable, semifixed, and semivariable costs?
- Identify, interpret, and construct graphs reflecting these four different types of costs?
- Define, calculate, and graph the break-even point?
- Define and determine a contribution margin?
- Calculate the revenues needed to earn a specific profit before taxes?
- Explain the assumptions underlying C/V/P analysis that must always be considered in long-range financial planning?
- Apply C/V/P analysis to determine the effect of certain actions on a company's profit plan?

The first chapter of *Management Accounting* focuses on these skills, introducing you to C/V/P analysis as a fundamental tool for financial planning.

1. Introduction. A critical step in developing a financial plan is to determine the level of activity at which you must operate to reach the business objective of profit. The technique of *cost/volume/profit analysis* (C/V/P) is a powerful tool for making decisions. C/V/P analysis allows you to evaluate, before the fact, the effects of selecting a particular volume level as your planning base, to determine how many units you need to produce and/or how much to charge per unit to meet your objectives.

> **C/V/P analysis** shows the interrelationships of:
>   **Costs**—expenses, such as supplies, material, labor, over-
>   head.
>   **Volume**—amounts, such as units produced, hours
>   worked, programs developed.
>   **Profit**—the "bottom line"; the difference between reve-
>   nues (dollar inflows) and expenses (dollar
>   outflows).

Example. A company spends $8,000 (costs) to produce 50 storage units (volume) that are sold for $200 each, leaving $2,000 (profit) after expenses are paid.

$$\text{volume of units} \times \text{price} = \text{revenues} \quad \text{and} \quad \text{revenues} - \text{costs} = \text{profits}$$

$$[50 \times \$200 = \$10,000 - \$8,000 \text{ (costs)} = \$2,000 \text{ (profit)}]$$

Exercise

Identify the costs, volume, and profit in the following situation: A publishing house sells 10,000 copies of a book for $5 each. Printing, binding, labor, and distribution costs are $50,000.

Costs   _____

Volume   _____

Profit   _____

- - - - - - - - - - - - - - -

Costs = $50,000; volume = 10,000 copies; profit = $0.

Any of the key factors in C/V/P analysis can be manipulated to achieve a desired outcome. A critical interrelationship, however, is that between costs and volume.

2. Cost/Volume Relationships. If you rent a chain saw for $5.00 for half a day to fell trees for firewood and you can fell 10 trees from which you can get 50 pieces of firewood each, each log costs you $0.01. If, however, a storm comes up and you only get 1 tree felled, your logs cost $0.10 each. Cost and volume are often closely related, a basic premise of C/V/P analysis.

> A basic concept underlying C/V/P analysis is **cost vari-ability**; that is, certain costs are directly affected by changes in volume.

You are probably already familiar with this concept from a buying perspective.

Example. If you were ordering stationery, you would probably find that the more you ordered, the less each piece would cost:

Price List

50 or less	$ 2.80
100	3.75
200	4.70
300	5.70
400	6.65
500	7.65
600	8.65
700	9.60
800	10.60
900	11.55
1000	12.55
Add'l 1000s	9.75

Exercise

1. Compute the cost per copy for 50 copies. _____
2. Do the same for 300 copies. _____ For 500 copies. _____
3. If you order a printing job where you want the copies folded and collated, which of these special service costs would change as the number of copies (volume) changes?

_____

Special Services

	500	1,000	1,500	2,000	2,500	3,000
Perforating and scoring $5.00 min. to 500 sheets $0.50/addl. 100	5.00	7.50	10.00	12.50	15.00	17.50
Padding		$1.00 plus $0.10 per pad				
Folding 1 or 2 parallel folds $2.50 min. to 500 sheets $0.25/addl. 100 sheets	2.50	3.75	5.00	6.25	7.50	8.75
Drilling $1.50 min. to 500 sheets $0.15/addl. 100 sheets	1.50	2.25	3.00	3.75	4.50	5.25
Collating—$2.50 min.		$4.50 per 1,000 sheets				

_ _ _ _ _ _ _ _ _ _ _ _ _ _

1. 5.6 cents.   2. 1.9 cents; 1.5 cents.   3. Both.

TYPES OF COSTS

You are likely to encounter *four classes of costs* in developing a financial plan:

1. Variable costs
2. Fixed costs
3. Semivariable costs
4. Semifixed costs

Each type of cost is important from a planning perspective.

3.   Variable Costs.   Some costs, such as materials costs, labor, and usage charges, go up or down as production goes up or down. The more units you produce, the more materials you use and the more labor-hours are expended.

> **Variable costs** are expenditures that *change in direct proportion* to some specific measure of volume, but these costs *remain constant per unit* as volume changes.

Example.   A small machine shop accepts an order for 1,000 metal fixtures. To produce the units, the materials will cost $2.00/unit and labor cost will be approximately $1.50/unit (15 minutes each at an average labor rate of $6.00/hour) plus $0.50/unit on a leased machine. Therefore, the variable costs include:

Materials	$2,000	($2/unit × 1,000)
Labor	1,500	($1.50/unit × 1,000)
Usage charge	500	($0.50/unit × 1,000)
Total	$4,000	variable costs

Dividing variable costs by the number of units produced gives a per unit cost of $4.00. This can be described graphically by plotting costs on the vertical (Y) axis and volume on the horizontal (X) axis:

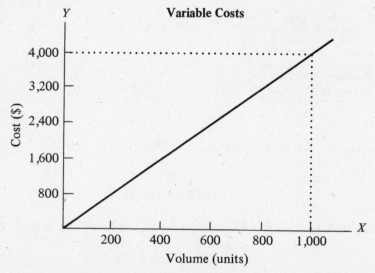

Notice that as volume increases, costs increase proportionally.

Exercise
1. Using the same figures of $2.00/unit for materials, $1.50/unit for labor, and $0.50/ unit use charge, calculate the variable costs for 600 units. _____
2. What is the cost per unit now? _____
3. Represent these cost and volume figures on the preceding graph. _____
   _____
4. What relationship exists between variable costs and changes in volume? _____
   _____
   In unit price? _____
5. Identify the variable costs in the following situation and calculate the cost per unit.
   The airlines prepare meals for many of their scheduled flights. Materials for the meals cost $1.25/meal and labor costs are $1.00/meal. If 1,000 meals are prepared, what is the variable cost? _____ What would the cost per unit be for the 1,000 meals? _____

- - - - - - - - - - - - - - - -

1. $2,400.
2. Still $4.00/unit.
3.

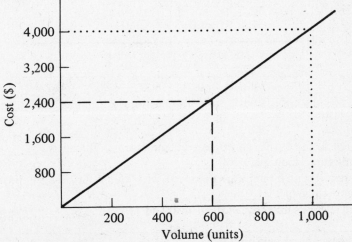

4. Variable costs change in direct proportion to volume; if volume increases, total variable costs increase. The cost per unit remains constant.
5. $2,250; still $2.25 per unit.

4.   Fixed Costs.   Other costs, such as machinery leases and yearly salaries, remain constant during an accounting period. The more you can produce, the "more you get for your money." By their nature, fixed costs are generally adjusted only when a specific management decision is made, for example, giving someone a raise. Therefore, these costs usually remain constant during a given planning period.

> **Fixed costs** are expenditures that are *unaffected* by changes in volume; that is, they *remain constant in total*. They *decline* on a *per unit* basis *as volume increases*.

Example. Suppose that the machine shop we talked of earlier was paying $200/month to lease the machine required to fill the order for the metal fixtures. Whether the shop produced 600 or 1,000 units, the lease rate remains $200. The per unit cost for the 1,000 units ordered would be $0.20/unit.

Graphically, fixed costs are represented by a straight line that parallels the volume (X) axis:

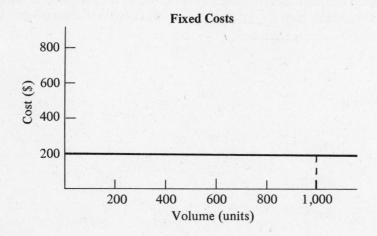

Fixed Costs

Exercise
1. Calculate the fixed cost per unit if only 600 units are produced. _____
   If 2,000 units are produced. _____
2. If a strike occurs, and no units are produced, what would the monthly fixed cost for leasing the machine be? _____
3. What is the relationship between fixed costs and volume? _____
   _____
   Between costs and per unit price? _____
   _____
4. Identify the fixed costs in the following example. Then graph these costs.
   A regional sales manager is paid $1,500 per month while serving as a company representative. His monthly office rent is $250, and phone service costs $50 per month. His sales range from 2,000 units to 6,000 units per month.

- - - - - - - - - - - - - -

1. 33⅓ cents per unit; 10 cents per unit.
2. The lease would still cost $200, even if no units were produced.
3. Fixed costs do *not* change as volume changes. However, per unit costs decline as volume increases. And per unit costs increase as volume decreases.
4. Fixed costs are $1,800 per month; these do not change even though volume increases.

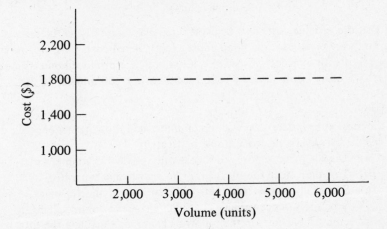

5.   **Semivariable Costs.**   Often, costs are not clearly variable or fixed, but are a combination of both. You are probably familiar with this type of cost when you rent a car and pay a flat fee (fixed cost) of say $20/day plus $0.25/mile (variable cost).

> **Semivariable costs** are expenditures containing both fixed and variable elements of cost.

Example.   Recall that there was a cost of $0.50 per unit produced for the leased machine used to produce the metal fixtures. This was in addition to the $200/month flat fee. The two costs combined are classified as semivariable and can be diagrammed as follows:

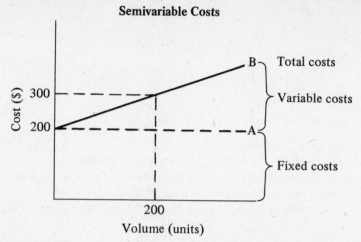

Semivariable Costs

Volume (units)

Notice that the variable costs now begin at the dollar figure of the fixed costs. Even though *no* units are produced, the fixed cost remains. Fixed costs plus variable costs give you the total costs for a project. Thus, where 200 units are produced on this machine in one period, total costs would be $350 ($200 fixed costs + 200 units at $0.50).

Exercise

1. Select the most appropriate response to complete the following sentence: In doing C/V/P analysis, semivariable costs should be treated:
   _____ (a) Together as one cost, since cost will not vary as volume varies.
   _____ (b) Together, since the two cannot be realistically separated.
   _____ (c) Separately, since fixed costs will change as volume changes.
   _____ (d) Separately, since variable costs will change as volume changes.
2. Identify the semivariable costs in the following example. Calculate the total cost when total sales by this individual are $10,000; $15,000. Then graph the semivariable costs for a given month's activities.

   A salesman works for a base salary of $1,000 per month, but he also receives a 10% commission on all sales that are completed.

1. You should have checked only (d). All the other statements are false.
2. Sales of $10,000 at a cost of $2,000; at $15,000 the cost would be $2,500.

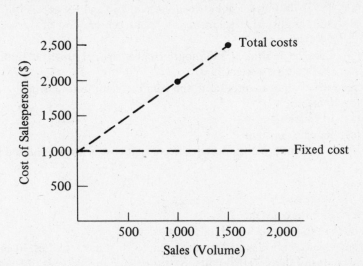

6.   Semifixed Costs.   A fourth type of cost frequently encountered in financial planning is a "one-time" expense incurred to fill a specific order or need. For example, you
may need to pay a setup charge for a printing job, or hire a consultant.

> **Semifixed costs** are basically fixed expenditures that can
> shift up or down when specific management decisions are
> made.

Example.   Suppose that the machine shop we have been discussing receives an order
for 500 standard metal fixtures and 500 fixtures requiring a specialized machining
process. To make the latter, an attachment must be added to the leased machine, increasing the monthly lease rate from $200 to $250. This reflects an upward change in a fixed
cost that will remain constant until another management decision is made.
Semifixed costs are represented graphically as follows:·

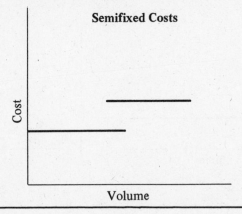

Exercise

1. Adding the special attachment means that management should
   _____ (a) Divide the extra cost between the standard and the specialized fixtures.
   _____ (b) Add the special attachment cost to the per unit cost of the specialized fixtures.
   _____ (c) Take the additional $50/month from a "special projects" fund, since it is a one-time expenditure.
2. As more specialized units are produced, the semifixed cost in total will
   _____ (a) Increase
   _____ (b) Decrease
   _____ (c) Remain constant
3. As more specialized units are produced, the per unit cost of the specialized fixtures will
   _____ (a) Increase
   _____ (b) Decrease
   _____ (c) Remain constant
4. Identify the semifixed costs in the following example.

   A toy manufacturer is planning for next year's Christmas activities. In an average month the company ships 50,000 units to its suppliers, and the cost of leasing a warehouse is $20,000. When volume increases above 50,000 units per month, however, added space must be leased at $5,000 per month. Signing the lease for added space is a top management decision.

- - - - - - - - - - - - - - - -

1. (b).   2. (c).   3. (b).   4. Added warehouse space @ $5,000/month.

7.   Summary: Types of Costs

1. Identify the type of cost represented in each graph and describe how cost and volume are related in each.

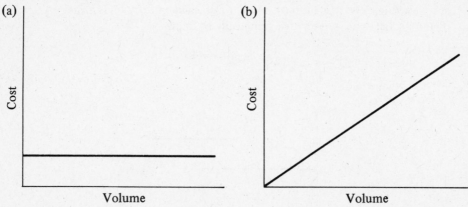

(a)

Cost

Volume

(b)

Cost

Volume

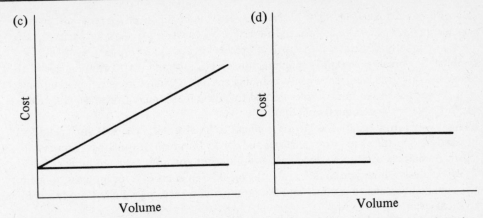

2. Examine the following situation and identify the types of costs involved. Calculate the cost for producing 1,000 brochures and the per unit cost. Do the same for 5,000 brochures. Which costs account for the difference in unit price?

You are working with a social group and have been asked to handle the advertising for an annual function. The Copy Shop advises you that a 1-page brochure has been used effectively in prior years. Paper costs $5.00 for each ream (500 sheets). Printing is $10.00 for the first 1,000 pages, and $2.50 for each additional 1,000 sheets. A one-time service charge of $30.00 is assessed for printing plates and other miscellaneous costs.

- - - - - - - - - - - - - - - - - -

1. (a) Fixed;   (b) variable;   (c) semivariable;   (d) semifixed.
2. Costs for 1,000 brochures would be $50 in total, or $0.05 per brochure. For 5,000 brochures the total cost is $100, or $0.02 per brochure. Paper costs are variable at $0.01 per sheet; printing costs are semivariable in nature; the service charge is a fixed cost.

	1,000	5,000
Paper	$10	$50
Printing	10	20 [$10 + (4 × $2.50)]
Charge	30	30
Total	$50	$100

8. **Break-even Analysis.** The analysis of cost/volume relationships is an important advance in management accounting. The resulting knowledge of behavior patterns, in turn, has directly contributed to the development of a useful technique, *break-even analysis*. The break-even point represents the level of revenues that corresponds in amount to all costs incurred. From a planning viewpoint, therefore, you can determine, before the fact, the volume of sales needed to ensure that required financial resources are available in the coming fiscal period.

You know from practical experience what "to break even" means. If you spend $5.00 on seeds and fertilizer to grow tomatoes and get $5.00 worth of tomatoes from the plants, you break even—you don't lose anything, but you don't gain anything either. C/V/P analysis allows you to determine the break-even point of your business, to identify the volume you need to produce and the revenues you need to generate from this volume to break even.

Break-even units are the number of units that must be produced and sold to generate revenues to cover all costs incurred during the accounting period. *Break-even revenues* are the level of sales dollars required to cover your costs during this accounting period. And the *break-even point* is that level of activity that generates revenues exactly sufficient to cover costs, yielding neither profit nor loss.

> The **break-even point**: total revenues = total expenses.

Example. In our machine shop example, if 1,000 units were produced at a cost of $4,200 and were sold for $4.20, the shop would break even. The break-even units would be 1,000, the break-even revenues would be $4,200, and the break-even point would be $4,200 in costs. The profit in C/V/P analysis would be zero.

Exercise

If Wearwell Shoe Repair fixes 200 pairs of shoes in a week and uses $50 worth of material and $350 in overhead, what dollar figure would represent the break-even revenues? _____ . This would mean that to break even, the average cost per repair would have to be _____ .

– – – – – – – – – – – – – – –

Break-even revenues would be $400. The average cost per repair would be $2.

9. **The Contribution Margin.** Applying the break-even technique requires the use of one technical measure, *contribution margin*.

> **Contribution margin** is the difference between sales revenues and variable costs.

Example. A company that sells 1,000 products for $1.50 per unit incurs a variable cost of $1.00 per unit. Total revenues for this company are $1,500. In this case the company's contribution margin is $500 ($1,500 in revenues − $1,000 in variable costs). Viewed in terms of each unit, the contribution margin is $0.50 ($1.50 sales price − $1.00 in variable costs) per unit.

Exercise

A local brother–sister team sell hot dogs at football games. They buy 100 hot dogs for $0.30 each and sell them for $0.40 apiece. If all the hot dogs are sold, what is the total contribution margin?

Total revenues = $40.00; total variable costs = $30.00; total contribution margin = $10.00 (100 × $0.10).

Two other descriptions of the contribution margin are sometimes used to develop information about a company's break-even volume of activity. Contribution margin can be expressed in terms of a *percentage*. Using the preceding example, the sales price per unit equals 100% of the revenues generated when the product is sold. Since the variable cost of each unit is $1.00, the variable cost percentage of the product is 66.7% ($1.00 in variable cost per unit divided by the $1.50 in sales price per unit). This measure remains constant for each unit sold.

The second description views contribution margin relative to *fixed costs*. In any case where a break-even volume is achieved, the contribution margin equals the fixed costs incurred.

Two different approaches can be used to determine a company's break-even point. Both are equally effective, and the underlying revenue and cost data are easily adjusted to provide the specific measures.

10.   Break-even in Units. One way to determine the break-even point states both revenue and cost figures on a per unit basis. The resulting measure of the break-even point is then stated in terms of units of sales required. A simple algebraic equation is used to determine the required break-even volume. The unknown (X) in the formula is the required volume in units at the break-even point.

$$\text{sales price}(X) = \text{fixed cost} + \text{variable cost}(X)$$

Example. Two college students decided to open a sandwich shop directly across the street from a University. They intended to offer a limited menu of sandwiches and soft drinks. As a starting point, they rented a small shop at an annual expense of $2,400. All other fixed costs were expected to be $400 per month.

Each menu item includes one sandwich and a soft drink. A sandwich is to be sold for $1.20 and each soft drink is $0.30, a total of $1.50 per menu item. Variable costs have been estimated at $1.20 per serving ($1.00 for each sandwich and $0.20 for the soft drink). When these students approached a banker for an initial loan, she requested that they provide an estimate of the operation's required break-even volume on a monthly basis.

In this case, the sales price for each menu item (sandwich and soft drink) is $1.50. The variable cost of each item is $1.20. Monthly fixed costs are expected to be $600. [Total fixed cost, of course, includes the rent of $2,400 (divided by 12 months) and all other fixed costs.] These data can be used in the break-even formula to determine the number of units that must be sold to break even:

$$\text{sales price}(X) = \text{fixed cost} + \text{variable cost}(X)$$
$$\$1.50(X) = \$600 + \$1.20(X)$$
$$(\$1.50 - 1.20)(X) = \$600*$$
$$\$0.30(X) = \$600$$
$$X = 2{,}000 \text{ (the break-even point in units)}$$

The solution can be verified by substituting the measure of break-even units into the original equation:

$$\$1.50(2{,}000) = \$600 + \$1.20(2{,}000)$$
$$\$3{,}000 = \$3{,}000$$

Thus total revenues of $3,000 equal the sum of fixed costs, $600, and total variable costs, $2,400.

Exercise

Use the break-even formula to obtain the measure of units that must be sold per month for revenues to equal total costs in the following situation.

A small businessman invested in new equipment that will cost his company $10,000 per year. The new products have a·selling price of $5.00 per unit, and their variable cost is $3.00 apiece.

- - - - - - - - - - - - - -

$$\$5.00(X) = \$10{,}000 + \$3.00(X)$$
$$X = 5{,}000 \text{ units per year}$$

---

*Recall from algebra that you can clear items from one side of an equation by performing the same operation on each side of the equation. In this case, you subtract $1.20($X$)$ from each side, leaving $0.30($X$)$ on the left side.

11.   Income Statements—Proofs of Break-even Measures.   The same relationships can be expressed in the form of an *income statement:*

> An **income statement** identifies:
>   Revenues (units X sales price)
>   Less variable costs (units X variable costs)
>   Contribution margin (revenues - variable costs)
>   Less fixed costs per month
>   Net income (loss)

Example.   An income statement from the sandwich shop previously described would include:

Revenues	$3,000
Less variable costs	2,400
Contribution margin	600
Less fixed costs	600
Net income (loss)	$ —0—

Note that the contribution margin equals the fixed costs when the break-even volume is attained.

Exercise

Make an income statement for the case illustrated in the preceding exercise if 5,000 units had been sold in the first year.

— — — — — — — — — — — — — —

Revenues (5,000 units X $5)	$25,000
Variable costs (5,000 units X $3)	15,000
Contribution margin	10,000
Fixed costs per year	10,000
Net income (loss)	$ —0—

Note that at sales above or below 5,000 units, the company does not operate at its break-even point.

12.   Break-even in Sales Dollars.   The second approach to determining an operation's break-even point also begins with an algebraic expression. The only major difference rests in the measures used. Specifically, the break-even point is stated in terms of total sales revenues rather than units of output. As a starting point, the unknown sales dollars at break-even are reflected at 100%(Y). Variable costs in turn are measured as a percentage of sales dollars. In other words, if a product sells for $1:00 and variable costs are $0.75, variable costs can be expressed as 75% of sales dollars.

$$100\%(Y) \qquad = \text{fixed cost} + \text{variable cost } \%(Y)$$
$$\text{(unknown sales dollars)}$$

Example.   In our sandwich shop case, recall that the sales price of each menu item was $1.50 (100%). Variable costs were $1.20 per menu item, or 80% of the total sales price. Fixed costs were $600 per month. Inserting these data into the formula results in:

$100\%(Y) = \$600 + 80\%(Y)$
$20\%(Y) = \$600$ (remember: you subtract 80%(Y) from each side of the formula)
$Y = \$3,000$ (break-even point in sales dollars)

Notice that the break-even volume in units (2,000 × $1.50/unit) is equal to the sales revenues measured using this approach. Again, you can verify the solution by substituting the break-even measure (sales revenue) into the basic equation:

$$100\% (3,000) = \$600 + (80\% \times 3,000)$$

An income statement can also be produced using this method.

Exercise
    Use the total sales revenues method to determine the break-even point in the preceding exercise (frame 10). Remember, variable costs per unit were $1.20 and the sales price was $1.50 per unit.

$100\%(Y) = \$600 + 80\%(Y)$
$20\%(Y) = \$600$
$Y = \$3,000$ or   2,000 units × $1.50 per unit

13. Graphing the Break-even Point. Some managers prefer to evaluate break-even considerations by using a graph rather than an algebraic formula. Such graphs are extremely useful in focusing attention on the basic cost/volume relationships.

One graphical format uses the semivariable cost pattern as its basis. Step 1 below shows variable costs added to fixed costs, thereby portraying an activity's total costs. In step 2, a third line representing revenues is imposed over the cost information. This line crosses the total cost line at the break-even point.

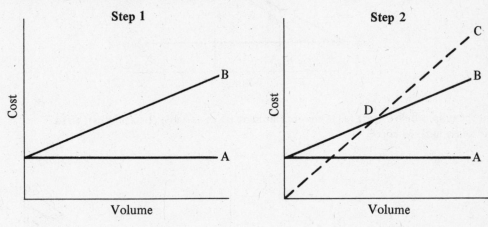

Exercise

Using what you have learned previously about graphing cost/volume relationships and the information immediately above, identify the following:

Line *A* represents _____

Line *B* represents _____

Line *C* represents _____

Point *D* represents _____

What does segment *C-D-B* represent? _____

— — — — — — — — — — — — — — — —

A = fixed costs; B = total costs; C = total revenues; D = break-even point; segment C-D-B = profit.

14. The break-even graph can be used as a tool for decision making. For example, you might want to change one variable: (1) sales price per unit, (2) variable cost per unit, or (3) fixed costs. If all other elements remain constant—a key assumption—the effects of a decision on the break-even volume can be depicted graphically.

Using the same graph, assume that the sales price per unit is increased. The revenue line shifts from C to C_1 and the break-even point moves to the left from D to D_1, reflecting a reduction in required units.

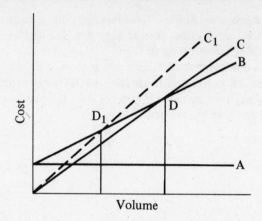

In the graphs below, part (a) represents an increase in variable costs and part (b) a decrease in fixed costs.

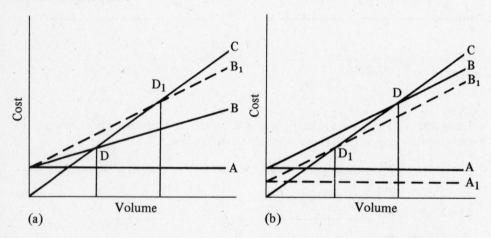

(a)   (b)

(a) What is the effect of increasing variable costs per unit on the volume required to break even? _____

(b) Does the break-even point shift to the right or left? _____

(c) What is the effect of decreasing fixed costs on the volume required to break even?

_____

(d) What direction is this move in break-even point on the graph? _____

— — — — — — — — — — — — —

(a) Increase volume.
(b) Right.
(c) Decrease volume.
(d) Left.

15.   The following graph shows the original problem.

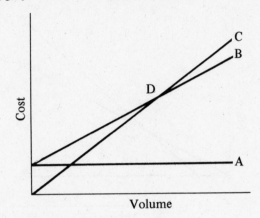

(a) Mark in a line to show a decrease in variable costs.

(b) What effect does this have on the volume required to achieve break even? _____

_____

(c) Which way does the break-even point shift? _____

— — — — — — — — — — — — — —

(a)

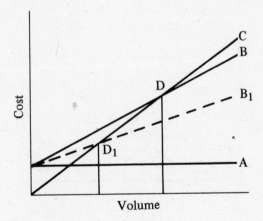

(b) Decrease.
(c) Left.

16. The original graph is shown once again.

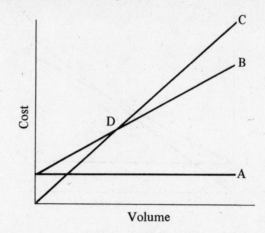

(a) Mark in lines to represent an increase in fixed costs, with a corresponding increase in total costs.

(b) What effect does this have on the volume required to achieve break even? _____

(c) Which way does the break-even point shift? _____

– – – – – – – – – – – – – – – –

(a)

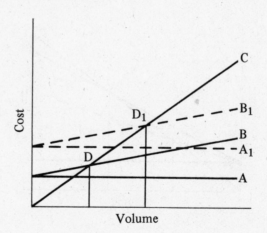

(b) Increase.
(c) Right.

17.   The Profit Dimension. Most people want to do better than simply break even. Fortunately, the break-even model can be expanded to allow evaluations of the possible effects of management decisions on levels of profitability. This profit dimension makes the model more powerful because its full capacity in cost/volume/profit analyses can be used.

Often, a business objective is to achieve a specified *net income*, an excess of revenues over costs that can be stated in terms of either before-tax or after-tax dollars. For the moment, we'll focus on before-tax dollars. The desired net income is frequently expressed as a *profit target*—management's desired level of profitability measured either in dollars or in terms of a specified financial ratio, such as a certain percent return on an investment.

Profit planning can be accomplished through either units or sales revenues, the two approaches to cost/volume analysis just presented.

Profit targets can be set by determining the **required volume in units**:

sales price(X) = fixed costs + profit target + variable costs(X)

Example. Returning to our sandwich shop example, assume that the students owning the sandwich shop want to earn \$300/month in net income before taxes. To include a profit-before-tax goal in the C/V/P framework, the amount of desired income before tax is treated like fixed costs. The required volume in units is determined as follows:

$$\$1.50(X) = \$600 + \$300 + \$1.20(X)$$

sales   fixed   profit   variable
price   costs   target   costs

$$\$0.30(X) = \$900$$

$$X = 3{,}000 \text{ units} \quad \text{(target volume to make \$300 profit)}$$

Exercise

Determine the sandwich shop's target volume in units if the owners wished to make

\$600 profit per month. _____ How much contribution margin is provided

by these extra units? _____

— — — — — — — — — — — — — — —

4,000 units (an additional 1,000 units). Each additional unit adds \$0.30 in contribution margin. The added 1,000 units thus produce the additional \$300 in desired profits before tax because fixed costs do not change.

18. The second approach to C/V/P analysis, percentage contribution margin, can also be modified to include targets of net income before taxes. The formula can be adjusted slightly from an algebraic viewpoint without changing the basic substance of the model:

$$Y = \text{volume in sales dollars needed to achieve the profit target}$$

Base formula: $100\%(Y)$ = fixed costs + net income before tax + variable costs $\%(Y)$

Subtract $vc\%(Y)$ from both sides:

$$100\%(Y) - vc\%(Y) = \text{fixed costs} + \text{net income before taxes}$$

Factor (Y): $Y(100\% - vc\%)$ = fixed costs + net income before taxes

Divide both sides by $(100\% - vc\%)$:

$$Y = \frac{\text{fixed costs} + \text{net income before taxes}}{100\% - vc\%}$$

$$\begin{array}{l} \text{desired} \\ \text{sales volume} = Y = \dfrac{\text{fixed costs} + \text{net income before taxes}}{100\% - \text{variable costs }\%} \\ \text{in dollars} \end{array}$$

Example. In our sandwich shop situation, the following computations are made:

$$\text{required sales revenues} = Y = \frac{\$600 + \$300}{100\% - 80\%}$$

$$Y = \frac{\$900}{20\%}$$

$$= \$4,500$$

Notice that if you multiply the 3,000 target units from the first method by $1.50 per unit, the result is also $4,500.

Exercise

Determine the required sales volume in dollars for the sandwich shop if the owners want to make $600 profit per month. _____

– – – – – – – – – – – – – – – –

$6,000 target sales revenues (equivalent to 4,000 units at $1.50).

19. A C/V/P Planning Problem. Management accounting techniques allow you to evaluate alternatives, that is, to consider different courses of action as you make financial plans. You can determine the effects of changing sales prices, reducing variable or fixed costs, or adjusting previous profit targets. However, C/V/P analysis also has some important limiting assumptions you must be aware of.

Perhaps most important, the C/V/P model operates on the assumption that fixed and variable costs are known and relatively predictable for coming periods. Underlying this assumption is the premise that these basic cost relationships will remain valid only within given ranges of volume. If output for a time period extends beyond this range, all important cost factors must be reevaluated.

In addition, assumptions are made regarding the stability of sales prices, the volume of various product lines, expected inventory levels, and even the technological state of the business. Although such topics are inappropriate at this introductory level, you should be aware of these limiting assumptions when you implement C/V/P analysis.

Finally, some managers see little value in learning management accounting techniques, relying instead on computers to provide their financial plans. Unquestionably, computers can be used effectively in financial planning and evaluating alternative courses of action. But only if you understand the algebraic and graphical approaches to C/V/P analysis can you use the full capacity of a computer.

The following management problem will give you a chance to assess how well you understand C/V/P analysis. Read the problem carefully before you answer the questions and make the needed computations.

Two enterprising students want to own their own automobile service company. Their shop instructor suggests that they gain some experience by beginning the service while still in school. They decide to offer automobile tune-ups for $20, with the unique feature that the service would be offered at the client's home. The person making repairs would receive $6 per call. The costs of parts for each tune-up will average $8. Tools leased from the school will cost $25/month, and truck rental will cost an additional $50/month. The students made 20 calls a month the first year.

1. Identify the fixed, variable, semifixed, and semivariable costs involved for 1 month and for the entire year.

2. What was the total revenue for the first year's operation?

3. What was the contribution margin?

4. Summarize the first year's financial data into an income statement reflecting the entire first year.

5. In the income statement, what percent is represented by revenues? By variable costs? By the contribution margin?

6. Once the historical data are summarized, what is the next step the students should take?

- - - - - - - - - - - - - - -

1. Fixed costs are $25/month for leasing tools and $50/month for leasing the truck, for a total of $75/month X 12 = $900/year.
   Variable costs are $6 per call plus $8 for parts for a total of $14 per call X 20 calls per month = $280/month X 12 = $3,360/year.
   There were no semifixed or semivariable costs involved.
2. Total revenue for the first year's operation was $4,800 ($400/month).
3. The contribution margin was $120/month ($400 – $280) or $1,440/year ($4,800 – $3,360).
4. Your income statement might look as follows:

Auto Services
Income Statement
for the Year Ended 19XX

Revenues (240 service calls at $20)	$4,800
Less variable costs (240 at $14)	3,360
Contribution margin	1,440
Less fixed costs	900
Net income	$ 540

5. Revenues represent 100% of total income. Variable costs equal 70%; the contribution margin = 30%.
6. The next step is to use the data to determine the minimum number of tune-ups they can provide in the coming year and achieve a break-even level, or the required sales revenue for the year to break even.

. . . .

7. Using either method, compute the break-even point for the auto service.

8. The two students would like to improve their profits in the coming year. Each wants to earn at least $50/month in profits, a total of $1,200 for the year. Assuming that all factors remain unchanged, how much dollar volume must they generate to achieve this goal?

– – – – – – – – – – – – – –

7. The break-even point is 150 tune-ups, or $3,000. $20(X) = $900 + $14(X)$.
8. The dollar volume to reach their profit target would be $7,000.

$$\frac{\$900 + \$1,200}{100\% - 70\%} = \frac{\$2,100}{30\%} = \$7,000$$

Note that at $7,000 in revenues, variable costs are $4,900 (70% X $7,000) and contribution margin is $2,100—the same as fixed costs.

. . . .

9. The students are concerned about their ability to increase revenues from last year's $4,800 to the $7,000 that is desired in the coming year. In a discussion with the shop instructor, they learn two additional facts. First, the fixed rental cost for tools must increase to $50/month, and, second, the costs of tune-up parts are likely to increase to $10 per service call. If the profit target of $1,200 is included, how many tune-ups are required to cover the increased costs and still achieve their financial objective?

10. Does this number seem realistic? What alternative comes to mind?

– – – – – – – – – – – – – –

9. 600 tune-ups would be required:

$$\$20(X) = \$1,200 + \$1,200 + 16(X)$$

$$\$4(X) = \$2,400$$

$$X = 600$$

10. This is probably unrealistic. An increase in price might be a logical alternative.

. . . .

11. After reviewing the data, the shop instructor does suggest that a normal price increase might be appropriate. He also observes, however, that their profit target is unrealistic because the students now earn $6 for each service call. After much discussion, the students reach a compromise. They will reduce their service charges to $4 per call because the time required is considerably less now due to their added efficiency. In addition, they will reduce their profit target to $300 each for the year. The students must determine their required volume (number of automobile tune-ups to achieve these financial objectives). Using the revised data, compute the required volume.

12. Then compute the required sales volume to achieve the profit target.

13. Finally, prepare a projected income statement to reflect the relevant cost/volume/ profit relationships for these student's service activities.

14. What assumptions did the students make that necessitated the change in profit target?

- - - - - - - - - - - - - -

11. 300 tune-ups to break even with the desired profit target included.

$$\$20(X) = \$1,200 + \$600 + \$14(X)$$
$$\$6(X) = \$1,800$$
$$X = 300 \text{ tune-ups}$$

12. \$6,000 (300 tune-ups X \$20)

$$X = \frac{\$1,200 + \$600}{100\% - 70\%}$$

$$= \frac{\$1,800}{30\%}$$

$$= \$6,000$$

13.

Sales revenues (300 X \$20)	\$6,000	100%
Less variable costs (300 X \$14)	4,200	70%
Contribution margin (300 X \$6)	1,800	30%
Less fixed costs	1,200	
Desired profit	\$ 600	

14. They had erroneously assumed that all costs from one accounting period would remain constant for the succeeding accounting period.

. . . .

   Before completing the Self-Test that follows, review the questions posed at the beginning of this chapter to be certain you can answer each question. If you are unsure of any of the answers, review the appropriate sections of the chapter before completing the Self-Test.

CHAPTER 1 SELF-TEST

1. Name and explain the three key variables involved in C/V/P analysis:
   (a)

   (b)

   (c)

2. What basic concept underlies C/V/P analysis?

3. Define and give at least one example of each of the four types of costs:
   (a) Fixed

   (b) Variable

   (c) Semifixed

   (d) Semivariable

4. Describe the following graphs in terms of costs:

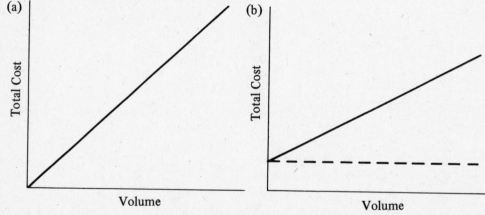

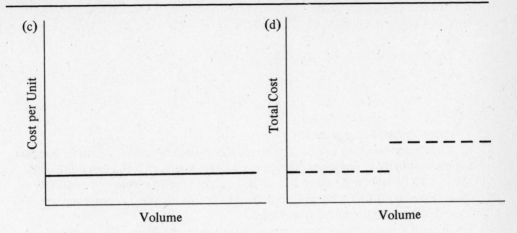

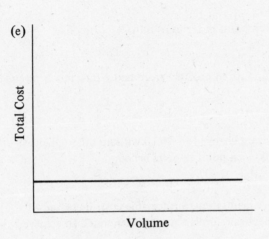

5. What is the break-even point and how is it determined?

6. What is a contribution margin and how is it determined?

7. What assumptions are made in C/V/P analysis?

8. Complete the following problem:

A company operating food and beverage concessions for athletic events is considering the possibility of implementing a new concept. A sandwich and soft drink menu
item would be sold for $1.00 and could be produced for a variable cost of $0.60 per
order. Fixed costs for each stand would be $1,000 per month. The company wants to
make $200/month in profit before taxes.

(a) What is this company's contribution margin per unit? Percentage per unit?

(b) What is this company's break-even point in terms of units?

(c) For this company to earn $200/month in profits before taxes, how much revenue
must be generated?

(d) If the price for each menu item were changed to $1.10 with no other changes,
what would the company's break-even point in units become?

(e) If the price remained at $1.00 per menu item, but variable costs increased to
$0.75 on each item sold, how many sales dollars must be generated to achieve
break even?

(f) Use the data in part (e) and the $200/month profit target to make a projected
income statement for this venture.

ANSWERS

1. C/V/P analysis shows the interrelationships of (a) costs—expenses such as supplies, material, labor, and overhead; (b) volume—amounts such as units produced, hours worked, programs developed; and (c) profit—revenue dollars left after expenses are paid; the difference between revenues and expenses. (frame 1, 6 pts)

2. A basic concept underlying C/V/P analysis is cost variability; that is, certain costs are directly affected by changes in volume. (frame 2, 2 pts)

3. (a) Variable costs are expenditures that change in direct proportion to some specific measure of volume; for example, hours worked, materials used. They remain constant per unit as volume changes. (frame 3, 2 pts)

   (b) Fixed costs are expenditures that are unaffected by changes in volume; that is, they remain constant in total: for example, lease payments, monthly phone bills, nonhourly salaries. Fixed costs decline on a per unit basis as volume increases. (frame 4, 2 pts)

   (c) Semivariable costs are expenditures containing both fixed and variable cost expenditures: for example, a leased machine (fixed) with a per use charge (variable). (frame 5, 2 pts)

   (d) Semifixed costs are basically fixed expenditures that can shift up or down when specific management decisions are made: for example, leasing a special attachment or hiring a consultant for a specific project. (frame 6, 2 pts)

4. (a) Variable costs; (b) semivariable costs; (c) variable costs; (d) semifixed costs; (e) fixed costs. (frames 3-7, 5 pts)

5. The break-even point is the level of activity that generates revenues exactly sufficient to cover costs, yielding neither profit nor loss. Total revenues equal total expenses. It is determined by first calculating the contribution margin and then applying an algebraic formula to determine the per unit contribution margin or the percentage contribution margin. (frames 8-12, 5 pts)

6. The contribution margin is the difference between sales revenues and variable costs. It can be expressed either in terms of a percentage or a per unit measure and is equal to fixed costs when the break-even point is achieved. (frames 9-11, 2 pts)

7. C/V/P analysis assumes that fixed and variable costs are known and are relatively predictable for coming periods as well as the stability of sales prices, that the proportion of each product line sales to total sales will be unchanged, that inventory levels will remain constant, and that technology doesn't change significantly. (frame 19, 2 pts)

8. (a) $0.40 per unit ($1.00 revenue less $0.60 variable costs). (frame 10, 5 pts)
       40% (100% revenue less 60% variable costs). (frame 12, 5 pts)

   (b) 2,500 units ($1,000 fixed cost divided by $0.40 contribution per unit. (frame 10, 5 pts)

   (c) $3,000 ($1,000 fixed costs + $200 profit divided by 40% variable cost). (frame 18, 5 pts)

   (d) 2,000 units ($1,000 fixed costs divided by $0.50 contribution per unit). (frame 17, 5 pts)

   (e) $4,000 ($1,000 fixed costs divided by 25% contribution margin). (frame 18, 5 pts)

(f)

Income Statement

Sales	$4,800	100%
Variable costs	3,600	75%
Contribution margin	1,200	25%
Fixed costs	1,000	
Net income before taxes	$ 200	

(frame 11, 5 pts)

Total possible points: 60. You should have scored at least 48 correct.

CHAPTER 2

Profit Planning

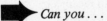 *Can you . . .*

- Use balance sheet and income statement data to develop a return-on-equity measure?
- Develop a projected income statement or a sales forecast?
- Identify factors to consider when developing a projected income statement?
- Determine and use the following measures: Return on sales? Return on assets? The current ratio? The debt-to-equity ratio?
- Identify cost components included in manufacturing costs? Materials costs?
- Estimate manufacturing costs?
- Obtain a measure of the cost of goods sold?
- Make a gross profit projection?
- Develop a monthly cost plan?
- Develop and use pro-forma financial statements?

After completing this chapter, you will be able to use the preceding skills to develop and assess your plans for making a profit.

A *profit plan* combines financial objectives, sales forecasts, production budgets, and other financial measures into an integrated projection of future financial conditions and requirements. The interrelationship of cost, volume, and profit (C/V/P analysis) provides the foundation for developing a profit plan. This chapter focuses on preparing various types of financial planning guidelines and using selected financial ratios to assess the possible results. After the profit objective or target is established, a sales forecast can be developed. Attention is directed to various product lines, estimated sales volumes and prices, and the time periods that comprise the planning period: for example, months or quarters. The sales forecast, in turn, is the foundation for operating plans and estimates of essential costs.

In a manufacturing operation, the sales forecast provides information to guide overall production planning. Detailed estimates of the cost of goods sold can then be prepared before the period begins, providing both purchasing and personnel functions with estimates of physical and financial requirements. Industries oriented to personal services, on the other hand, use the sales forecast as the basis for hiring and scheduling personnel. Both types of operating environments, manufacturing and service industries, are discussed in this chapter.

DEVELOPING AND ASSESSING THE PROFIT TARGET

The starting point for the profit planning process is to determine the desired return on investment. This profit target can then be incorporated into the C/V/P model to generate a volume goal in terms of sales dollars. Other return ratios relating net income to either sales or assets can then be used to evaluate the reasonableness of the profit objective.

The following case presents a reference point for developing and assessing profit objectives.

Thoroughbred Computer Services, Inc., provides a broad range of data analyses and technical programming services for its clientele. Business has been expanding in recent years, and the company's owners are now evaluating the need for additional processing equipment. Their banker has requested a brief summary of their sales and profit potential for the coming 3 years.

1. **Return on Investment.** The starting point for the profit planning process is to determine the desired return on investment *after* taxes. This measure is also called *return on equity.*

Return on investment is the relationship between net income after taxes and an organization's financial resource base in terms of the owner's investment. Balance sheet and income statement data are used to determine the return on investment:

1. Multiply owner's equity (from the balance sheet) by the desired profit target in after-tax dollars.
2. Convert after-tax dollars to before-tax dollars by using the formula

$$\text{net income before taxes} = \frac{\text{net income after taxes}}{100\% - X\% \text{ tax rate}}$$

3. Use this net-income-before-tax target in the C/V/P model to determine the required sales volume to achieve your target.

Example. In preparing data for the banker's review, a *profit target* of 12% in return on equity was considered reasonable. The company's balance sheet reflects the following financial information at the end of its most recent year.

Thoroughbred Computer Services, Inc.
Balance Sheet
December 31, 19XX

Current assets	$ 80,000	Current liabilities	$ 40,000
Long-term assets	160,000	Long-term liabilities	100,000
		Owner's equity	100,000
Total assets	$240,000	Total liabilities and equity	$240,000

Thoroughbred Computer Services, Inc.
Income Statement
for the Year Ended December 31, 19XX

Sales	$150,000	100%
Variable costs	90,000	60%
Contribution margin	$ 60,000	40%
Fixed costs	48,000	
Net income before taxes	$ 12,000	
Taxes (40%)	4,800	
Net income after taxes	$ 7,200	

As the first step, the owner's equity in the balance sheet ($100,000) is multiplied by the return-on-equity criterion of 12% to obtain the desired profit target of $12,000 in *after-tax* dollars.

To convert the C/V/P model from a technique for break-even analysis to one for profit planning, desired profit before taxes must be added to the fixed costs. In Thoroughbred's situation, the target income was initially stated in terms of after-tax dollars. Consequently, this measure must now be converted into before-tax dollars for this particular model to produce accurate results. The income statement shows that Thoroughbred's tax rate is 40%. Inserting this rate into the conversion formula, a measure of the target net income before taxes can be computed:

$$\text{net income before taxes} = \frac{\$12,000 \text{ (net income after taxes)}}{100\% - 40\% \text{ tax rate}} = \frac{\$12,000}{60\%}$$

$$= \$20,000$$

Now, using this net-income-before-tax target of $20,000, the C/V/P model can be used to compute the required sales volume:

$$\text{required sales volume} = \frac{\text{fixed cost} + \text{net-income-before-tax target}}{100\% - \text{variable cost \%}}$$

$$= \frac{\$48,000 + \$20,000}{100\% - 60\%}$$

$$= \frac{\$68,000}{40\%}$$

$$= \$170,000$$

Exercise

1. Assume that Thoroughbred expected only 10% return on investment. What would the required sales volume be? _____

2. If Thoroughbred wanted to achieve a 15% return on investment, what would the required sales volume be? _____

3. If Thoroughbred kept its original target of 12% return on investment, but its tax rate were reduced from 40% to 35%, what would the required sales volume be?

_____

— — — — — — — — — — — — — —

1. $161,667 (desired profit = $10,000; net income before taxes = $16,667).
2. $182,500 (desired profit = $15,000; net income before taxes = $25,000).
3. $166,153 (desired profit = $12,000; net income before taxes = $18,461).

2.   Projected Income Statements.   As the name implies, a projected income statement uses the data from C/V/P analysis and the cost data from the current income statement to describe the expected revenues for the upcoming year.

Projected income statements contain the following entries:		
Sales revenues	$XXX	100%
Less variable costs	$XXX	X%
Equals contribution margin	$XXX	
Less fixed costs	$XXX	
Equals net income before taxes	$XXX	
Less taxes (X%)	$XXX	
Equals income after taxes	$XXX	

Example.   Assuming that both the variable-cost percentage and fixed costs for Thoroughbred Computer Services, Inc., remain the same, their projected income statement would look like this:

Thoroughbred Computer Services, Inc.
Projected Income Statement
for the Year Ended December 31, 19XX

Sales revenue	$170,000	100%
Variable costs	102,000	60%
Contribution margin	$ 68,000	40%
Fixed costs	48,000	
Net income before taxes	$ 20,000	
Tax (40%)	8,000	
Net income after taxes	$ 12,000[a]	

[a]Note that the net income after taxes equals the measure for profit-after-tax target obtained by using the C/V/P model.

Exercise

1. On a separate sheet of paper, prepare a projected income statement for Thoroughbred Computer Service that reflects an anticipated 15% return on investment. (Use the figures from the second answer in frame 1.)
2. Then prepare a projected income statement for Thoroughbred reflecting a reduction in tax rate from 40% to 35%. (Use the figures from the third answer in frame 1.)

_ _ _ _ _ _ _ _ _ _ _ _ _ _ _ _

1.			
Sales revenue	$182,500	100%
Variable costs	109,500	60%
Contribution margin	73,000	40%
Fixed costs	48,000	
Net income before taxes	25,000	
Taxes (40%)	10,000	
Net income after taxes	$ 15,000	

2.			
Sales revenue	$166,153	100%
Variable costs	99,692	60%
Contribution margin	66,461	40%
Fixed costs	48,000	
Net income before taxes	18,461	
Taxes (35%)	6,461	
Net income after taxes	$ 12,000	

3. Assessing Assumptions. The past year's performance and the desired results that are reflected in the projected income statement can then be compared to assess whether the selected profit target is reasonable. In this assessment, two critical factors should be considered.

To assess the reasonableness of your target profit, consider:
1. Is the projected annual growth rate reasonable?

$$\% \text{ annual growth rate} = \frac{\text{expected \$ increase}}{\text{last year's sales \$}}$$

2. Are fixed costs likely to remain the same? If not, revise your projected income statement to reflect anticipated changes.

Example. Thoroughbred's projected annual growth rate is 13.3% ($20,000/$150,000). If their past performance showed a similar rate of growth, the projected growth would be reasonable.

Thoroughbred's owners determine that fixed costs might increase by $6,000 in the third year of the plan. If sales for Thoroughbred Computer Service do increase by

$20,000 per year, fixed costs increase by $6,000, and variable costs as well as tax rates remain the same, the estimated profit for the third year can be reflected in a revised projected income statement for the company's *third* year:

Thoroughbred Computer Services, Inc.
Income Statement
for the Year Ended December 31, 19XX

Sales revenue	$210,000	100%	($170,000 + $20,000 + $20,000)
Variable costs	126,000	60%	
Contribution margin	$ 84,000	40%	
Fixed costs	54,000		($48,000 + $6,000)
Net income before taxes	$ 30,000		
Taxes (40%)	12,000		
Net income after taxes	$ 18,000		

Exercise

A bicycle sales and repair shop is growing rapidly. The owner's investment is now $30,000 and he desires a return of 12%. He expects to invest an additional $20,000 at this time. Current sales of $60,000 annually should increase to $100,000 in the next 3 years, but variable costs should remain at about 60%. Fixed costs are now $1,500 per month but will increase to $2,500 in the future. Prepare a projected income statement for the third year that will show the banker the progress that is expected. This company's tax rate is 40%.

Income Statement

	Current	Percent	Projected	Percent
Sales	$60,000	100	$100,000	100
Variable costs	36,000	60	60,000	60
Contribution margin	$24,000	40	$ 40,000	40
Fixed costs	18,000		30,000	
Net income before taxes	$ 6,000		$ 10,000	
Taxes (40%)	2,400		4,000	
Net income after taxes	$ 3,600		$ 6,000	

Four additional measures—return on sales, return on assets, the current ratio, and a measure relating long-term debt-to-equity—can be used to reflect the financial improvements that can be expected if a profit plan is successfully executed.

4. Return on Sales

Return on sales is the financial relationship of net income after taxes to the company's net sales for the accounting period.

$$\text{return on sales} = \frac{\text{net income after taxes}}{\text{sales}}$$

Example. For Thoroughbred, return on sales for the year just ended would be 4.8% ($7,200/$150,000) (from income statement given as the example in frame 1).

Exercise
1. What would Thoroughbred's return on sales be for the first year of the plan? (Use the income statement given as the example in frame 2.) _____
2. What would it be in the third year of the plan? (Use the income statement given as the example in frame 3.) _____

- - - - - - - - - - - - - - - - -

1. 7.1% $\left(\dfrac{\$12,000}{\$170,000}\right)$

2. 8.6% $\left(\dfrac{\$18,000}{\$210,000}\right)$

5. Return on Assets

Return on assets is the financial ratio of net income after taxes to the organization's asset base.

$$\text{return on assets} = \frac{\text{net income after taxes}}{\text{total assets}}$$

Example. Recall that Thoroughbred's total assets were $240,000. Combining this information with the net income after taxes for the past year of $72,000, the company's return on assets for the year was 3% ($7,200/$240,000). Using the data from the projected income statement for the first year of the new profit plan, with a $12,000 net income after taxes (assuming no change in total asset position), Thoroughbred's return on assets increases to 5% ($12,000/$240,000).

Exercise

1. Assuming no change in Thoroughbred's total asset position, what would the return on assets be in the third year of the plan? (Use the data from the income statement given as an example in frame 3.) _____

2. If Thoroughbred's total assets increased to $260,000, what would the return on assets be in the third year of the plan? _____

- - - - - - - - - - - - - -

1. 7.5% $\left(\dfrac{\$18,000}{\$240,000}\right)$

2. 6.9% $\left(\dfrac{\$18,000}{\$260,000}\right)$

6. Current Ratio

> **Current ratio** is the financial relationship between current assets and current liabilities. It serves as a means of assessing an organization's ability to satisfy its short-term obligations. Improvement occurs as the ratio *increases.*
>
> $$\text{current ratio} = \frac{\text{current assets}}{\text{current liabilities}}$$

Example. Recall that in the past year Thoroughbred's current assets were $80,000 and its current liabilities $40,000. This would give them a current ratio of 2 to 1, that is,

$$\frac{\$80,000}{\$40,000} = \frac{2}{1} \quad \text{or} \quad 2{:}1, \text{ as it is often expressed}$$

If Thoroughbred's current assets increased to $100,000 with current liabilities remaining constant, the current ratio would *increase* to a level of 2.5 to 1 ($100,000/$40,000). This increase reflects improvement. If, on the other hand, current assets remained the same and current liabilities were to increase to $50,000, the current ratio would be 1.6 to 1 ($80,000/$50,000), a *decrease* that could indicate a problem.

Exercise

The bicycle shop mentioned earlier now has current assets of $20,000 and current liabilities of $8,000. The owner has considered borrowing $10,000 from the bank on a short-term note. What is the shop's present current ratio? _____What will this ratio be if the loan is obtained? _____

- - - - - - - - - - - - - - - -

Present current ratio: $\dfrac{\$20,000}{\$8,000} = 2.5$ to 1

After loan: $\dfrac{\$30,000}{\$18,000} = 1.67$ to 1

7. Long-Term Debt-to-Equity Ratio

> **Long-term debt-to-equity ratio** is the financial relationship between an organization's long-term debt to outsiders and the amount of owner's investment; this ratio serves as a means of assessing long-range financial stability. Improvement occurs when the ratio *decreases* to a level below 1 to 1.
>
> $$\text{debt-to-equity ratio} = \frac{\text{long-term debt}}{\text{owner's equity}}$$

Example. In the current year, Thoroughbred's long-term debt as shown on the balance sheet (frame 1) was $100,000 and the owner's equity was $100,000 giving a debt-to-equity ratio of 1 to 1 ($100,000/$100,000). If Thoroughbred's owners were able to reduce their long-term debt to $80,000, the ratio would change to 0.8 to 1 ($80,000/$100,000), representing an improvement in their long-range financial stability.

Exercise

A large manufacturing firm has consistently maintained a ratio of 1.2 to 1 in terms of long-term debt to equity. At the present time, its debt is $2,400,000 and equity is $2,000,000. The owners are considering investing an additional $2,000,000 in the business. What will the long-term debt-to-equity ratio be at that time? _____
How much added debt can they incur and still maintain a 1 to 1 ratio? _____

- - - - - - - - - - - - - - -

$$\frac{\$2,400,000}{\$4,000,000} = 0.6 \text{ to } 1.$$

They could borrow an added $1,600,000 in long-term funds:

$$\$4,000,000 \text{ debt}/\$4,000,000 \text{ equity} = 1 \text{ to } 1$$

Cautions

In spite of the usefulness of the preceding measures, you should recognize that there are no absolute criteria for the most desirable financial ratios. Each measure can serve as a guideline and, considered in combination, can be used to compare prior-year data with current-year and projected measures to assess where improvements are occurring and where major problems might exist.

In addition, even the most carefully constructed profit plan has little chance of success if certain fundamental conditions are lacking. First, management must be fully willing to *commit sufficient resources* to execute each segment of the plan. Second, all relevant information must be *communicated* in a timely manner to those authorized to make decisions. Third, the responsibility for *coordinating* diverse, yet interrelated activities must be clearly assigned to specific individuals. And fourth, *control* must be exerted by monitoring progress throughout each phase of the operating period. If these four fundamental conditions exist, the plan *can* be successfully implemented.

PROFIT PLANNING IN A MANUFACTURING COMPANY

After establishing a profit target that seems realistic, attention is directed to developing a comprehensive profit plan. These plans will vary somewhat depending on whether the business is a manufacturing or a service company. We'll look first at developing a profit plan for a manufacturing company, Delta Manufacturing Company, as a basis for our discussion. Although a variety of time frames could be used to prepare operational plans, this section illustrates the planning of profits for one quarter.

8. Sales Forecasting. Personnel involved in forecasting generally find it more effective to prepare a comprehensive sales forecast for each product. In this way, quarterly revenue and unit estimates are available when needed for management.

> A **sales forecast** is a projection of expected revenues by major business segment (e.g., product lines, divisions) for coming periods. To develop a sales forecast:
> 1. Determine anticipated unit volume per quarter.
> 2. Convert unit volume into financial projections.

Example. Delta Manufacturing Company is preparing a sales forecast for its major new product line, food processors for household kitchens. The product is produced in three models: compact, standard, and deluxe. Sales prices are $20, $30, and $50, respectively. Management expects that 8,000 units can be sold during the first year. Of these sales, the standard model should comprise 50% of the total in each of the four quarters; the other models should generate 25% of the sales. The total volume of sales is likely to occur in the following manner: 20% of total sales during the first quarter, 25% of total sales during both the second and third quarters, and 30% of total sales during the fourth quarter.

As a foundation for the entire plan, forecast data concerning volume for the year are first developed:

Quarter	Percentage of Total	(25%) Compact	(50%) Standard	(25%) Deluxe	(100%) Total
First	20	400	800	400	1,600
Second	25	500	1,000	500	2,000
Third	25	500	1,000	500	2,000
Fourth	30	600	1,200	600	2,400
Total units	100	2,000	4,000	2,000	8,000

These unit data are then converted into financial projections:

Quarter	($20) Compact	($30) Standard	($50) Deluxe	Total
First	$ 8,000[a]	$ 24,000	$ 20,000	$ 52,000
Second	10,000	30,000[b]	25,000	65,000
Third	10,000	30,000	25,000[c]	65,000
Fourth	12,000	36,000	30,000	78,000[d]
Total	$40,000	$120,000	$100,000	$260,000

[a] 400 units X $20.
[b] 1,000 units X $30.
[c] 500 units X $50.
[d] (600 X $20) + (1,200 X $30) + (600 X $50).

Exercise

Prepare a sales forecast based on the following situation.

X Manufacturing Company produces two products in its auto supply division: radios and stereo units. Radios sell for $100 and stereos for $200. Expected sales for the coming year of 10,000 units should be distributed as follows: 20% of the total in the first and fourth quarters and 30% in the other quarters. Radios comprise 60% of total sales and stereos the remaining 40%.

Unit Sales Forecast

Quarter	Radios	Stereos	Total
First	1,200	800	2,000
Second	1,800	1,200	3,000
Third	1,800	1,200	3,000
Fourth	1,200	800	2,000
Total	6,000	4,000	10,000

Revenue Sales Forecast

Quarter	Radios	Stereos	Total
First	$120,000	$ 80,000	$ 200,000
Second	180,000	120,000	300,000
Third	180,000	120,000	300,000
Fourth	120,000	80,000	200,000
Total	$600,000	$400,000	$1,000,000

9. **Manufacturing Costs per Unit.** Once you know what revenues can be expected from specific products, the next step is to determine the cost incurred in manufacturing them. Manufacturing costs are usually the most significant portion of the outlays required to produce and sell a product. Therefore, the cost of manufacturing each unit must be estimated and then used as a guideline for the total cost plan.

Manufacturing costs are expenses incurred to produce goods and services for resale to customers. Manufacturing costs include:
—**Materials costs**—expenses incurred to acquire the resources to be used in the production process.
—**Labor costs**—expenses incurred to acquire personnel resources to produce goods and services. This measure includes only production employees who are directly involved in producing the goods.
—**Overhead costs**—all production expenses other than materials and labor that are specifically attributable to the end product. These include items such as inexpensive supplies, the costs of production support activities and supervisory personnel, and so on.
These cost data can be summarized as follows:

Manufacturing Cost per Unit

Raw materials
—	$
—	$
—	$
	$
Direct labor	$
Overhead	
Variable	$
Fixed	$
Total	$

Example. The manufacturing costs for the deluxe product line of Delta Manufacturing unit might appear like this:

Manufacturing Cost per Unit

Raw materials		
Plastic frame	$ 4.50	
Electric motor	12.50	
Other parts	4.00	
Supplies	2.00	$23.00
Direct labor—assembly (1 hour at $4.00)		4.00
Manufacturing overhead		
Variable costs (50% of direct labor per unit)		2.00
Fixed costs ($1.00 per unit)		1.00
Total		$30.00

Exercise

The materials for X Manufacturing Company's car radios cost $26. Direct labor is $30 per unit. The manufacturing overhead is computed as follows: variable overhead is 60% of direct labor costs and fixed overhead is $6 per unit. Determine X's total cost for each car radio.

- - - - - - - - - - - - - - - -

Manufacturing Cost per Unit

Raw materials	$26
Direct labor	30
Variable overhead (60% of $30)	18
Fixed overhead	6
Total	$80

10.   Manufacturing Costs per Quarter. Once the manufacturing cost per unit is determined, this cost can be combined with data on the desired raw materials inventory and the finished goods inventory and the sales forecast to determine the manufacturing costs for the quarter.

The **raw materials inventory** includes all products that have been purchased and are being stored for use in the production process.

The **finished goods inventory** includes only products immediately available for sale to customers. Estimated manufacturing costs can then be summarized:

Estimated Manufacturing Costs
for the Quarter Ended March 31, 19XX

Beginning inventory—raw materials	$ _____
Plus materials purchased	_____
Equals raw materials available for use	_____
Less ending inventory—raw materials	_____
Equals raw materials costs	_____
Plus direct labor costs	_____
Variable manufacturing costs	_____
Fixed manufacturing costs	_____
Total manufacturing costs	_____

Example. Delta Manufacturing maintains a sufficient raw materials inventory at all times to allow production of at least 200 units. Thus its beginning raw materials inventory for the deluxe model was $4,600 (200 units X $23.00) at the beginning of the planning period. In addition, the finished goods inventory is also maintained at 200 units, a valuation of $6,000 (200 X $30) at January 1, 19XX. Since Delta plans to produce and sell 400 deluxe units during the first quarter, the quarterly cost of materials must next be determined:

400 Deluxe Units—Inventory

Plastic frames	400 at $ 4.50	=	$1,800
Electric motors	400 at 12.50	=	5,000
Other parts	400 at 4.00	=	1,600
Supplies	400 at 2.00	=	800
Total purchases			$9,200

Next, the direct labor cost, variable, and fixed costs are determined, and the data are summarized into a manufacturing expense plan for the deluxe model.

Estimated Manufacturing Costs
Deluxe Model
(400 units)
for the Quarter Ended March 31, 19XX

Beginning inventory—raw materials (200 units at $23)	$ 4,600
Plus materials purchased (see preceding data)	9,200
Equals raw materials available for use	13,800
Less ending inventory—raw materials (200 units at $23)	4,600
Equals raw materials costs—deluxe model	9,200
Plus direct labor costs (400 hours at $4.00/hour)	1,600
Variable manufacturing costs (50% of direct labor)	800
Fixed manufacturing costs ($1.00/unit)	400
Total manufacturing costs	$12,000

Although in this example the beginning and ending inventories are the same, this is not always the case; that is the reason they must be included in the data. At the end of a given quarter, there may be no raw materials left—therefore, no beginning inventory for the following quarter. Unless inventory changes are considered, one quarter may appear to be much more profitable than any other and incorrect decisions might result.

All these data—production requirements to satisfy sales forecasts and all planned inventory changes—are combined as the basis for a company's overall production budget. The budget identifies specifically the types and numbers of products that are to be produced during specific future time periods.

Exercise

The X Manufacturing Company has generally maintained sufficient raw materials to produce 500 units of its radios. These materials cost $26 per unit. In one month, however, the company purchased materials to produce 1,000 units, but only 900 units were actually completed. How much inventory was on hand at month's end?
_____ Prepare a schedule to show total manufacturing costs for the month's production. (See Exercise—frame 9.)

— — — — — — — — — — — — —

600 units are on hand at month's end; total manufacturing costs are:

Direct materials (900 units at $26)	$23,400
Direct labor (900 units at $30)	27,000
Variable overhead (60% of direct labor)	16,200
Fixed overhead (900 units at $6)	5,400
Total manufacturing costs	$72,000

11.   Cost of Goods Sold.   To obtain a measure of cost of goods sold, manufacturing expenses are combined with information about changes in the finished goods inventory. Again, if the amounts of inventory change, the cost-of-goods-sold measure is affected.

Information on **cost of goods sold** can be depicted as follows:

Cost of Goods Sold
for the Quarter Ended March 31, 19XX

Beginning finished goods inventory	$ _____
Plus total manufacturing costs	_____
Goods available for sale	_____
Less ending finished goods inventory	_____
Cost of goods sold	$ _____

Example. For Delta Manufacturing's deluxe model, the information would appear like this:

Cost of Goods Sold
Deluxe Model
for the Quarter Ended March 31, 19XX

Beginning finished goods inventory	$ 6,000
Plus total manufacturing costs	12,000
Goods available for sale	18,000
Less ending finished goods inventory	6,000
Cost of goods sold—deluxe model	$12,000

Exercise

X Manufacturing Company's beginning inventory of finished goods includes 1,000 radios at $80 and 1,200 stereo units at $140. In a given month, 500 units of each product are produced; the company sold 800 radios and 600 stereo units.

Determine the cost of goods sold for each product line.

- - - - - - - - - - - -

Flows of Inventory

	Radios	Stereos
Beginning inventory	1,000	1,200
Production	500	500
Units available for sale	1,500	1,700
Sales	800	600
Ending inventory	700	1,100

Cost of Goods Sold

	Radios	Stereos	Total
Beginning inventory	$ 80,000	$168,000	$248,000
Production	40,000	70,000	110,000
Goods available for sale	$120,000	$238,000	$358,000
Ending inventory[a]	56,000	154,000	210,000
Cost of goods sold	$ 64,000	$ 84,000	$148,000

[a] Note: The cost-of-goods-sold measure reflects the fact that 800 radios were sold at a cost of $80 each, and 600 stereos were sold at a cost of $140 per unit.

12.   Gross Profit Projection. Once the cost of goods sold is estimated, the cost can be compared to the forecasted revenues, both in dollars and as a percentage. In this way the product line manager can compare planned performance with those of prior years. If changes in either revenues or costs are required to achieve desired profit targets, the plans can be adjusted as needed.

Gross profit is computed by subtracting the cost of goods sold from the expected revenues for the quarter. It is usually depicted as follows:

Gross Profit Projection
for the Quarter Ended March 31, 19XX

Expected revenues	$ _____
Less cost of goods sold	_____
Gross profit	$ _____

Example. Delta's gross profit projection would appear like this:

Gross Profit Projection
Deluxe Model
for the Quarter Ended March 31, 19XX

Expected revenues—deluxe model	$20,000
Less cost of goods	12,000
Gross profit	$ 8,000

Exercise

X Manufacturing Company expects to sell 400 radios and 500 stereos in the coming month. They will produce exactly these quantities, so there will be no change in inventory. What is the month's projected gross profit from these sales?

- - - - - - - - - - - - - - -

	Radios	Stereos	Total
Revenues	$40,000	$100,000	$140,000
Cost of sales	32,000	70,000	102,000
Gross profit	$ 8,000	$ 30,000	$ 38,000

13.   Support Costs; Monthly and Quarterly Cost Plans. The study of costs involved in manufacturing products for sale serves as a brief example of one approach to developing an operating cost plan. Attention must now be directed to the remaining costs, those incurred to facilitate production activities.

Support costs are expenditures for administration, marketing, research and development, occupancy costs (rent, utilities, etc.), and others of a comparable nature. Both variable costs (in % of sales dollars) and fixed costs are identified, and a monthly cost plan developed:

Monthly Cost Plan

	Variable Costs	Fixed Costs
Administration	%	$
Marketing	%	$
Research and development	%	$
Occupancy	%	$
Total	%	$

The totals are then multiplied by *three* for the *quarterly costs.*

Example. The top management of Delta Manufacturing, Inc., used their computer to analyze thoroughly each of the nonmanufacturing cost classifications over a 3-year period. These measures were reevaluated and updated each quarter as the operating environment underwent changes. Their monthly cost plan for the first quarter might look like this:

Delta Manufacturing
Monthly Cost Plan

	Variable Costs[a]	Fixed Costs
Administration	2%	$ 800
Marketing	3%	500
Research and development	2%	400
Occupancy	3%	300
Total	10%	$2,000

[a]% of sales dollars.

Remember that variable costs are a certain percentage of total sales. The sales forecast for Delta for the first quarter indicated expected revenues for *all* products of $52,000. Given these data, the first quarter's variable cost for administration would be $1,040 (2% X $52,000). Carried further, total variable costs should approximate $5,200 (10% X $52,000). To this total 3 months of fixed costs must be added, that is, $6,000. Thus Delta's first-quarter support costs could be summarized like this:

Projected First-Quarter Support Costs

Administration	$1,040	$2,400	$ 3,440
Marketing	1,560	1,500	3,060
Research and development	1,040	1,200	2,240
Occupancy	1,560	900	2,460
Total	$5,200	$6,000	$11,200

Do not be misled into thinking that the $11,200 support costs exceed the anticipated gross profit for the quarter on the deluxe model ($8,000). The previous gross profit analysis considered only the deluxe product line. Gross profits from all three product lines will clearly exceed the nonproduction costs incurred.

Exercise

X Manufacturing Company estimates that its variable support costs are 15% of sales; the fixed portion is $9,000 per month. Using the data from the preceding exercise (frame 12), compute this company's net income for the month.

- - - - - - - - - - - - - -

X Manufacturing
Income Statement

Sales		$140,000
Cost of sales		102,000
Gross profit		$ 38,000
Other costs		
Variable support	$21,000	(15% X $140,000)
Fixed support	9,000	given
Total		30,000
Net income before taxes		$ 8,000

14. Summary: Manufacturing Profit Planning. Manufacturing profit plans proceed from the profit target to establishing a sales forecast for the total volume of sales required for the time period converted into a financial projection or revenue plan. Then manufacturing costs per unit are determined, including costs of material, labor, and overhead. These costs are extended for a 3-month period and combined with the raw materials inventory and the finished goods inventory to obtain manufacturing costs for the quarter. Next, the cost of goods sold is determined, taking into consideration the finished goods inventory to be maintained. Then a gross profit projection is calculated by subtracting the quarterly cost of goods sold from the financial projection for the quarter. Finally, support costs are calculated.

Exercise

Delta Manufacturing Company's accounting records reveal the following data for one quarter.

Sales	$60,000
Purchases of materials	22,000
Direct labor	10,000
Variable manufacturing overhead	5,000
Fixed manufacturing overhead	3,000
Variable support	10,000
Fixed support	7,000

Also provided are data concerning changes in inventory during the quarter.

Inventory	Beginning	Ending
Raw materials	$ 8,000	$12,000
Finished goods	$10,000	$ 9,000

(a) How much in raw materials were used during the quarter? _____

(b) What is the amount of total manufacturing cost? _____

(c) How much was Delta's cost of goods sold? _____

(d) Prepare an income statement from these data.

- - - - - - - - - - - - - -

(a)
Beginning materials inventory	$ 8,000
Purchases of materials	22,000
Available for use	$30,000
Ending materials inventory	12,000
Raw materials used	$18,000

(b) Materials used $18,000 (from A)
Direct labor   10,000
Variable manufacturing overhead   5,000
Fixed manufacturing overhead   3,000
     Total manufacturing costs $36,000

(c) Beginning finished goods inventory $10,000
Total manufacturing costs   36,000[a] (from B)
Goods available for sale $46,000
Ending finished goods inventory   9,000
Cost of goods sold $37,000

[a]This illustration assumes that all production is completed at the end of each day; thus there are no partially completed units in the production area when a new shift begins.

(d) Sales $60,000
Cost of sales   37,000
Gross profit $23,000

Support costs
     Variable $10,000
     Fixed   7,000
     Total   17,000
Net income before taxes $ 6,000

PROFIT PLANNING IN A SERVICE COMPANY

Profit planning procedures vary among companies because operating environments differ. Service industries, for example, focus on the use of personnel time and effort to satisfy the needs of customers, whereas manufacturing industries focus on a product for consumer satisfaction. For this discussion we consider the profit planning process as it exists in a hypothetical hospitality service industry firm, The Congenial Motor Inn.

15. Sales Forecasting

> To develop a **sales forecast** in a service company:
> 1. Identify the number of days per month the service will be provided and multiply that by the level or volume of service expected.
> 2. Convert this forecast into projected revenues for each month of the quarter.
> 3. Determine the total revenues anticipated from all services.

Example. The Congenial Motor Inn is a 200-unit motor hotel with a restaurant seating 60 customers. The average revenue for each room is $20 per night, and this facility generally enjoys an occupancy rate of 70% (i.e., on an average night, 140 of its rooms are occupied). Food and beverage revenues, on the other hand, are generally estimated to approximate 40% of each day's room revenues.

The owner/manager of Congenial is preparing a sales forecast for one quarter's activities (April, May, and June). A brief schedule has been prepared to provide necessary information for the forecast.

Congenial Motor Inn
Motel Occupancy Forecast

Month	Days	Available Rooms	Occupancy Rate
April	30	200	70%
May	31	200	70%
June	30	200	70%

These basic data provide a means of forecasting the Motor Inn's occupancy in room-days:

Congenial Motor Inn
Forecasted Room-Days
for the Quarter Ended June 30, 19XX

Month	Operating Days	Occupancy[a]	Forecasted Room-Days
April	30	140	4,200
May	31	140	4,340
June	30	140	4,200
Total room-days for quarter			12,740

[a] 200 rooms at the 70% occupancy rate.

The *revenue forecast* is merely an extension of these occupancy data in terms of average revenues:

Congenial Motor Inn
Forecasted Room Revenues
for the Quarter Ended June 30, 19XX

Month	Forecasted Room-Days	Estimated Average Room Rate	Estimated Room Revenue
April	4,200	$20	$ 84,000
May	4,340	20	86,800
June	4,200	20	84,000
Estimated total revenue			$254,800

These revenue estimates are used as the basis for projecting the same quarter's revenues from the restaurant operations as summarized in the following schedule of forecasted data:

Congenial Motor Inn
Forecasted Restaurant Revenues
for the Quarter Ended June 30, 19XX

Month	Forecasted Room Revenue	Percent Room Revenue	Forecasted Restaurant Revenue
April	$84,000	40%	$ 33,600
May	86,800	40%	34,720
June	84,000	40%	33,600
Estimated restaurant revenue			$101,920

Finally, the revenues anticipated from the rooms and the restaurant can be combined to produce the projected quarterly revenues:

Congenial Motor Inn
Forecasted Revenues
for the Quarter Ended June 30, 19XX

Month	Estimated Room Revenue	Estimated Restaurant Revenue	Total Estimated Revenue
April	$ 84,000	$ 33,600	$117,600
May	86,800	34,720	121,520
June	84,000	33,600	117,600
Total	$254,800	$101,920	$356,720

Exercise

A snack bar at the local university serves three meals per day, 7 days per week. Its average daily dinner revenue on Monday through Thursday is $1,000. On Friday, Saturday, and Sunday, daily revenue increases to $1,500. Revenue forecasts use these data as a base; breakfasts average 40% of dinner revenues and lunches 60%. Prepare a forecast for 1 week's revenue in this snack bar.

Day of the Week	Breakfast	Lunch	Dinner	Total
Sunday	$ 600	$ 900	$1,500	$ 3,000
Monday	400	500	1,000	1,900
Tuesday	400	500	1,000	1,900
Wednesday	400	500	1,000	1,900
Thursday	400	500	1,000	1,900
Friday	600	900	1,500	3,000
Saturday	600	900	1,500	3,000
Total	$3,400	$4,700	$8,500	$16,600

16. Cost Analysis. Just as in manufacturing companies, managers involved in service industry activities are responsible for developing cost plans. Some differences in approach exist, however, because the nature of their efforts are different.

> Using historical data, identify major costs in providing each service. Then determine what percent of revenues generated each of these costs represents.

Example. A review of Congenial Motor Inn's past cost data for the restaurant reveals that three types of costs must be considered—food costs, beverage costs, and service personnel costs (salaries and wages). These represent classes of expenditures that should be monitored almost continually. Thus the manager's attention must be directed primarily to these areas as cost plans are developed.

When Congenial's historical data were analyzed, the following cost percentages were developed: food costs generate approximately 40% of total food revenues, beverage costs are approximately 30% of beverage revenues, and personnel costs are generally 30% of each revenue category. A plan was constructed based on the assumption that the food revenues for the second quarter would be 75% of total restaurant revenues and beverages would comprise the remainder.

Congenial Motor Inn
Estimated Food and Beverage Revenue
for the Quarter Ended June 30, 19XX

Month	Total Restaurant Revenue	Food Revenue (%)	Beverage Revenue (%)
April	$ 33,600 (100%)	$25,200 (75%)	$ 8,400 (25%)
May	34,720	26,040	8,680
June	33,600	25,200	8,400
Total	$101,920	$76,440	$25,480

Then, in estimating the *costs* of food and beverages that are likely to be incurred, develop a schedule to combine the food/beverage revenue estimates with available historical cost percentages. Using April data, you can see the uses of these data in preparing *gross profit estimates* for both food and beverages in this service industry setting:

Congenial Motor Inn
Estimated Gross Profits[a]
Foods and Beverages
for April 19XX

	Food	Beverage	Total
Revenue	$25,200 (75%)	$8,400 (25%)	$33,600
Costs			
Food	10,080 (40%)		10,080
Beverages		2,520 (30%)	2,520
Personnel	7,560 (30%)	2,520 (30%)	10,080
Total costs	$17,640	$5,040	$22,680
Gross profit	$ 7,560	$3,360	$10,920

[a]Rounded to the nearest whole dollar.

The final service classification to be considered relates to costs incurred in the rooms segment. Personnel costs include the front desk area and all other expenditures directly involved with serving the Inn's clientele. Generally, this cost factor comprises 40% of rooms' revenues. Thus the cost plan for this segment in April merely translates estimated room revenues of $84,000 into costs by applying the percentage factor. Total personnel costs for the rooms segment are thus expected to be $33,600 ($84,000 × 40%).

Exercise

The snack bar's combined food and beverage costs approximate 60% of its revenues, and personnel costs represent about 30% of revenues. Using these data and those developed in the preceding example (frame 15), you can determine the snack bar's estimated weekly contribution margin from each meal period.

		Breakfast		Lunch		Dinner
Weekly revenue		$3,400		$4,700		$8,500
Estimated costs						
Food and beverages	$2,040		$2,820		$5,100	
Personnel	1,020		1,410		2,550	
Total		3,060		4,230		7,650
Contribution margin		$ 340		$ 470		$ 850

17.   High–Low Two-Point Cost Analysis of Mixed Costs. In Chapter 1 four basic types of costs were discussed: fixed, variable, semivariable, and semifixed. Sometimes, however, costs are so interrelated that they cannot be clearly identified as being fixed or variable without further analysis. If a computer is available, it can easily be programmed to separate these *mixed costs.* If no computer is available, however, a technique called the *high–low two-point method of cost analysis* can be used. The method is inexpensive, but has limited accuracy. Nevertheless, resulting data offer small businesses a useful framework for planning and controlling important cost categories.

The steps to follow in isolating mixed costs are presented directly below. Do not be concerned if on first reading you are not sure how to perform the technique. Go on to the example and review each step in the boxed material as it is presented in the example.

To analyze mixed costs, use the **high–low two-point method of cost analysis**:

1. Identify all other costs and determine if they are variable, fixed, or mixed.
2. Identify high and low volume periods. For each period, find variable costs per volume measure and fixed costs per quarter.
3. Subtract the low month figures from the high month figures for both volume measures and fixed costs per quarter.
4. Divide the difference between the average monthly cost by the difference between the volume measure to determine the estimated variable costs.
5. Multiply the variable cost by the volume. Then subtract the total estimated variable costs from the total mixed costs to determine the estimated fixed costs.

   total mixed costs – estimated variable costs = estimated

   fixed costs

6. Finally, determine total mixed costs by using the formula

mixed costs = (variable cost rate × volume measure) + fixed costs

Example. As you read the following example, compare the steps taken at Congenial Motor Inn with the summary of steps presented in the preceding box.

Four other cost classifications have been identified for attention as Congenial's management completes its profit plan. These expenses, common to the hotel/restaurant industry, are: administrative and general; advertising and sales promotion; heat, light, and power; and repairs and maintenance. Since each is a significant cost factor, each must be analyzed in detail before making a plan.

Because Congenial's manager does not have access to a computer, the more simplified approach of the high–low two-point method of cost analysis was used.

1. As a starting point, the manager reviewed costs of prior months and analyzed specific documents that had been paid. He identified some costs that were clearly variable and others that were clearly fixed. The remaining costs, however, could not be separated any further. These were classified as *mixed costs* for planning purposes. A schedule was developed to summarize the available cost data:

Congenial Motor Inn
Other Monthly Operating Costs
(Developed from Historical Data)

Expenses	Variable Costs[a]	Fixed Costs	Mixed Costs
Administrative and general	1%	$2,000	$ 3,000
Advertising and sales promotion	2%	1,000	1,000
Heat, light, and power	1%	1,000	4,000
Repairs and maintenance	2%	1,000	2,000
Total	6%	$5,000	$10,000

[a]Percentage of revenues.

2. After reviewing historical data regarding volume, a high- and a low-volume period were identified. The volume of service provided and the average monthly cost for both the high and low months were also determined:

Congenial Motor Inn
Other Monthly Operating Costs
High and Low Months

Selected Period	Volume Measure (Room-Days)	Average Monthly Costs
High month	3,000	$12,000
Low month	2,100	9,300

3. Subtracting the low-month figures from the high-month figures shows a difference in volume of 900 room-days and a difference in costs of $2,700. It can be assumed that the increase in volume caused the increase in costs, and the only costs that change as volume changes are variable costs.

4. These two factors, changes in room-days and changes in costs, can be combined to obtain a measure of Congenial's *variable cost per room-day* simply by dividing cost by the volume. The variable cost per room-day for Congenial would be $3.00 ($2,700 ÷ 900 room-days).

5. This measure of variable cost per room is then used to identify the fixed costs that Congenial should expect to incur. By multiplying the estimated variable cost per room-day by the volume for the month, the total estimated variable costs for the month can be identified. These can then be subtracted from total mixed costs, leaving an estimate of the fixed costs for the month:

total mixed costs − estimated variable costs = estimated fixed costs
$12,000   − $9,000   = $3,000
(3,000 room-days × $3)

This same analysis can be applied to the lowest month of activity:

$9,300 − $6,300   = $3,000
(2,100 room-days × $3)

Notice that the fixed-cost estimate for both the high and low months remains the same, $3,000. This result is consistent with our definition of fixed costs, that is, those not expected to change even though volume may increase or decrease. The variable costs of $3.00 per room-day also satisfy the earlier definition framework, costs that are constant per unit of activity. The high- and low-volume levels, in turn, are presumed to indicate the relevant range of activity for this motor inn.

6. The mixed cost estimates are combined to serve as the basis for Congenial Motor Inn's overall cost plan. At a volume level of 4,200 room-days, total mixed costs can be computed as follows:

mixed costs = (variable cost rate × volume measure) + fixed costs
$15,600   =   (4,200 days   × $3)   + $3,000

These data can then be combined to develop a budget for other operating costs. Since April revenues are expected to be $84,000 for the volume of 4,200 days, total other costs can be computed in the following manner:

other costs =   variable costs   + mixed costs + fixed costs
$25,640   = (6% × $84,000) + $15,600   + $5,000

When combined with previously developed revenue and departmental information, the profit plan can be constructed for any given month. In this way, too, a set of financial guidelines are developed to facilitate the control process. Specific targets thus serve to guide management decision making.

Exercise

The manager of a local fast-food outlet is troubled with her inability to monitor mixed costs that are incurred on a monthly basis. One of her part-time employees, a student in a management accounting course, suggested that they attempt to use the high–low method of cost analysis. The following data have been developed for these purposes.

	Meals Served	Total Costs
High	11,400	$15,600
Low	9,200	14,500

(a) What are the variable costs per meal served? _____
(b) What are the monthly fixed costs? _____
(c) If the outlet serves 10,000 meals next month, what should their budgeted mixed costs be if this method is used? _____

- - - - - - - - - - - - - - -

(a)

	Meals	Costs
High	11,400	$15,600
Low	9,200	14,500
Changes	2,200	$ 1,100

Variable costs are $1,100 divided by 2,200, or $0.50 per meal.

(b) In the high month, 11,400 meals at $0.50 per meal results in total variable costs of $5,700. Subtracting these from total costs, we can determine fixed costs.

Total costs	$15,600
Total variable costs	5,700
Fixed costs	$9,900

In the low period, the same method applies:

$$\$14,500 - (9,200 \times \$0.50) = \$9,900$$

(c) If 10,000 meals are served, budgeted costs would be

$$\text{total budgeted costs} = \$9,900 + (10,000 \times \$0.50) = \$14,900$$

18.   Projected Income Statement. The data from cost analysis can be integrated into a monthly projected income statement so that management can evaluate the reasonableness of the projected income for the planning period. If changes in the profit plan are needed, the appropriate decisions can be made before the month begins.

Use a **projected income statement** such as the one below to compile the relevant financial information in summary form for use in profit planning in a service industry:

Service Industry X
Projected Income Statement
Month Ending Date, Year

	Component A	Component B	Component C	Total
Revenues	$ _____	$ _____	$ _____	$ _____
Direct costs	_____	_____	_____	_____
Gross profit	_____	_____	_____	_____
Other costs				_____
Planned profit				_____
Corporate fixed costs				_____
Estimated net income				$ _____

Example. Congenial's projected income statement would appear as follows:

Congenial Motor Inn
Projected Income Statement
Month Ending April 30, 19XX

	Rooms	Foods	Beverages	Total
Revenue	$84,000	$25,200	$8,400	$117,600
Direct costs	33,600	17,640	5,040	56,280
Gross profit	$50,400	$ 7,560	$3,360	$ 61,320
Other operating costs				$ 25,640
Planned profit from operations				$ 35,680
Corporate fixed costs				25,000
Estimated net income				$ 10,680

Exercise

The fast-foods outlet manager now can project both costs and income for the coming month. Revenues are expected to be $30,000. Variable costs should be 22% of revenues and fixed costs are $5,000 per month. They expect to serve 11,000 meals and the mixed-cost formula (frame 17) is used to project mixed costs. Develop the projected income statement for the coming month.

- - - - - - - - - - - - -

Revenues		$30,000
Costs		
Variable costs	$6,600	
Fixed costs (given)	5,000	
Mixed costs—variable		
(11,000 × $0.50)	5,500	
Mixed costs—fixed	9,900	
Total		27,000
Net income		$ 3,000

Note: Contribution margin could be provided by subtracting variable costs from revenues ($30,000 - $12,100 = $18,900) if the manager desired these data.

PRO-FORMA FINANCIAL STATEMENTS

Pro-forma or *projected financial statements* are used to assess the potential financial effects of management decisions. As a starting point, a set of financial targets are specified. With these guidelines, you can evaluate the financial results of each major decision in terms of whether major targets are likely to be achieved. Projected financial statements allow you to preview the company's likely financial status at the end of the planning period.

Previous examples in this chapter referred to one organization providing tangible outputs, manufactured products, and another offering services. Pro-forma statements can be prepared for each of these companies using the data developed. Profit planning techniques apply effectively to all types of operations. For our discussions of preparing pro-forma statements, a department store, Diversified, is used to illustrate the procedures used.

19.   **Financial Targets.** Different types of targets have already been discussed. As one example, we consider one owner who wants to realize a certain percent return on investment. Other targets must also be established before pro-forma statements can be prepared.

As a base for **pro-forma statements**, determine financial targets such as:

Financial position targets

Cash	$ amount
Merchandise inventory	X months' cost of sales
Building and equipment	$
Accounts receivable	% of a month's sales
Other assets	$
Accounts payable and other current liabilities	%
Long-term debt	%
Return on equity	%

Monthly operating targets

Sales	$
Cost of sales	X% of sales
Operating expenses	X% of sales
Net income before tax	X% of sales
Expected tax rate	%

Example. Diversified is the only department store in a small Midwest community. It had been family-owned and -operated until recently, but a large organization now holds the controlling interest. After working closely with the family, the following general financial targets were established to guide activities during time periods when the ownership change was being executed.

Financial position targets

Cash	$60,000
Merchandise inventory	2 months' cost of sales
Building and equipment	$130,000
Accounts receivable	¼ month's sales
Other assets	$20,000
Accounts payable and other current liabilities	50% current assets
Long-term debt	100% owner's equity
Return on equity	12%

Monthly operating targets

Sales	$100,000
Cost of sales	70% of sales
Operating expenses	26% of sales
Net income before tax	4% of sales
Expected tax rate	50%

20.   Projected Income Statements.   Using the targets and financial relations, you can construct a projected set of financial statements. The first step is to develop an income statement for the coming year.

Proposed income statements can be prepared on a schedule such as this:

Proposed Income Statement
for the Year Ended December 31, 19XX

	Dollars	Percent of Sales
Sales	$ _____	_____
Cost of sales	$ _____	_____
Gross profit	$ _____	_____
Operating expenses	$ _____	_____
Net income before taxes	$ _____	_____
Income taxes	$ _____	_____
Net income after taxes	$ _____	_____

Example.   Since Diversified expects a monthly sales volume of $100,000 or an annual total of $1,200,000, and has developed other financial targets, their statement would look something like the following:

Diversified
Proposed Income Statement
for the Year Ended December 31, 19XX

Sales	$1,200,000	100%
Cost of sales	840,000	70%
Gross profit	$ 360,000	30%
Operating expenses	312,000	26%
Net income before taxes	$ 48,000	4%
Income taxes	24,000	2%
Net income after taxes	$ 24,000	2%

Exercise

Delta Manufacturing projects its quarterly income on the basis of predetermined percentage targets. Cost of goods sold are estimated at 60% of sales; other operating costs are separated into variable (20% of sales) and fixed ($4,000 per month). If quarterly sales are estimated at $80,000, develop an appropriate projected income statement.

- - - - - - - - - - - - - - -

Delta Manufacturing
Projected Income Statement

Sales		$80,000
Cost of sales (60% of sales)		48,000
Gross profit		$32,000
Other costs		
Variable (20% of sales)	$16,000	
Fixed costs	12,000	
Total		28,000
Net income before taxes		$ 4,000

21. **Balance Sheet.** The next step is to construct a balance sheet.

A balance sheet summarizes total assets, liabilities, and owner's equity and might contain the following information:

Projected Current Assets

Cash	$ _____
Accounts receivable	_____
Inventories	_____
Total current assets	$ _____

Projected Total Assets

Current assets	$ _____
Building and equipment	_____
Total assets	$ _____

Projected Liabilities and Owner's Equity

Accounts payable and other	
current liabilities	$ _____
Long-term debt	_____
Owner's equity	_____
Total liabilities and equity	$ _____

Example.   The desired year-end cash balance for Diversified is established as $60,000. The outstanding balance in accounts receivable should not exceed 1 month's sales ($100,000). Merchandise inventories, on the other hand, should not exceed 70% of 2 months' sales ($140,000). Using these targets, Diversified's schedule of current assets was prepared.

Diversified
Projected Current Assets

Cash	$ 60,000
Accounts receivable	100,000
Inventories	140,000
Total current assets	$300,000

Next, Diversified's total asset position is summarized.

Diversified
Projected Total Assets

Current assets	$300,000
Building and equipment	150,000
Total assets	$450,000

Finally, total liabilities and owner's equity are itemized.

Accounts payable and other current liabilities	$150,000
Long-term debt	150,000
Owner's equity	150,000
Total liabilities and equity	$450,000

Notice that total assets equal liabilities plus owner's equity. A further comment is needed here regarding the relationship between current assets and current liabilities. The difference between these two measures is termed "working capital." In this case, Diversified's working capital is $150,000: current assets of $300,000 less current liabilities of $150,000. The working-capital concept will be discussed in more depth in a succeeding chapter.

Exercise
Delta's management has established a current asset target of $300,000 to be maintained at all times. Of these amounts, the cash position should be 15%, accounts receivable 25%, and inventories 60%. Fixed assets are carried on the balance sheet at $200,000. Current liabilities are maintained at approximately 50% of current assets, and the long-term debt-to-equity ratio must be 1 to 1. Project a balance sheet from these data.

- - - - - - - - - - - - - - -

Delta Manufacturing Company
Projected Balance Sheet

Assets		Liabilities	
Current assets		Current liabilities	$150,000
Cash	$ 45,000		
Accounts receivable	75,000	Long-term debt	175,000[a]
Inventory	180,000	Equity	175,000[a]
Total	$300,000		
Fixed assets	200,000		
Total assets	$500,000	Total liabilities	$500,000

[a]Since long-term debt and equity must be equal, as the 1-to-1 ratio states, the remaining $350,000 is divided equally.

22. Evaluating Pro-Forma Statements. As a final step in preparing pro-forma financial statements, recheck all figures and then test each projected measure for reasonableness. Most important, the targets established must be attainable.

> **Evaluate pro-forma statements** by determining return-on-equity ratio. Other measures to evaluate targets can include the return on sales, the return on assets, the current ratio, and the debt-to-equity ratio.

Example. Diversified established a 16% return-on-equity target, meaning that their annual net income after taxes must represent that proportion of the owner's equity at the end of the planning period. In this planning period Diversified's ratio was:

$$\frac{\$24,000 \text{ (net income after taxes)}}{\$150,000 \text{ (owner's equity)}} = 16\% \quad \text{(return on equity)}$$

Their target appears to be reasonable for the coming planning period.

Exercise

Delta's management desires a return on equity of 12%, a return on sales of 5%, and a current ratio of at least 1.8 to 1. Are these goals satisfied if the projected balance sheet is achieved and if net income after taxes for the year is $25,000 on annual sales of $400,000?

_ _ _ _ _ _ _ _ _ _ _ _ _ _ _ _

Return on equity	$25,000 ÷ $175,000 = 14.3%; yes
Return on sales	$25,000 ÷ $400,000 = 6.3%; yes
Current ratio	$300,000 ÷ $150,000 = 2 to 1; yes

Many different approaches can be used to develop pro-forma financial statement data. However, whatever approach you select, the financial statement data, whether projected or historical, must be supported by accurate computations and careful documentation. The supporting information is an important foundation for management decision making.

Before completing the Self-Test that follows, review the questions posed at the beginning of the chapter. If you are uncertain of any answers, reread the appropriate pages.

CHAPTER 2 SELF-TEST

1. Matching – Terminology/Concepts

Match the following terms to the definitions.

1. Debt to equity	8. Production budget
2. Current ratio	9. Profit plan
3. Finished goods inventory	10. Raw materials inventory
4. Labor costs	11. Return on assets
5. Manufacturing costs	12. Return on investment
6. Materials costs	13. Return on sales
7. Overhead costs	14. Sales forecast

_____ (a) The relationship between net income after taxes and an organization's financial resource base in terms of the owner's investment.

_____ (b) The financial relationship between an organization's debt to outsiders and the amount of owner's investment; used to assess long-range financial stability.

_____ (c) Expenses incurred to acquire personnel resources to produce goods and services, including both production employees and support personnel.

_____ (d) Combines financial objectives, sales forecasts, production budgets, and other asset-base items.

_____ (e) The relationship between net income after taxes and an organization's financial resource base in terms of the owner's investment.

_____ (f) Products that are immediately available for sale to customers.

_____ (g) All products that have been purchased and are being stored for use in the company's production process.

_____ (h) The financial relationship between current assets and current liabilities, used to assess an organization's short-term stability.

_____ (i) All production expenses other than materials and labor that are specifically identifiable in the end product.

_____ (j) Projection of expected revenues by major business segments for coming periods.

2. Profit Planning Formulas

The ABC Company earned net income after tax of $120,000 during its past operating year. Its contribution margin rate is 40%, and the company incurred $600,000 in fixed costs. ABC's tax rate is 40%.

(a) What is the company's target in net income before taxes?

(b) If all factors remain the same in the coming year, how much in sales revenue must this company generate to achieve a profit level of $120,000 after taxes?

(c) Assume further that management changed its profit expectations for the coming year. The profit plan now calls for a return on investment of 15%. The investment base is $1,600,000 and the tax rate will remain at 40%. Fixed costs, however, will increase to $720,000. How many dollars of revenue must be generated to achieve the required revenue target?

3. Sales Forecast

The director of profit planning for the X Company has been asked by the president to develop information on the coming year's profit plan. The following data have been developed for two of the company's primary product lines, A and B, in response to this request.

	Per Unit	
	A	B
Sales price	$20	$10
Cost of goods sold	14	7
Gross profit	$ 6	$ 3

Other information indicates that selling and administrative expenses should be $9,000 per month for these lines. In addition, other general expenses should be $6,000 per month.
(a) A sales forecast has been prepared for developing the profit plan.

Product	Annual Sales (Units)	Quarterly Sales Percentage				
		1	2	3	4	Total
A	12,000	25	25	25	25	100
B	20,000	20	30	30	20	100

Present a schedule to reflect expected product line gross profits for the first quarter.

(b) Given the sales forecast information just developed, determine the number of product A and product B units that must be produced to satisfy sales requirements. By policy, beginning finished goods inventories are maintained at 20% of the next quarter's sales. Consequently, product A and B inventories at the beginning of the year were 600 units and 800 units, respectively. How many units of A and B must be produced during the first quarter if the company will sell 3,000 units of A and 4,000 units of B?

(c) Assume that the company must produce 3,000 units of A and 5,000 units of B during a specified quarter. The following cost data are provided to use in determining manufacturing costs for this period.

	Product A	Product B
Materials, per unit	4 lb at $2/lb	2 lb at $3/lb
Labor, per unit	1 hr at $4/hr	3 hr at $2/hr
Overhead, per unit	50% labor costs	50% labor costs

Using these data, determine the manufacturing costs that will be incurred during this quarter.

4. Pro-Forma Statements

The projected asset position of X Company at its upcoming year-end date is presented in the following schedule:

Current assets	$ 500,000
Long-term assets	1,000,000
Total assets	$1,500,000

Using these data as a reference point, construct a pro-forma balance sheet and income statement for this company that will reflect accomplishment of the following financial targets:

(a) Current ratio, 2 to 1
(b) Total debt-to-equity ratio, 1 to 1
(c) Long-term debt-to-equity ratio, 1.5 to 1 or 60% long-term debt to 40% equity
(d) Return on assets, 12%
(e) Return on sales, 3%
(f) Gross profit percentage, 40%

ANSWERS

1. Matching – Terminology/Concepts

(a) 12 (frame 1, 1 pt)   (b) 1 (frame 7, 1 pt)   (c) 4 (frame 9, 1 pt)
(d) 9 (frame 1, 1 pt)   (e) 11 (frame 5, 1 pt)   (f) 3 (frame 10, 1 pt)
(g) 10 (frame 10, 1 pt)   (h) 2 (frame 6, 1 pt)   (i) 7 (frame 9, 1 pt)
(j) 14 (frame 15, 1 pt)

2. Profit Planning Formulas [frames 1–7, 9 pts total (3 pts each part)]

(a) $\dfrac{\$120,000}{100\% - 40\%} = \dfrac{\$120,000}{60\%} = \$200,000$

(b) $\dfrac{\$600,000 + \$200,000}{0.40} = \$2,000,000$

Revenues	$2,000,000
Variable costs (60%)	1,200,000
Contribution margin	$ 800,000
Fixed costs	600,000
Net income before taxes	$ 200,000
Taxes 40%	80,000
Net income after taxes	$ 120,000

(c) Return on investment 15% × $1,600,000 = $240,000
Target income before taxes

$$\dfrac{\$240,000}{100\% - 40\%} = \underline{\$400,000}$$

Revenue target

$$\dfrac{\$720,000 + \$400,000}{0.40} = \underline{\$2,800,000}$$

3. Sales Forecast [frames 8–14, 12 pts total (4 pts each part)]

(a)

	Product A	Product B	Total
Sales revenue	$60,000 (3,000 × $20)	$40,000 (4,000 × $10)	$100,000
Cost of goods sold	42,000 (3,000 × $14)	28,000 (4,000 × $ 7)	70,000
Gross profit	$18,000 (3,000 × $ 5)	$12,000 (4,000 × $ 3)	$ 30,000

(b)

	Product A	Product B
Sales requirement	3,000 units	4,000 units
Plus: Ending inventory requirements		
Product A—20% × 3,000	600 units	
Product B—20% × 6,000		1,200 units
	3,600 units	5,200 units
Less: Beginning inventory	600 units	800 units
Required production	3,000 units	4,400 units

(c)

	Product A	Product B
Materials	$ 8	$ 6
Labor	4	6
Overhead	2	3
Manufacturing cost per unit	$14	$15
Units produced	3,000 units	5,000 units
Total manufacturing costs	$42,000	+ $75,000 = $117,000

4. *Pro-Forma Statements* (frames 19-21, 6 pts)

Balance Sheet
for the Period Ended XXXX

Current assets	$ 500,000	Current liabilities	$ 250,000
Long-term assets	1,000,000	Long-term liabilities	500,000
		Equity	750,000
Total assets	$1,500,000	Total liabilities	$1,500,000

Income Statement

Sales	$6,000,000
Cost of goods sold	3,600,000
Gross profit	$2,400,000
Operating expenses	2,220,000
Net income (12% × $1,500,000)	$ 180,000

Total possible points: 37. You should have scored at least 30.

CHAPTER 3

Cash Budgeting

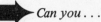 *Can you . . .*

- Identify cash inflow and outflow for a specific project, product, or service?
- Prepare a schedule of payments for a loan?
- Analyze cash sales and accounts receivable?
- Convert a budgeting schedule into a schedule of expected cash flows?
- Develop a schedule for accounts receivable? Collection?
- Budget operating costs such as personnel expenses? Administrative expenses? Selling expenses? Occupancy expenses?
- Use cash disbursement budgets for decision making?
- Estimate capital expenditures and evaluate your working-capital position?
- Develop a comprehensive cash budget?

After completing this chapter, you should have the skills required for effective financial planning.

Financial planning begins with assessing cost/volume/profit relationships. The second phase of financial planning is developing a profit plan, including various financial targets. Financial plans are incomplete, however, without careful assessments of cash flows and requirements, or cash budgeting, the third basic component of financial planning.

Cash budgeting focuses on projecting cash inflows and cash outflows for specified future periods of time. It is a technique designed to determine possible effects of planned actions on a company's available financial resources. Detailed analysis of cash inflows from sales and collections of receivables is the initial reference point. Cash outflows are then analyzed to determine whether sufficient liquid resources are available. To the extent that additional cash is needed, the marketable securities position can be adjusted. In some cases, added funds are acquired through borrowing. The key to success rests in the fact that cash needs are known well before problems are expected to arise.

Cash budgeting is an integral part of management accounting. Data developed during the application of the C/V/P model are used as the basis for profit planning. Estimates from the profit plan, in turn, serve as a foundation for many of the specific cash budgets.

Cash flow analyses similarly affect capital budgeting procedures, discussed in Chapter 9. Taken together, these techniques provide the financial information base essential to management's planning decisions.

A series of different practical environments are used in this chapter as reference points to demonstrate the versatility of management accounting techniques. Their capacity for use in any environment is a major strength.

THE CASH BUDGET

Cash budgeting is an important management tool in all environments. Although applications are most often discussed in terms of profit-oriented enterprises, cash flow plans are also essential in not-for-profit endeavors. Our first illustrative case, a special funding project in a hospital, is an example of one such project.

Community Hospital, located in a small town, provides health care services that are a significant resource to both local citizens and those in surrounding localities. A major problem exists, however, because Community's x-ray equipment is old and somewhat outdated. A group of the town's businesspeople have now started a program to finance the $25,000 in funds that are needed for new equipment. As a starting point, 40 families have pledged $250 to this cause. These funds are to be received in less than 30 days. Additional pledges were received from 70 individuals in the amount of $100 each; these funds are to be received in 90 days. The remainder is to be borrowed to ensure that the equipment can be obtained as soon as possible. In order to repay the loan, $2.50 will be charged for each patient who requires x-rays. The hospital's staff predicts that at least 100 patients will use these services monthly; thus the loan will be repaid in a timely manner.

The local banker is willing to loan funds for this worthwhile cause. Bank policy, however, requires a cash budget in support of all loan applications.

1. Schedule of Cash Inflows

> The first step in preparing a cash budget is to determine
> expected cash inflows or receipts. **Cash receipts** are all
> inflows into a company for goods and services provided to
> customers as well as collections on account and amounts
> obtained from investors (owners) or borrowings (creditors).

Example. Community Hospital will receive $10,000 in 30 days from the 40 families who have pledged $250 each. It will receive another $7,000 in 90 days from 70 other individuals who have pledged $100 each, making a total of $17,000. Since they need $25,000 for the x-ray machine, they need to borrow $8,000. This loan is to be repaid by an inflow of $250 per month receipts from charges for use of the machine, or $3,000 a year. This information was summarized in a cash budget as follows:

	Year				Total
	1	2	3	4	
Cash receipts					
Pledges	$17,000				$17,000
Loan	8,000				8,000
Operations	3,000	$3,000	$3,000	$3,000	12,000
Total	28,000				37,000
Available cash	$28,000				$37,000

(Ignore for the moment the totals for years 2, 3, and 4.)

Exercise

The Research Institute at a major private university is in the process of accumulating funds for a new research project. They have received $300,000 in pledges that are to be received in equal quarterly payments over a 3-year period. In addition, they have borrowed an additional $520,000 from local banks; 50% of these funds are to be received immediately and the remaining 50% at the end of the first year. The administrator expects to receive $5,000 each month (for 36 months) in added miscellaneous funds from their contributors.

(a) How much in total funding should be received in the next 3 years? _____
(b) Prepare a cash receipts (inflows) budget for the four quarters of the first year's activities.

- - - - - - - - - - - - - - - -

(a) The institute should receive $1,000,000: $300,000 in pledges, $520,000 in loans, and $180,000 in miscellaneous contributions.

(b)

	First	Second	Third	Fourth	Total
Pledges	$ 25,000	$25,000	$25,000	$ 25,000	$100,000
Loans	260,000			260,000	520,000
Other funds	15,000	15,000	15,000	15,000	60,000
Total by quarter	$300,000	$40,000	$40,000	$300,000	$680,000

2. Loan Schedules. Before the cash outflows can be determined, you must know what the payments on any loan will be.

> **Loan schedules** incorporate a constant payment on principal
> with interest computed on the outstanding balance for a
> given time period. Each month the interest decreases.

Example. The banker for Community Hospital has suggested a note for the $8,000
loan with quarterly payments of $500 over a 4-year period at an *annual* interest rate of
8%. To determine if the $12,000 inflow from the services provided by the x-ray machine
are sufficient to repay the note, a loan schedule is developed:

Quarter	Principal	Principal Payment	Interest Payment
1	$8,000	$500	$160[a]
2	7,500	500	150
3	7,000	500	140
4	6,500	500	130
5	6,000	500	120
6	5,500	500	110
7	5,000	500	100
8	4,500	500	90
9	4,000	500	80
10	3,500	500	70
11	3,000	500	60
12	2,500	500	50
13	2,000	500	40
14	1,500	500	30
15	1,000	500	20
16	500	500	10

[a] $8,000 × 8% × ¼ year = $160.

In the first quarter, the initial balance of $8,000 remains outstanding for the first 3
months. Interest, at 8% annually, is $640 for a full year, or $160 ($640 × ¼ year) for one
quarter. By paying $500 on the principal, the balance due at the end of the first quarter
is reduced to $7,500. Interest in the second quarter is $150, and the schedule continues
in the same manner for each succeeding quarter.

Exercise

The Institute borrowed $520,000 to meet its expected requirements in a 10-year
program. They have agreed to retire the loan in 6 years. Payments on the principal will
be $20,000 per quarter with a final payment of $40,000 at the end of the sixth year.
Annual interest at 10% is computed on the balance outstanding at the beginning of each
quarter; the quarterly principal and interest are paid on the last day of each 3-month
period. Compute the interest that the Institute must pay for the first quarter.
_____ The second quarter. _____

First quarter: $520,000 × 10% × ¼ = $1,300.
Second quarter: $500,000 × 10% × ¼ = $1,250.

Note: The Institute paid $20,000 on the outstanding loan at the end of the first quarter.

3. Schedule of Cash Outflows

> After cash inflow is budgeted and a payment schedule is
> prepared for any loans anticipated, determine expected
> cash outflow or disbursements. **Cash disbursements** en-
> compass all cash payments for goods and services acquired
> from suppliers, employers, or any other entity, including
> reductions of debt and commitment of resources to long-
> term projects.

Example. Community Hospital can anticipate $2,000 payments on principal for the
first year in addition to interest expenses of $580, for a total outlay of $2,580. Each
year can be analyzed in the same way and put into the form of an outflow budget:

		Year			
	1	2	3	4	Total
Cash disbursements					
Equipment purchase	$25,000				$25,000
Payments—principal	2,000	$2,000	$2,000	$2,000	8,000
Payments—interest	580	420	260	100	1,360
Total disbursements	$27,580	$2,420	$2,260	$2,100	$34,360

Exercise
The Research Institute (exercise in frame 2) is now preparing a total cash disbursements
for its first year of activities. Develop a schedule of first-year requirements for payments
on the loan balance and interest due.

Quarter	Beginning Principal	Payment on Principal	Interest	Total Cash Outlay
1	$520,000	$20,000	$13,000	$ 33,000
2	500,000	20,000	12,500	32,500
3	480,000	20,000	12,000	32,000
4	460,000	20,000	11,500	31,500
		$80,000	$49,000	$129,000

4. Analyzing Data and Decision Making

> Compare expected cash inflow with expected cash outflow
> to determine if adequate financial resources are available
> for the plan under consideration.

Example. Once Community Hospital has budgeted expected cash outflow, its ability to meet this commitment can be assessed by looking at the budgeted cash inflow:

	Year			
	1	2	3	4
Beginning cash balance	—0—	$ 420	$1,000	$1,740
Plus cash receipts (frame 1)	$28,000	3,000	3,000	3,000
Available cash	28,000	3,420	4,000	4,740
Less cash disbursements (frame 3)	27,580	2,420	2,260	2,100
Ending cash balance	$ 420	$1,000	$1,740	$2,640

Notice that in the first year Community Hospital has $28,000 inflow and only $27,580 outflow for this particular project, leaving a beginning cash balance of $420 for the second year. The same analysis is performed for years 3 and 4, providing data to determine that the overall plan *is* sufficient to satisfy Community Hospital's financial needs.

Exercise

The Research Institute expects its operating costs to be $6,000 per month in the first year. The cash flow plan operates on the assumption that inflows from pledges and miscellaneous contributions (exercise in frame 1) will be sufficient to cover operations as well as the loan principal and interest obligations. Develop a cash flow budget to determine if inflows are sufficient to satisfy these demands during the first year.

- - - - - - - - - - - - -

Year 1: Cash inflows

Loan	$520,000
Pledges	25,000
Other contributions	15,000
Total	$560,000

Cash outflows

Operations	$ 18,000
Principal and interest	129,000
Total	$147,000

Excess (inflows over outflows)	$413,000

BUDGETING CASH RECEIPTS

Frequently, budgeting cash receipts involves predicting *when* payments will be made. For our more thorough discussion of budgeting cash receipts, a retail TV store's system will be analyzed.

The Roberts own and operate a small Television Sales and Service Center. Business has increased steadily during the past 2 years. Nevertheless, if working space can be expanded, the store's service effort can be improved considerably. Plans for remodeling are now being developed. The major question to be resolved, however, is whether the necessary cash will be available when construction begins in early July. A cash budget for the second quarter must be developed as a basis for these plans. Preliminary estimates indicate that approximately $3,000 in cash will be needed to complete the project. Below are selected account balances from the Center's balance sheet at March 31, 19XX.

Cash in bank		$2,200
Accounts receivable		
January sales	$ 300	
February sales	800	
March sales	2,600	

5. Estimating Amount and Type of Inflow

> Use historical data and projected income statements to esti-
> mate the amount of inflow and whether it will be cash or
> credit.

Example. Roberts TV developed the following information:

	Cash Sales	Credit Sales	Total Sales
Actual data			
January	$1,900	$3,000	$4,900
February	2,900	4,400	7,300
March	3,100	5,200	8,300
Estimated data			
April			$6,000[a]
May			$8,000[a]
June			$5,000[a]

[a] On the average 40% of the company's sales are
cash and the remaining 60% are on credit.

Using expected cash sales as their starting point, they started the cash budgeting process
by developing the following schedule:

Anticipated cash sales

April	40% X $6,000	=	$2,400
May	40% X $8,000	=	3,200
June	40% X $5,000	=	2,000

Estimated cash inflows from sales $7,600

Exercise

A small jewelry store has been operating for less than a year. Upon evaluating his sales
activities, the owner determined that cash sales represented only 40% of his total
revenues. If he expects to sell an average of $10,000 per month in merchandise during the
coming year, how much cash inflow should he receive during the coming year?

– – – – – – – – – – – – – –

$48,000   ($10,000 X 12 months X 40% cash sales).

6.   **Establishing Collection Patterns**

> Study past collection patterns to predict when credit sales
> will be paid. Develop a summary budgeting schedule in
> percentages of accounts receivable.

Example. The Roberts studied historical data and determined that the following
collection patterns were likely to occur:

> 50% of total credit sales are collected in the month of the sale.
> 30% of total credit sales are collected in the first month after the month of the sale.
> 10% of total credit sales are collected in the second month after the month of the
> sale.
> 10% of the total credit sales are collected in the third month after the month of the
> sale.

Notice that the Roberts anticipate no uncollectible accounts. They expect all credit sales
to be collected in 3 months. In developing their second-quarter budget, the Roberts
prepared a summary schedule in percentages:

Expected Collection Patterns

Credit Sales	April	May	June	Subsequent Months
April	50%	30%	10%	10%
May		50%	30%	20%
June			50%	50%

Exercise

The owner of the jewelry store next analyzed the patterns of his collections on
account. Of these receivables, 50% is collected in the month after the sale and the remaining 50% in the next succeeding month. Develop a schedule in percentage terms to reflect
these expected collection patterns for the first quarter.

Expected Collection Pattern

Month of Sale	January	February	March
January		50%	50%
February			50%
March			

Note: This schedule refers only to the credit sales, not to total sales.

7.   **Developing a Schedule of Expected Cash Inflows from Credit Sales**

> Convert the schedule of expected collection patterns to a schedule of expected cash inflows.

Example. The Roberts developed the following schedule for their company:

Expected Cash Inflows

| | Credit | Month of Collection | | | Outstanding |
Month of Sale	Sales (60%)	April	May	June	at June 30
April	$ 3,600	$1,800	$1,080	$ 360	$ 360
May	4,800	–0–	2,400	1,440	960
June	3,000	–0–	–0–	1,500	1,500
Total	$11,400	$1,800	$3,480	$3,300	$2,820

Exercise

The jewelry store's total sales for the first quarter are forecasted as follows: January, $8,000; February $10,000; and March, $12,000. Prepare a schedule of cash receipts from accounts receivable for the quarter from these data and the previous information on collection patterns.

- - - - - - - - - - - - - - -

| | Credit | Month of Collection | | |
Month of Sale	Sales	January	February	March
January	$4,800	—	$2,400	$2,400
February	$6,000	—	—	$3,000
March	$7,200	—	—	—

8. Developing a Schedule of Accounts Receivable Collections

> Use historical data to determine what amounts were out-
> standing at the close of the period and are expected to be
> collected in the upcoming period.

Example. Having projected cash inflows that should be received from second quarter sales, the Roberts turned their attention to collections from accounts that were out-standing at March 31, 19XX. They expected to collect these balances no later than June, as reflected in the following schedule of expected accounts receivable collections:

Month of Sale	Outstanding Balance	Collections April	May	June
January	$ 300	$ 300		
February	880	440	$440	
March	2,600	1,560	520	$520
Total	$3,780	$2,300	$965	$520

Collection of the outstanding balance from January represents only 10% of that month's sales. It is expected that the entire balance of $300 will be collected in April, the third month after the sale. Since the unpaid balance from February sales represents 20% of that month's sales, a portion ($440) is collected in April and the remaining $440 in May. Of the unpaid balance from March, 30% or $1,560 should be collected in April, the first month after the sale. Each of the remaining 2 months in the schedule includes planned receipts of 10%, or $520. Thus these accounts will be completely collected at the end of this quarter.

Exercise

The jewelry store's owner is discussing the June 30 financial statements with his banker. The accounts receivable balance at that date is $8,400. May total sales were $12,000 and June total sales were $8,000. Determine the months when the receivables will be collected by using information from the previous frames.

- - - - - - - - - - - - - - -

Month	Total Sales	Credit Sales	Collections May	Collections June	Collections July	Collections August
May	$12,000	$7,200	—	$3,600	$3,600	
June	8,000	4,800	—	—	2,400	$2,400
Accounts receivable on June 30 — $8,400			$3,600	$6,000	$2,400	

9. Establishing Cash Reserves and Analyzing Data

> Establish a minimum cash reserve — **desired ending balance** — and then combine anticipated inflow with anticipated outflow to determine if sufficient cash is available for a planned project.

Example. The Roberts estimate that cash outlays for operations will be approximately $5,000 per month. They also want to have at least $1,000 in the cash account at all times. To determine whether cash will be available to accomplish the July construction project, they prepared the following schedule from the data previously developed:

Month	Cash Sales	Collections on Account Current Month	Collections on Account Prior Months	Total
April	$2,400	$1,800	$2,300	$ 6,500
May	3,200	3,480	960	7,640
June	2,000	3,300	520	5,820
Total	$7,600	$8,580	$3,780	$19,960
Less: operating expenses (quarter)				15,000
Less: desired ending balance				1,000
Total cash available for project				$ 3,960

Since the project requires only $3,000, the estimated ending cash balance indicates that the Roberts will have sufficient funds to complete the project. Had the estimated ending cash balance indicated a shortage, the Roberts would have time to make other plans, such as increasing sales, obtaining a bank loan, or postponing the project. In any event, such needs can be carefully defined well before the fact. Herein lies the real value of cash budgeting and all other planning techniques.

Exercise
The jewelry store's cash balance is $5,000 at July 1, and the owner desires to maintain the balance at this level at all times. If July sales are $10,000 and operating expenses for that month require $9,000 in cash outlays, can the minimum cash balance be maintained? Use the cash receipts data from frame 8 in this solution.

Beginning cash balance		$ 5,000
Cash receipts		
July cash sales	$4,000	
Accounts receivable	6,000	10,000
Available cost		$15,000
Cash disbursements—operations		9,000
Projected ending cash balance		$ 6,000

Yes, the minimum balance can be maintained if results occur as they are projected.

BUDGETING CASH DISBURSEMENTS

Efforts required to develop a cash disbursements budget are similar to those for cash receipts budgets. First, identify types of outlays during each period and group them into common classifications; second, estimate the amounts of each expenditure; and finally, consider the requirements in terms of specific dates or time periods. Taken together, these elements comprise a cash disbursements budget.

The central component of a cash disbursements budget for business organizations usually revolves around its operating expenses, including personnel, selling, administrative, and occupancy expenses.

Travels & Tours, Inc., is a medium-sized travel agency, offering a useful practical situation for studying cash disbursements budgets. Agencies operate on a weekly-period basis because of airline reporting requirements. For this reason, cash budgets are prepared for each 4-week period, a total of 13 times each year. Jane Anderson, the owner/manager of Travels & Tours, Inc., is well aware of the need for effective cash control. Proceeds from air tickets sales are deposited into a separate account established for this purpose. The weekly air report serves as a basis for remitting funds to the appropriate air carrier, and the remaining funds are transferred to the operating account when needed for agency expenses. Generally, funds are transferred to this account at the beginning of each 4-week period to cover estimated cash outlays. The problem confronting Jane stems from her desire to invest excess cash (funds in excess of weekly requirements) in short-term certificates of deposit. The interest income is used to purchase additional publications for the agency library, an important priority from Jane's viewpoint. The cash disbursements budget is a key tool, therefore, because it allows her to estimate all financial requirements for at least 4 weeks and perhaps longer.

Although Travels & Tours' most important expenditure is its weekly payment to airlines, this is handled in a separate account. The following discussion refers to budgeted expenses in the agency's operating account.

Travel agencies incur four types of operating costs: personnel, selling, administrative, and occupancy expenses.

10.   Personnel Expenses. Personnel expenses include more than salaries and wages. They also include F.I.C.A. payments, unemployment taxes, and fringe benefits. In addition, some personnel expenses may be expressed in percentages, for example, a certain percentage of an employee's compensation may be budgeted as an administrative cost.

> **Personnel expenses** include all costs incurred to obtain employee services *other than* those specifically identified as administrative, a classification particularly important for nonmanufacturing companies.

Example. Travels & Tours, Inc., employs one part-time and two full-time sales counselors. Full-time employees receive $190 per week, paid biweekly. The part-time person is paid $3.50 per hour and works 20 hours per week. Jane, the owner/manager, earns $250 per week in addition to a profit-sharing bonus at the end of the year. Of this salary, 60% is considered a selling expense; the remaining 40% is administrative. Payroll taxes are remitted at the end of each 4-week period and amount to 10% of salaries and wages. An additional 15% of the salaries and wages budget is paid into a fringe benefit fund each 4 weeks. The following schedule summarizes the budgeting of personnel expenses for Travels & Tours:

Counselor A (full-time)	$190 × 4 weeks	$ 760
Counselor B (full-time)	$190 × 4 weeks	760
Counselor C (part-time)	$ 70 × 4 weeks	280
Owner/manager (60% × $250)	$150 × 4 weeks	600
Total wages and salaries		2,400
Payroll taxes (10% × $2,400)		240
Fringe benefit fund (15% × $2,400)		360
Total personnel expenses		$3,000

Exercise

The jewelry store employs two employees. One full-time salesperson is paid $560 per month. A part-time employee works 80 hours per month at a rate of $3 per hour. Payroll taxes and fringe benefits are estimated at 25% of the total monthly payroll. How much in personnel expenses should be budgeted for the coming month?

Personnel	Costs/Month
Full-time employee	$ 560
Part-time employee	240
Total wages	$ 800
Other payroll costs	200
Total personnel costs	$1,000

11. Selling Expenses

> **Selling expenses** include all costs relating to activities oriented to supporting selling efforts, for example, incentive commission plans, advertising, and promotion.

Example. Travels & Tours' advertising and sales promotion budget is established at the beginning of each year. During the coming year $400 is committed for payment at the beginning of each 4-week period. A fund of $100 per week is established to facilitate other sales promotion activities. Automobile and telephone expenses each average $50 per week, paid at the end of each period. These data are summarized in the agency's selling expenses budget as follows:

Selling Expenses	Each 4-Week Period
Advertising and sales promotion	$ 400
Other promotional activities	400
Telephone expenses	200
Automobile expenses	200
Total selling expenses	$1,200

Exercise

The jewelry store's manager estimates all support expenses in terms of personnel costs. He feels that the store should spend at least 40% of the amount paid for personnel on advertising, promotion, and related support activities. Of these expenditures, advertising and promotion represent one-half; the other half is divided evenly between telephone and other miscellaneous selling costs. Prepare a selling expense budget from this information.

- - - - - - - - - - - - - -

The total selling expense budget should be $400 (40% × $1,000 in personnel costs).

	Budgeted Expenses
Advertising and promotion (50%)	$200
Telephone (25%)	100
Other selling expenses	100
	$400

12. Administrative Expenses

> **Administrative expenses** include all costs associated with compensating and supporting personnel who are involved in managing the activities of an organization or unit as well as costs associated with discretionary decisions to obtain specialized services such as legal counseling.

Example. Travels & Tours' administrative expenses include a salary of $150 per week for a receptionist/bookkeeper as well as 40% of the owner/manager's salary. Equipment rental contracts (typewriters, etc.) require outlays of $1,950 per year, paid in equal installments at the beginning of each 4-week period. Office supplies average $25 per week. These data serve as the basis for preparing a schedule of the agency's administraive expense budget:

Administrative Expenses	Each 4-Week Period
Receptionist/bookkeeper	$ 600
Owner/manager salary (40% × $250)	400
Payroll taxes (10%)	100
Fringe benefits (15%)	150
Equipment rental	150
Office supplies	100
Total administrative expenses	$1,500

Exercise

The owner of the jewelry store draws an administrative salary of $1,000 per month. Secretarial and bookkeeping functions cost this company an additional $250 per month. Supplies and other general expenses approximate $100 per month. Prepare a budget for these administrative expenses. Remember that payroll taxes and fringes represent 25% of total salaries.

- - - - - - - - - - - - - - - -

Administrative Expenses	Budgeted Expenses
Owners' salaries (including fringes)	$1,250
Secretarial and bookkeeping services	250
Other general expenses	100
Budgeted monthly expenses	$1,600

13. Occupancy Expenses. The final category of costs, occupancy expenses, are easily budgeted because they are relatively fixed in nature.

> **Occupancy expenses** are costs associated with providing and maintaining a facility such as a plant or office building for operations, including rent, utilities, insurance, maintenance, and other related expenses.

Example. The rental cost for Travels & Tours' location is $5,200 per year, or $400 each operating period. Utilities average $50 per week, paid at the end of each 4 weeks. A contingency fund of $25 is set aside for necessary repairs and maintenance. The agency occupancy expense budget is developed in the following format:

Occupancy Expenses	4-Week Period
Rental	$400
Utilities	200
Repairs and maintenance	100
Total occupancy expenses	$700

Exercise

The jewelry store incurs a monthly rental cost of $600. Utilities cost $200 per month, repairs and maintenance $200 per month. How much in annual occupancy costs must be budgeted for this store's operations? _____

- - - - - - - - - - - - - -

$12,000 in annual costs ($1,000 per month).

14.   Decision Making.   The central focus of cash budgeting is directed at estimating the timing and amounts of cash inflows and outflows and to then relate these data to planning decisions.

> Integrate cash inflow and outflow data into an understand-
> able form for decision making.

Example.   Travels & Tours' owner/manager wants to invest excess funds in short-term securities. By integrating cash inflow and outflow data, she can readily determine the amount available for short-term investment purposes:

Beginning cash balance		$ 4,000
Plus: expected cash receipts		6,000
Available cash		$10,000
Less: expected cash disbursements		
Personnel	$3,000	
Selling	1,200	
Administration	1,500	
Occupancy	700	
Total disbursements		6,400
Cash balance (period end)		$ 3,600
Less: desired cash balance		2,000
Available for short-term investment		$ 1,600

Exercise

The jewelry store owner is preparing a quarterly cash flow analysis. His beginning cash balance is $6,000. Expected receipts for the coming quarter (sales and collections of receivables) total $15,000. In addition to the operating expenses budgeted in the preceding frames—personnel, selling, administrative, and occupancy—the owner must pay at least $1,000 per month in principal and interest on an outstanding loan. What is the maximum amount that he can pay on the loan and still retain a $5,000 cash balance at the end of the quarter?

- - - - - - - - - - - - - -

Quarterly Budget
of Cash Flows

Beginning cash balance		$ 6,000
Expected cash receipts		15,000
Total available cash		$21,000
Budgeted cash disbursements		
Personnel	$3,000	
Selling	1,200	
Administrative	4,800	
Occupancy	3,000	12,000
Cash available for use		$ 9,000
Less minimum desired cash balance		5,000
Cash available for loan payment		$ 4,000

15. A Comprehensive Cash Budget. The mechanics of cash budgeting are simple. However, do not underestimate the potential power of this tool. This type of advance planning is critical to business success. Frequent comparisons of actual cash inflows and outflows to those in the budget are equally important. In this way you become immediately aware of significant changes that may have occurred and can resolve problems in a timely manner.

Planning for cash requirements requires an evaluation of a company's working-capital position.

Working capital is the difference between an organization's current assets and current liabilities; this measure serves as an indication of available financial resources at a given date that can be used in operations.

Example

Thoroughbred Computer Services, Inc.
Balance Sheet
December 31, 19XX

Current assets	$80,000	Current liabilities	$ 40,000
Long-term assets	160,000	Long-term liabilities	100,000
		Equity	100,000
Total assets	$240,000	Total liabilities and equity	$240,000

Thoroughbred Computer Services has $40,000 in working capital at this year-end date. Historical data were used to obtain the figures for this balance sheet. Data from cash budgeting assist in developing this measure because cash represents a major portion of most companies' working-capital position.

Exercise

The following exercise integrates all the components of cash budgeting. Read the description of the manufacturing company that serves as the basis of study for the exercise and then complete the steps requested.

The DLM Company is a small manufacturing company that specializes in producing handcrafted picture frames. A significant business opportunity has been presented to DLM's management; thus both future cash flows and working-capital requirements are now primary concerns. A regional department store chain is interested in contracting to purchase picture frames on a monthly basis to support its operations in a six-state region. The data below reflect DLM's estimated working-capital position of $20,000* at the date when the new contract is to become effective. Both accounts receivable and inventory data reflect operations during the last week of the current year. Relevant collections, usage of inventory, and payments to suppliers will occur during the first weeks of the next year.

DLM Manufacturing Company
Working-Capital Position

Current Assets		Current Liabilities	
Cash	$18,000	Accounts payable	$1,000
Accounts receivable	3,000	Notes payable	—0—
Inventory	—0—	Other liabilities	—0—
Prepaid expenses	—0—		
Total	$21,000		$1,000

Other elements in the contract will also have impact on DLM's cash and working-capital position. The company is required to maintain an inventory of finished goods (picture frames ready for delivery) equal to 50% of the next month's sales volume. Sales will be billed on the 15th and 30th of each month. Thus 50% of revenues are collected in

*Current assets of $21,000 less current liabilities of $1,000.

the month of sale and the remainder in the succeeding month. Purchases of raw materials (wood for the frames) are made in the month prior to production. Similarly, 50% of these costs are paid in cash at the time of purchase. The remaining payment is made in the next month. All other costs are processed as immediate cash disbursements. Specifically, these include the rental of space and other related occupancy expenses, a total of $1,400 per month. Details of the sales contract indicate that the department store chain will purchase the following quantities of picture frames each month.

Style	Monthly Volume (Units)	Sales Price
A (ornamental)	200	$15
B (standard)	600	10
C (miniature)	1,000	5

DLM's management has decided to produce 50% of a month's supply prior to accepting the contract. In this way, product costs can be estimated beforehand, and the contractual requirement for finished goods inventory (50% of a month's sales) can be satisfied. These products could be sold to other customers if this contract is rejected.

Production costs have been developed for each style of frame:

Style	Materials	Labor	Overhead	Total
A	$5	$3	$2	$10
B	3	2	1	6
C	1	1	1	3

In addition, a prepayment on the machine leased to produce the frames is required in the amount of $900. The DLM Company is concerned at the onset with determining the amounts of funds that must be committed and whether their working capital is sufficient to undertake this contract. Therefore, they analyze each of the accounts included in working capital.

15A

1. The first step is to determine the initial investment in the *finished goods inventory*. Develop a schedule reflecting the finished goods inventory (use a separate sheet of paper). What is the total amount of the investment required for this purpose? _____

2. Next determine the initial investment in the *raw materials inventory*. Develop a schedule for this investment. What is the total amount of investment required? _____

3. What other expenses will be incurred before any revenues are generated from the contract? _____

4. Taking these data together, DLM is required to make an initial outlay of _____ .

5. If the contract is accepted, management must be willing to commit these resources. Since all such expenditures require cash outlays, the net-working-capital position would not be affected. Look at the original working-capital position on page 102 and then revise this schedule to reflect the changes required by accepting the contract.

Current Assets		Current Liabilities	
Cash	_____	Accounts payable	_____
Accounts receivable	_____	Notes payable	_____
Inventories			
Finished goods	_____		
Raw materials	_____		
Prepaids	_____		
Total	_____	Total	_____

- - - - - - - - - - - - - -

1. $4,300.

Finished Goods Investment

Style	Desired Inventory[a]	Product Costs	Total Valuation
A	100	$10	$1,000
B	300	6	1,800
C	500	3	1,500
	Total costs		$4,300

[a]50% of monthly sales volume.

2. $3,800.

Raw Materials Investment

Style	Sales Volume (First Month)	Materials Costs	Total Costs
A	200	$5	$1,000
B	600	3	1,800
C	1,000	1	1,000
	Initial investment		$3,800

3. $900 prepayment on the leased machine.

4. $9,000.

5.

Current Assets			Current Liabilities	
Cash	$ 9,000		Accounts payable	$1,000
Accounts receivable	3,000		Notes payable	−0−
Inventories				
Finished goods	4,300			
Raw materials	3,800			
Prepaid expenses	900			
Total	$21,000		Total	$1,000

Note: Net working capital remains at $20,000 because cash was reduced by $9,000 and then current assets increased in total by the same amount.

15B. The next step is to prepare a cash inflow budget. The new contract promises sales of a constant volume each month, simplifying planning greatly. Thus DLM's management can obtain a useful estimate of future cash flows by reviewing probable results for the first quarter. As you analyze the cash receipts, recall that only 50% of the sales will be collected in the month of sale.

1. First, develop a schedule of total monthly revenues. (Use your own paper for this.) What are the total anticipated revenues for the month? _____
2. Using your schedule of total monthly revenues as a basis, prepare a cash receipts budget, showing expected collecting from accounts for the first quarter. What are the anticipated total cash receipts during the first quarter? _____

- - - - - - - - - - - - - - -

1. $14,000.

Style	Sales Volume	Sales Price	Total Revenues
A	200	$15	$ 3,000
B	600	$10	6,000
C	1,000	$ 5	5,000
Total revenues			$14,000

2. $35,000.

Expected Collections from Accounts

	January	February	March	Total
Total revenues	$14,000	$14,000	$14,000	$42,000
Cash collections				
January (50% sales)	7,000			7,000
February (50% Jan. sales)		7,000		7,000
(50% Feb. sales)		7,000		7,000
March (50% Feb. sales)			7,000	7,000
(50% Mar. sales)			7,000	7,000
Total cash receipts	$ 7,000	$14,000	$14,000	$35,000

In developing the overall cash budget, remember that the beginning accounts receivable balance of $3,000 will be collected in early January. At the end of the quarter, in turn, the accounts receivable balance consists of 50% of March sales, or $7,000.

15C. Again using the contractual sales volume as a basis, determine cash disbursements.

1. Develop a schedule for the quarter for disbursements for materials. What is the total required for materials for the quarter? _____
2. Develop a schedule for direct labor costs for 1 month. What is the monthly cash disbursement for labor? _____
3. Develop a similar schedule for monthly overhead. What is the total? _____
4. Now, combine the cash disbursements data into a comprehensive schedule for total production costs for the quarter. What will the total cash outflow during the quarter be? _____

- - - - - - - - - - - - - -

1. $11,400.

Materials Purchases: Cash Requirements

	January	February	March
January production			
50% Jan. requirements	$1,900		
50% Feb. requirements	1,900		
February production			
50% Feb. requirements		$1,900	
50% Mar. requirements		1,900	
March production			
50% Mar. requirements			$1,900
50% Apr. requirements			$1,900
Total	$3,800	$3,800	$3,800

As was the case in the earlier computations, the budget must reflect the fact that accounts payable at the beginning of the period, $1,000, will require a cash outlay in early January. Likewise, 50% of March materials purchases, $1,900, is the accounts payable balance at the end of the quarter.

2. $2,800.

Direct Labor

Style	Units Produced	Labor Cost per Unit	Total Labor Costs
A	200	$3	$ 600
B	600	2	1,200
C	1,000	1	1,000
Total direct labor			$2,800

3. $2,000.

Overhead

Style	Units Produced	Labor Cost per Unit	Total Labor Costs
A	200	$2	$ 400
B	600	1	600
C	1,000	1	1,000
Total overhead			$2,000

4. $30,000.

Total Costs

	January	February	March	Total
Raw materials	$ 3,800	$ 3,800	$ 3,800	$11,400
Direct labor	2,800	2,800	2,800	8,400
Overhead	2,000	2,000	2,000	6,000
Occupancy costs	1,400	1,400	1,400	4,200
Total disbursements	$10,000	$10,000	$10,000	$30,000

15D. The final step in the cash budgeting process is to combine all relevant cash receipts and disbursements data so they can be used in making decisions. The following schedule incorporates all cash flow data related to acceptance of the proposed contract. Using your previous calculations, complete this schedule:

DLM Manufacturing Company
Cash Budget
First Quarter, 19XX

	January	February	March
Beginning cash balance	$18,000	_____[a]	_____
Cash receipts			
Cash sales	_____	_____	_____
Collections (A/R)	_____	_____	_____
Total	_____	_____	_____
Available cash	_____	_____	_____
Cash disbursements			
Current month	_____	_____	_____
Prior month (A/P)	_____	_____	_____
Total	_____	_____	_____
Ending cash balance	_____[a]	_____	_____

[a] The beginning balance for February is the same as January's ending balance.

	January	February	March
Beginning cash balance	$18,000	$ 8,000	$12,000
Cash receipts			
Cash sales	7,000	7,000	7,000
Collections	3,000	7,000	7,000
Total	10,000	14,000	14,000
Available cash	$28,000	$22,000	$24,000
Cash disbursements			
Current month	10,000	10,000	10,000
Prior month	1,000	–0–	–0–
Initial investment	9,000	–0–	–0–
Total disbursements	$20,000	$10,000	$15,000
Ending cash balance	$ 8,000	$12,000	$14,000

15E. Now evaluate the impact of the first quarter's cash flows on the company's working-capital position. Use the ending cash balance you determined in the preceding schedule. Use the other schedules as appropriate. Keep in mind that raw materials inventory relates directly to next month's sales requirements, and that finished goods must equal 50% of these sales estimates.

DLM Manufacturing Company
Working Capital Position
March 31, 19XX

Current Assets		Current Liabilities	
Cash	$ _____	Accounts payable	$ _____
Accounts receivable	_____	Notes payable	_____
Inventory		Other liabilities	_____
Raw materials	_____		
Finished goods	_____		
Prepaid expenses	_____		
Total current assets	_____	Total current liabilities	_____

Current Assets		Current Liabilities	
Cash	$14,000	Accounts payable	$1,900
Accounts receivable	7,000	Notes payable	–0–
Inventory		Other liabilities	–0–
Raw materials	3,800		
Finished goods	4,300		
Prepaid expenses	900		
Total current assets	$30,000	Total current liabilities	$1,900

This information serves effectively as the basis for DLM management's decision making. Most important, the data are developed *before* a commitment to the contract is made. If cash flows are not sufficient to justify accepting the contract, the responsible executive can attempt to negotiate more favorable terms. At minimum, however, potential future problems are avoided by evaluating data before major decisions are reached.

Before taking the Self-Test that follows, review the questions posed at the beginning of the chapter. If you are unsure of any answers, reread the appropriate pages.

CHAPTER 3 SELF-TEST

1. Matching – Terminology/Concepts

Match the following terms to the definitions.

1. Administrative expenses	6. Depreciation
2. Cash budgeting	7. Occupancy expenses
3. Cash disbursements	8. Personnel expenses
4. Cash receipts	9. Selling expenses
5. Capital expenditures	10. Working capital

_____ (a) All inflows of cash into a company for goods and services provided to customers as well as collections on account, amounts obtained from investors, or borrowings.

_____ (b) The difference between an organization's current assets and current liabilities.

_____ (c) Techniques designed to focus on projecting cash inflows and cash outflows for specified future periods of time.

_____ (d) Cash outlays required to acquire long-term resources or to complete related projects.

_____ (e) Encompasses all cash payments for goods and services acquired from suppliers, employees, or any other entity, as well as reductions of debt and commitments of resources to long-term projects.

2. Accounts Receivable Collections

(a) Company X is estimating its cash receipts for the next quarter. Significant proportions of these inflows are obtained from collections of accounts receivable. On the average, 60% of sales on credit are collected in the month of sale; 25% are collected in the second month, and 10% are collected in the third month. Carried further, approximately 75% of this company's sales are made on credit. The following sales projections have been developed:

January	$100,000
February	120,000
March	160,000

Collections from prior sales are expected to be $30,000 per month in the first quarter. Using these data, develop projections of cash receipts for each month in the first quarter of the coming year.

(b) Using the preceding data and assuming that all receivables from prior-year credit sales have been collected or written off, what is the company's accounts receivable balance at March 31?

3. Accounts Payable Analysis

(a) This company purchases all its raw materials on credit. In general, 50% of the purchases result in cash disbursements in the month of purchase, with the remaining 50% remitted the next month. Planned purchases for the first quarter of the coming year are as follows:

January	$ 70,000
February	110,000
March	120,000

The accounts payable balance for purchased raw materials at the end of the preceding year was $50,000. What is the total amount of cash disbursements for purchase that should be expected for the company in the first quarter?

(b) What is the company's expected balance in accounts payable at March 31 for materials purchased during the first quarter of the coming year? (2 points)

4. Cash Budgeting

The company is preparing a cash budget for one of its divisions for the coming month of January. Activities in this organizational unit are restricted to the production and sale of one product line. Data are provided to assist in developing this month's cash budget.

Cash sales	$120,000
Credit sales	80,000
Raw materials purchases	90,000
Labor costs	60,000
Overhead costs	30,000
Other cash expenses	10,000
Beginning cash balance	20,000
Accounts receivable—December sales	40,000
—November sales	30,000
Accounts payable beginning balance	100,000
Loans payable (including interest)	
due this month	11,000

Use the following information to develop a cash budget. Sales on credit are generally collected over a 3-month period: 60% in the month of sale and 20% in each of the two succeeding months. Raw materials are always purchased on credit with 50% of the cost paid in the month of purchase; 50% in the succeeding month. Included in overhead costs above is a $5,000 monthly charge for depreciation. Finally, management wants to keep a minimum of $15,000 in its cash account. Funds are borrowed in multiples of $1,000 to ensure that the minimum balance is maintained. These loans are repaid in the next month.

(a) Estimate the company's cash receipts for the coming month.

(b) Estimate the company's cash disbursements for the coming month.

(c) Prepare a complete schedule of cash receipts to determine the amount that must be borrowed, if any, to satisfy the company's minimum-cash-balance policy. Use your data from parts (a) and (b).

ANSWERS

1. Matching – Terminology/Concepts

(a) 4 (frame 1, 1 pt)   (b) 10 (frame 1, 1 pt)   (c) 2 (frame 1, 1 pt)
(d) 5 (frame 10, 1 pt)   (e)   3 (frame 3, 1 pt)

2. Accounts Receivable Collection [frames 6-8 and 15, 12 pts total (a, 8 pts; b, 4 pts)]

(a)

	January	February	March
Credit sales	$75,000	$ 90,000	$120,000
Prior-year collections	$30,000	$ 30,000	$ 30,000
Collections – January sales	45,000	22,500	7,500
– February sales		54,000	27,000
– March sales			72,000
Total cash receipts	$75,000	$106,500	$136,500

(b)

	Receivable Balance
January sales	$ –0–
February sales	9,000
March sales	48,000
Balance	$57,000

3. Accounts Payable Analysis [frames 10-15, 8 pts total (a, 6 pts; b, 2 pts)]

(a)

Cash Disbursements	January	February	March
Accounts payable balance	$50,000		
January purchases	35,000	$35,000	
February purchases		55,000	$ 55,000
March purchases			$ 60,000
Total cash disbursements	$85,000	$90,000	$115,000

(b) $60,000 (50% × $120,000 – March purchases).

4. Cash Budgeting [frames 1-5 and 15, 15 pts total (a and b, 6 pts each; c, 3 pts)]

(a)
Cash sales	$120,000
Collections of credit	
Sales – January sales	48,000
– December sales	20,000
– November sales	30,000
Total cash receipts	$218,000

The $30,000 in accounts receivable from November will be collected in January. Since $40,000 in accounts receivable is from December sales, the collections will be spread equally over the two succeeding months, January and February.

(b) Raw materials purchases $ 45,000 (50% of current month's purchases)

(b)		
Raw materials purchases	$ 45,000	(50% of current month's purchases)
Labor costs	60,000	
Overhead (less depreciation)	25,000	
Other cash expenses	10,000	
Accounts payable	100,000	
	$240,000	
Plus: Notes payable due	11,000	
Total cash disbursements	$251,000	

(c)	
Beginning cash balance	$ 20,000
Plus: Cash receipts (4a)	218,000
Cash available	$238,000
Less: Cash disbursements (4b)	251,000
Cash deficit	$ 13,000
Minimum balance requirement	15,000
Required borrowing	$ 28,000

Total possible points: 45. You should have scored at least 36.

SECTION TWO

The Cost Accounting Framework: A Basis for Control

The use of management accounting in various dimensions of planning was discussed in Section One. Plans and their corresponding budgetary guidelines are meaningless, however, unless you can use them to assess and control an organization's progress.

> **Cost accounting** is the process that traces costs directly to projects, jobs, or units of product.

Section Two focuses on procedures for tracing cost data to factors influencing achievement of goals and evaluating progress. The foundation for cost accounting is *cost traceability*. Specifically, traceability means assigning selected operating costs to units in production. Production costs are "attached" to units as the various production steps are accomplished. Included in these costs are manufacturing expenditures such as materials, labor, and overhead.

First, attention is directed to *job-order cost accounting systems*, where costs are traced to individualized customer orders (Chapter 4). Next, costs incurred in *process costing systems* are discussed. Here costs are traced to specialized departments and then to basically similar products, with each unit considered in terms of its average production cost (Chapter 5). Finally, *standard costing* is analyzed. Standard costing systems compare actual costs incurred to those that were predetermined as appropriate for the production process involved. Many consider standard costing to be the most effective of management approaches to controlling operating costs (Chapter 6).

CHAPTER 4

Cost Accounting: A Job-Order Approach

Can you . . .

- Identify prime costs and overhead costs for specific jobs and record them properly in the accounting system?
- State what documentation is required for specific costs incurred?
- Predetermine an overhead rate and enter it properly in the accounting records?
- Compare overhead incurred with overhead applied and evaluate the effects of differences between the two measures?
- Trace costs using a T-account model?
- Demonstrate the impact of costs on formal financial statements?

Job-order costing traces production expenditures directly to specific projects or customer orders as a basis for management planning and control decisions.

Job-order costing focuses on prime costs and indirect overhead costs. *Prime costs* are the combined expenditures for direct materials and direct labor. As you recall, *direct materials costs* are all costs associated with materials used to produce goods or services. These expenditures are easily traced to output. Similarly, *direct labor costs* are all costs associated with personnel specifically involved in the production process. These expenditures are also easily traced to units of output. *Indirect overhead costs* are those expenditures other than direct materials and direct labor that are incurred in producing units of output.

These costs are entered into the accounting system and must be carefully documented. Their impact upon the company's financial position (balance sheet) and performance (income statement) must also be analyzed and evaluated.

RECORDING AND DOCUMENTING COSTS

Job-order costing systems trace expenditure flows in producing specialized items. Since the outputs from these systems are tailored to predetermined specifications, procedures for costing are often unique. Materials may be transferred from one department to another or purchased from outside sources; labor may be existing personnel or outside consultants. Each type of expense requires accurate recording in the accounting system and accompanying documentation.

As an illustrative case, consider the situation of a company involved in completing one particular job.

Custom Homes, Inc., although having been in business for many years, has recently accepted a contract to develop a contemporary, solar energy home. Because of the experimental nature of this endeavor, the president requested that specific records be used to measure the total costs of the project. All relevant expenditures were to be assigned to job 1. The project was expected to take 6 months. Although some of the basic raw materials could be obtained from Custom's general inventory, most items were specialized and had to be purchased under separate contract. Similarly, the job required substantial amounts of highly skilled labor, the services of an innovative superintendent, and the use of specialized construction equipment in certain instances. Taken together, the need for a flexible and well-designed job-order costing system was apparent to the president of Custom Homes, Inc.

The job progressed according to schedule through its first 4 months. At this point, the president was required to present a progress report to the board of directors regarding the experimental solar project. The following data were developed:

Cost Classifications	April	May	June	July	Total
General raw materials	$ 4,000	$ 6,000	$ 4,000	$ 8,000	$22,000
Specialized raw materials	2,000	4,000	1,000	5,000	12,000
General labor	3,000	3,000	4,000	6,000	16,000
Contract labor	—	—	2,000	5,000	7,000
Superintendent salary	1,000	1,000	2,000	2,000	6,000
Rental (specialized equipment)	—	1,000	2,000	—	3,000
Miscellaneous costs	1,000	1,000	1,000	1,000	4,000
Total	$11,000	$16,000	$16,000	$27,000	$70,000

Original cost estimates for the total contract were $80,000. Expenditures to date of $70,000 seemed reasonable because costs for the next 2 months should approximate only $10,000. The president was pleased with the profitability prospects for this job because the contract price was $100,000.

1.　Materials Transferred from Inventory.　Often, materials needed for a particular job are already on hand and simply need to be transferred from existing inventory. When this is done, however, you must also assure that the cost of the materials is transferred to the specific project for which they were used.

> **To record materials transferred from inventory:**
> - Enter a debit to show an increase in costs associated with the specific job.
> - Enter a credit to show a decrease in the amount of general inventory available.

Example. Custom Homes used general raw materials from existing inventory for use in job 1 — the experimental solar project. In April $4,000 worth of general raw materials were transferred and used, so the following entries were made:

	Debit	Credit
Job 1 — direct materials	$4,000	
Raw materials inventory		$4,000

This entry reflects a transfer of raw materials in the amount of $4,000 from Custom's general raw materials inventory to job 1 in progress. The debit reflects an increase in costs associated with completing job 1, and the corresponding credit reflects a decrease in the amount of general inventory available for future use.

Exercise. Make the appropriate entry for transfer of materials in July.

- - - - - - - - - - - - - - -

	Debit	Credit
Job 1 — direct materials	$8,000	
Raw materials inventory		$8,000

2. Materials Purchased. When materials are purchased, the costs are reflected either as an increase in accounts payable, if the materials are purchased on credit, or as a decrease in cash (assets), if the materials are paid for on delivery.

> **To record materials purchased for a specific job:**
> - Enter a debit to show an increase in costs associated with the job.
> - Enter a credit to show a decrease in cash if paid for immediately.
> - *Or*, enter a credit to show an increase in the accounts payable liability account if items are purchased on credit.

Example. Custom Homes purchased specialized materials separately from a supplier. If the purchase was on credit, the entry would be:

	Debit	Credit
Job 1 – specialized materials	$2,000	
Accounts payable – supplier A		$2,000

The debit reflects an increase of $2,000 in the jobs-in-progress inventory account. The credit entry reflects an increase in the accounts payable liability account. If the materials had been paid for upon delivery rather than charged, the entry would be:

	Debit	Credit
Job 1 – specialized materials	$2,000	
Cash		$2,000

In this entry the credit reflects a *decrease* in cash assets.

Exercise

Assume that the $4,000 in specialized raw materials was purchased on credit from supplier B in May and that the $1,000 of specialized raw materials was bought from supplier C and paid for in June. Make the appropriate entries:

- - - - - - - - - - - - - - - -

	Debit	Credit
Job 1 – specialized materials (May)	$4,000	
Accounts payable – supplier B		$4,000
Job 1 – specialized materials (June)	$1,000	
Cash		$1,000

3. Documenting Costs Incurred for Materials. Formal documentation is the basis for all effective cost accounting systems. Only in this way can cost flows be traced from their incurrence to the job or unit under consideration.

> **Materials requisition forms** authorize transfer of materials in-house.
>
> **Purchase orders** authorize purchase of materials.
>
> **Receiving slips** indicate that purchased materials have been received.

Examples

No. _____			
Materials Requisition			
Date _____			
Project No. _____			
Type of Project _____			
Authorized by _____			
Quantity	Description	Unit Cost	Total Cost
	Invoice Total		

No. _____

Purchase Order

Date _____

Supplier _____

_____

_____

Estimated Delivery _____

Date Needed _____

Authorized by _____

Program Number _____

Quantity	Description	Unit Cost	Total

Purchases Total

No. _____

Date _____

Materials Receiving Slip

Responsible Person _____

Supplier _____

Description	Date Received	Quantity	Date Tested	Results of Tests

Exercise

1. What form would Custom Homes use to obtain the specialized raw materials required for job 1? _____
2. What form would it use to obtain the general raw materials required? _____
3. For which materials would a receiving slip be completed when the materials were obtained? _____

- - - - - - - - - - - - - -

1. Purchase order.
2. Materials requisition.
3. Specialized (purchased) materials.

4.   Direct General Labor Costs.   Direct labor costs are expenditures paid to personnel involved directly in completing a specific job. The term *direct* identifies costs specifically traceable to a segment of activity within an organization. Cost data in this category include actual wages, fringe benefits costs, and the employer's portion of payroll taxes (F.I.C.A., unemployment taxes, etc.). In some systems separate entries are required to record these items.

> **To record direct general labor costs:**
> - Enter a debit to show an increase in costs associated with a specific job.
> - Enter a credit to show an increase in the accrued payroll —general labor liability.

Example.   In April, Custom Homes, Inc., incurred costs of $3,000 in general labor on job 1. These costs would be recorded as follows:

	Debit	Credit
Job 1 in progress	$3,000	
Accrued payroll—general labor		$3,000

The debit reflects an increase in costs accumulated for job 1. The credit reflects the liability incurred for general labor costs on this job.

Exercise

Make the appropriate entry for general labor costs in July on job 1.

- - - - - - - - - - - - -

	Debit	Credit
Job 1 in progress	$6,000	
Accrued payroll—general labor		$6,000

5.   Direct Contract Labor Costs. As with materials, sometimes a company must go outside its own organization to obtain the services of specialized personnel. Expenses incurred for contracted labor are recorded like outside purchases, with the credit dependent on whether cash is paid immediately or the job is on a periodic billing basis.

To record direct contract labor costs:
- Enter a debit to show an increase in costs associated with a specific job.
- Enter a credit to show either a decrease in cash or an increase in the accounts payable liability account.

Example. In June, Custom Homes incurred $2,000 expenses in contract labor for job 1. If they paid cash for these services, the costs incurred would be recorded as follows:

	Debit	Credit
Job 1 in progress	$2,000	
Cash		$2,000

The credit entry reflects a *decrease* in cash assets. Had the contractor billed Custom Homes for the services, the credit would have been to accounts payable.

Exercise

In July Custom Homes incurred $6,000 in contract labor. Assume that these services were billed. Record the appropriate entry for this expense.

Does the credit entry reflect an increase or decrease in the account involved?

_____

_ _ _ _ _ _ _ _ _ _ _ _ _ _ _

	Debit	Credit
Job 1 in progress	$6,000	
Accounts payable		$6,000

The debit is an increase in an inventory account for job costs incurred; the credit entry reflects an increase in the accounts payable liability.

6.   Documenting Labor Costs. Again, documents must support the specific costs incurred for labor.

Job time tickets are used to record hours worked and rate.

Personnel records are used to record payroll rates and tax information.

Invoices submitted by the contractor are used to record specialized contract labor.

Examples

Week Ended _____

Job Time Ticket

Employee Name _____

Employee No. _____ Department _____

Description of Work Performed _____

_____

Job Number	Hours Worked	Rate	Total Cost

Personnel Record

Employee Name _____ Date Hired _____

Employee's Number _____ Department _____

Current Job Classification _____ Wage (Salary) _____

Performance Information

Date	Job Description	Pay Rate	Annual Performance Rating	Recommended for Promotion

---

Contract Labor Invoice

Contract No. _____   Date _____

Project No. _____

Type of Project _____

Authorized by _____

Date   Hours Worked

Total Hours _____

The subcontractor's invoice is signed by the superintendent responsible for the job after the work is successfully completed.

Exercise

1. What two forms would contain information related to general labor costs incurred by Custom Homes on job 1? _____

2. What form would be required for the contract labor used on job 1? _____

_____

– – – – – – – – – – – – – – – –

1. Job time tickets for general labor hours worked and personnel records for payroll rates and related tax data would be needed for general labor costs.
2. A subcontractor's invoice signed by the superintendent responsible for the job would be needed to support expenditures for specialized contract labor.

7.   Overhead Costs. In addition to direct costs, most jobs incur indirect overhead costs, all expenditures not directly traceable to a particular job. Such costs often include administrative salaries, equipment rental, and other miscellaneous costs. In practice, these costs would have been charged initially to other expense accounts, such as the administrative salaries account, an equipment rental account, or a general expense account.

> **To record indirect overhead costs:**
> - Enter a debit to reflect an increase in costs associated with the specific job.
> - Enter a credit to reflect a reduction in the specific account initially charged for the expense.
>
> Such cost allocations may require a corporate *authorization form* or *memo*.

Example. The superintendent's salary for Custom Homes would probably be charged initially to an overall administrative salaries account for the entire company. In this case, one-half of his time was spent on job 1 in the first 2 months and full time in both June and July. An entry to assign his salary for June to his job would be:

	Debit	Credit
Job 1 in progress	$2,000	
Administrative salaries		$2,000

The debit reflects the proportion of his total salary assignable to job 1. The credit reflects a reduction in the corporate administrative salaries account. (Since these types of costs are somewhat indirect in terms of a particular job, they are generally classified as overhead costs. In many cost systems, indirect or overhead costs are assigned to jobs or products through an allocation procedure similar to this. Specifically, the percentage of a manager's time devoted to a project is estimated so that appropriate amounts can be assigned to the jobs or products through journal entries.) The amount involved in this transaction would be supported by a written memorandum stating the proportion of time spent by the superintendent on job 1. Had the overhead costs been general (miscellaneous) costs, a cost allocation authorization form would probably be required:

No. _____

**Authorization Form
Cost Allocation**

Date _____

Project No. _____

Type of Project _____

Authorized by _____

- -

A. Reason for Cost Allocation

B. Amounts of Costs Involved

C. Program Accounts to Be Debited

D. Accounts to Be Credited

Exercise

1. Custom's president had decided before accepting the contract for the solar home that selected pieces of specialized equipment should be leased from the manufacturer annually to avoid committing significant capital to an experimental project. The corporation executed the lease contract and was responsible for the payments. Each manager could rent the equipment at $25/hour. Project 1 required 40 hours of service in May ($1,000). Record the appropriate entry for this cost.

2. The final cost involved in the Custom Homes project was an arbitrary $1,000/month charge assigned by the corporation for costs incurred in staff time and effort. This type of charge is sometimes found in experimental projects where many uncertainties are involved. These charges are assigned because corporate management wants all superintendents to be aware of the many costs incurred as concepts are designed and the contract negotiated. They are similar to research and development costs and can be appropriately charged to jobs such as this experimental contract activity. The entry to record the July charge for miscellaneous costs would be:

3. What form is likely to be required for these miscellaneous costs to be authorized?

_ _ _ _ _ _ _ _ _ _ _ _ _ _ _

1.

	Debit	Credit
Job 1 in progress	$1,000	
Equipment rental payable—corp. hdqtrs.		$1,000

The debit reflects an increase in inventory cost and the credit reflects an increase in the liability due to corporate headquarters for equipment rental.

2.

	Debit	Credit
Job 1 in progress	$1,000	
Corporate general expense		$1,000

The debit assigns costs to the job in question and the credit serves to reduce the total amount of corporate general expenses that is unallocated to specific activities.

3. Documentation for the entry is provided in the form of a corporate policy that allows $1,000 charge for all similar experimental projects. Generally, however, some type of corporate authorization form is used to explain the reasons for such cost allocations.

After all the preceding entries have been made, the entire 4 months' costs of $70,000 will have been charged to job 1. On July 31, these costs are carried in an inventory account on the balance sheet, jobs in progress. Ultimately, the costs will appear in the cost-of-sales section in the income statement of Custom Homes, Inc.

PROGRAM COSTING AND OVERHEAD RATES

The basic job-order costing system described in the preceding section can be expanded to facilitate more complex, realistic conditions where more than one job is in progress at a given time. For purposes of this discussion, consider the following hypothetical case.

A major state university became involved in developing a continuing education program. Each of its programs required that similar classes of costs be incurred. During the first year, the program director created a framework for a job-order costing system. His emphasis during the early stages was directed to developing forms for tracing the flow of costs. Similarly important was the need to develop an equitable procedure to assign overhead charges to programs to create measures of profitability. Profits were important in that the university's administration believed that this segment of activity should become financially self-sufficient in less than 5 years.

The center presented over 100 programs in its first year, most 2 days long with 6 hours of educational activity each day. In total, the director estimated that approximately 1,000 hours of continuing education would be offered that 12-month period. The following policy guidelines were established to facilitate program costing:

Materials: All principal educational materials costs were to be borne by the respective programs.

Teachers: These personal service costs were based on daily honorarium rates to be determined as contracts were negotiated.

Overhead: Administrative and other overhead costs were to be assigned to each program according to a predetermined overhead rate based on the number of program hours involved.

The center estimated its annual overhead costs in terms of expected monthly expenditures as follows:

Cost Classifications	Annual Costs
Administrative salaries ($6,500/month)	$ 78,000
Office expenses ($500/month)	6,000
Computer charges ($300/month)	3,600
Office rental ($900/month)	10,800
Miscellaneous expenses (annual)	1,600
Total	$100,000

During December, plans had been made to conduct three seminars. The first two programs were 2 days long; the final seminar, however, required 4 weeks, with 3 weeks' instruction to be given in December and the final week in January. The following cost data were available as a basis for evaluating programs started in December.

Program 12-1	2 Days	20 Attendees
Revenues—program fees		$3,000
Direct materials costs		200
Direct personal services costs		1,200
Estimated overhead (12 hours at $100)		1,200

Program 12-2	2 Days	18 Attendees
Revenues—program fees		$2,700
Direct materials costs		300
Direct personal services costs		1,000
Estimated overhead (12 hours at $100)		1,200

Program 12-3	20 Days	15 Attendees
Revenues—program fees		$30,000
Direct materials costs		2,000
Direct personal services costs		8,000
Estimated overhead (120 hours at $100)		12,000

All revenues were collected in advance for each program. When programs exceeded 1 week, teaching costs were incurred in installments, with 40% paid at the beginning and the remainder on the program's completion. All other costs were paid when appropriate bills were received.

8.   Program Costing Forms.   The first step in establishing a job-order costing system is to develop program costing forms to summarize relevant expenditures.

> **Program costing forms** specify the name and number of a given program and allow an accumulation of all expenditures assigned to the program. Included are costs incurred for materials with purchase order numbers and dates of order, labor costs with contract numbers and dates, and overhead costs based on a measure of activity and an appropriate application rate.

Example.   The director of the university's continuing education center developed the following form for use with his program:

Program Costing Sheet

Program No. _____

Program Title _____

Dates (Inclusive) _____

Number of Attendees _____

Location _____

Educational Materials

Date	Materials P.O. Form No.	Description	Cost
		Total	_____

Personal Services

Date	Contract No.	Name	Cost
		Total	_____

Overhead

Date	Program Hours	Rate per Hour	Cost
		Total	_____

Total Program Costs _____

Exercise

Use the preceding form to record the following data for Program 12-1 from the continuing education program.

1. Cost data on Program 12-1 included the purchase of binders for $150 authorized by purchase order 7542 dated 12/1/XX and printed materials for $50 authorized by purchase order 7546 dated 12/3/XX.
2. Two instructors worked as a team in delivering Program 12-1. Professor X taught for 8 hours at $100/hour. Professor Y taught 4 hours at the same rate. The contracts authorizing their services were numbered 124 and 125, respectively, and were both dated 12/5/XX. The program was offered on December 15-16.
3. The overhead costs were assigned to each program according to the number of educational hours involved. For Program 12-1, 6 hours were taught each day, December 15 and 16. The overhead rate was $100/hour.
4. Net income for this program is anticipated at $3,000. What profit will be earned?

_ _ _ _ _ _ _ _ _ _ _ _ _ _ _

Program Costing Sheet

Program No. 12-1

Program Title Continuing Education–XXX
Dates (Inclusive) December 15-16, XX
Number of Attendees 20
Location X Hall

1. *Educational Materials*

Date	Materials P.O. Form No.	Description	Cost
12/1/XX	#7542	Binders	$150
12/3/XX	#7546	Printed mat.	50

		Total	$200

2. *Personal Services*

Date	Contract No.	Name	Rate	Cost
12/15-16	124	Prof. X	$100	$800
12/15-16	125	Prof. Y	100	400

		Total	$1,200

3. *Overhead*

Date	Program Hours	Rate per Hour	Cost
12/15	6 hours	$100	$600
12/16	6 hours	100	600

	Total	$1,200

Total Program Costs — $2,600

4. Profit for this program is $400.

Note: Had this program been incomplete at period end, revenues would be classified as "unearned" and would appear as a liability on the balance sheet. The costs incurred, on the other hand, would be classified as programs in progress, an inventory account in the current assets section of the balance sheet for the center. When the program is completed in the succeeding period, the revenue and expenses would appear as income statement accounts.

9.   Predetermined Overhead Rates. Establishing predetermined overhead rates is a significant element in a job-order costing system. Underlying the need for such cost estimates is the fact that actual cost information is received only after the accounting period is completed. Actual data, therefore, are of little use in making major planning and control decisions.

An important step in establishing a predetermined overhead rate is to select an *activity measure* that effectively represents the nature of the operation. In some cases, activity is measured in terms of outflows—units produced, sales volume, and so on. In other situations, however, the inflows of resources are more critical to operating success—labor-hours used, machine-hours used, direct labor costs incurred, and so on. Since each approach is sometimes effective in a specific practical setting, both are considered entirely appropriate for cost accounting purposes.

Carried further, a predetermined overhead rate reflects the relationship between two factors: the measure of activity and the estimated overhead cost for the planning period. Where it is possible to estimate annual overhead costs with reasonable accuracy, use of yearly data is most acceptable. If significant cost variations are expected within the year, however, either a monthly or a quarterly rate is usually superior for decision making.

A **predetermined overhead rate** is the relationship between estimated overhead costs and expected levels of production output:

$$\frac{\text{anticipated costs}}{\text{measure of activity}}$$

Rates are used for assigning overhead costs to units of output, to jobs in process, ongoing programs, or production departments during an accounting period.

Example. The continuing education center estimated its overhead costs at $100,000 a year. Next, an activity measure needed to be selected. After discussing this problem with directors at comparable institutions, three activity measures seemed appropriate: (1) number of programs expected to be offered in the coming year, (2) number of attendee hours of education, and (3) number of educational hours delivered. The center expected to offer 100 educational programs during its first year. Using programs as the selected activity measure, the predetermined overhead rate was computed as follows:

$$\frac{\text{estimated annual overhead costs}}{\text{planned number of programs}} = \frac{\$100,000}{100 \text{ programs}} = \$1,000 \text{ per program}$$

Exercise

1. The second possible measure referred to output, the number of attendee-hours expected to be generated. If a program has 20 attendees for 2 days (12 contact hours), the program would generate 240 hours of educational output. The director estimated that the center's programs would generate approximately 20,000 continuing education hours during the coming year (100 programs × 10 hours × 20 attendees). Use these data to compute a predetermined overhead rate.

2. The third possible activity measure was the number of educational hours expected to be delivered in the planned programs. The best estimate is that each of the 100 planned programs will generate about 10 continuing education hours. Using these data, compute a predetermined overhead rate.

- - - - - - - - - - - - - - - -

1. $\dfrac{\text{Estimated annual overhead costs}}{\text{Estimated continuing education hours}} = \dfrac{\$100,000}{20,000 \text{ hours}} = \$5 \text{ per student-hour}$

Note: This measure poses a minor problem in that the number of actual program hours generated may be difficult to compute. If attendees leave early or fail to attend particular sessions, for example, the basic measure is somewhat inaccurate.

2. $\dfrac{\text{Estimated annual overhead costs}}{\text{Estimated number of program hours}} = \dfrac{\$100,000}{1,000} = \$100 \text{ per program-hour}$

Note: Although this measure is used frequently, it is difficult to estimate accurately on an annual basis. Nonetheless, the director elected to use this activity measure, program hours, as the basis for determining overhead rates.

10. Applied and Incurred Overhead Costs. Using predetermined overhead rates simplifies the cost-tracing process, but this procedure is not without some complexity. In most cases, the estimates developed at the beginning of any year differ from costs actually incurred. Since profits ultimately should reflect actual costs and revenues, period-end adjustments are usually required.

> **Overhead costs applied** include indirect production costs *assigned* to units of output on the basis of a predetermined overhead rate. To apply this rate, record a debit to reflect the assignment of costs to the program and a credit to an overhead costs applied account.
>
> **Overhead costs incurred** include indirect production costs *actually expended* during an accounting period. To apply this rate, record a debit to an overhead costs incurred account and a credit to cash or the appropriate expense or liability accounts.

Example. In the center's case, the actual number of program hours offered was 1,100. Multiplying this activity measure by the overhead rate of $100/hour, the total overhead charges applied to programs during the year was $110,000. The entry to reflect the assignment of these costs is as follows:

	Debit	Credit
Programs in progress	$110,000	
Overhead costs applied		$110,000

The actual overhead incurred for the year was $105,000. Of this total, $75,000 was paid in cash; the remaining $30,000 was assigned from other areas in the university and thus served to reduce expenses incurred directly by those units. The entry to reflect assignment of these costs is as follows:

	Debit	Credit
Overhead costs incurred	$105,000	
Cash		$75,000
Payables to other departments		$30,000

Exercise

An automobile repair shop uses a predetermined overhead system as a basis for assigning costs to jobs completed. The shop estimated its monthly overhead rate at $10,000. In total, direct labor employees (mechanics) were scheduled to work 1,000 hours per month. In one month's operations a total of $11,500 in overhead was actually incurred, and a total of 1,100 hours of charges were accumulated and assigned to specific jobs.

1. Compute the predetermined overhead rate for this repair shop. _____
2. Make the entry to record overhead costs applied.

3. If all overhead costs are paid in cash, make the entry to record overhead costs incurred.

----

1. $10,000 ÷ 1,000 = $10 per direct labor-hour.

2.

	Debit	Credit
Jobs in progress	$11,000	
Overhead costs applied		$11,000

	Debit	Credit
3. Overhead costs incurred	$11,500	
Cash		$11,500

11.   Over- and Underapplied Overhead Costs.   Frequently, the predetermined overhead costs applied and the actual overhead costs incurred differ. If costs incurred exceed the costs applied, the difference is termed *underapplied overhead costs;* this means that some proportion of the actual costs were not assigned to programs because of judgment error during the estimation process. Conversely, if overhead costs applied exceed those incurred, the difference is called *overapplied overhead costs.* Thus the amount of overhead assigned to programs was more than actually incurred. Again, the initial estimates were inaccurate to some extent, a problem almost always encountered in practical situations. The issue to be resolved is how this difference is treated from an accounting viewpoint.

The treatment of over- and underapplied overhead differs from company to company. Nevertheless, one approach used frequently is to assign the amount directly to the organization's cost-of-sales account. Simply stated, this entry is made when the accounts are closed to assign over- or underapplied overhead directly to programs completed during the year. If a large number of programs or jobs were incomplete at year end, allocation of the over- or underapplied overhead measure might be necessary to accomplish more effective reporting. If a large part of the difference can be identified as relating to particular programs, however, these costs could be charged directly to the specific programs involved.

	Debit	Credit
The least complicated approach to recording over- and underapplied overhead costs is to record the data by closing out the period account balance as follows:		
Overhead costs applied	_____	
Cost of sales		_____
Overhead costs incurred		_____

Example.   The center's overhead costs incurred ($105,000) was less than the overhead costs applied ($110,000). These data would be recorded as follows:

	Debit	Credit
Overhead costs applied	$110,000	
Cost of sales		5,000
Overhead costs incurred		$105,000

Note that the overhead applied account is debited in this entry. This account is thus closed, and the measure reflects the summation of the period's applications of overhead costs to programs then in progress. The credit to the overhead incurred account similarly closes out its balance at period-end. The difference, overapplied overhead in this case, is credited to cost of sales. The credit of $5,000 reduces the cost-of-sales account. The reduction occurs because applied program costs exceed those incurred. Thus the cost-of-sales account normally is assumed to carry a debit balance.

Exercise

Data for the repair shop were given in the preceding frame.

1. Make the entry to record under- or overapplied overhead in this case.

2. Was the overhead for the repair shop underapplied? _____ Overapplied?
_____

3. Is cost of sales increased or reduced by the entry to record the difference? _____
_____

- - - - - - - - - - - - - - - -

1.   Debit   Credit

	Debit	Credit
Overhead costs applied	$11,000	
Cost of sales	500	
Overhead costs incurred		$11,500

2. Underapplied.

3. Cost of sales is increased by the entry because more costs were incurred than were applied to jobs through the predetermined rate system.

12.   Tracing Cost Flow—The T-Account Model. The concept of cost traceability is a key element in the overall structure of cost accounting. Significant benefits are gained by observing cost flows through accounts in an operating system. For the discussion of tracing cost flows, consider the following hypothetical situation.

The Quality Publishing Company has a long-standing reputation as one of the best firms in its industry. One of its divisions specializes in publishing paperback books for management training courses throughout the country. A review of this division's operating history suggests that three to five books will be in production during any one accounting period. The month of April 19XX is a representative month. At the beginning of this month, three separate books are being produced. These printing projects are numbered 14, 15, and 16, respectively. Cost data have been accumulated as these jobs progressed during previous months. At the beginning of April, job costing sheets revealed the following beginning-of-the-month cost balances:

Job 14:	Materials	$1,800
	Labor	1,200
	Overhead	1,200
	Total	$4,200

Job 15:	Materials	$4,200
	Labor	2,800
	Overhead	2,800
	Total	$9,800

Job 16:	Materials	$ 400
	Labor	200
	Overhead	200
	Total	$ 800

During April, jobs 14 and 15 were completed; the revenues from these jobs were $10,000 and $15,000, respectively. Job 14 was delivered to the customer, but the delivery date for job 15 is May 10. This particular job, therefore, is classified as finished goods inventory at month-end to reflect the fact that the job is completed and awaiting delivery to the customer. Job 16 is approximately 30% complete at April 30 and will require at least 2 more months for production to be complete.

The following information reflects Quality's costing transactions for April:

Purchases of paper		
Job 14	$2,000	
15	400	
16	600	
17–20	8,000	
Indirect materials	3,000	
Total		$14,000

Labor costs		
Job 14	$ 700	
15	1,200	
16	2,000	
17–20	–0–	
Indirect labor	2,200	
Total		6,100

Other overhead costs (actually incurred)	2,400

Quality Publishing has had great success in estimating its overhead costs as a percentage of direct labor costs. For the current year, the predetermined rate is established at 100% of labor costs; that is, for every $1.00 in direct labor incurred on a particular job, 100%, or $1.00, in overhead cost is also assigned.

Direct materials and direct labor (prime costs) are accumulated weekly. Materials are maintained in the company's warehouse until requested. Labor costs generally include the hourly wages paid to printers and machine operators in the binding department. All other costs are treated as overhead, and charges are assigned to jobs either at the end of each month or at the completion date, whichever is appropriate.

The challenge to management accounting is to keep the costs of each job order separate, to trace them from the beginning of the job through to finished goods and revenues. All data must be recorded, posted to the appropriate accounts, and then traced.

> To trace cost flows, design a **T-account model of accounts** in the system. Record and post all transactions during the month to the appropriate account to reflect debits and credits incurred in each account (e.g., cash, accounts receivable, accounts payable, materials inventory, jobs in progress, finished jobs inventory, overhead costs incurred and applied, corporate payroll, cost of sales, and sales).

Example. The T-account model for Quality Publishing would appear as follows:

Cash	Accounts Receivable	Accounts Payable
$12,000*	$15,000*	$7,000*

Materials Inventory	Jobs-in-Process Inventory	Finished Jobs Inventory
$5,000*	Detailed information from this account is posted directly into accounts for each specialized job.	

Job 14 in Process	Job 15 in Process	Job 16 in Process
$4,200*　(7)	$9,800*	$800*

*Asterisks indicate beginning balance in the account.

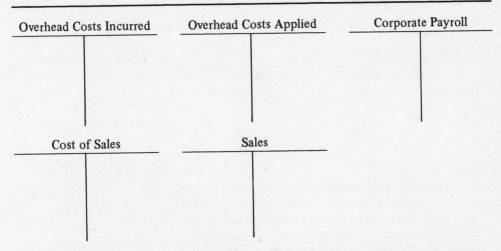

After beginning balances are entered, each transaction for specific jobs can be entered.

1. Transaction 1 — paper stock costing $11,000 was purchased for jobs to be produced in April and May. The paper is purchased on account; payment is to be made in early May. In addition, indirect materials costing $3,000 were purchased on account. The purchase of paper and indirect supplies would be recorded as follows:

	Debit	Credit
Materials inventory	$14,000	
Accounts payable		$14,000

It would then be entered into the T-account model as follows:

Accounts Payable		Materials Inventory	
	$ 7,000*	$ 5,000*	
	(1) 14,000	(1) 14,000	

(The reference number in parentheses reflects the transaction number and helps trace monetary amounts through the system.)

2. Transaction 2 — direct materials were transferred to the managers responsible for producing jobs. Job 14 received $2,000. This would be recorded as follows:

	Debit	Credit
Job 14 in progress — materials	$2,000	
Materials inventory		$2,000

It would then be entered into the T-account model as follows:

Materials Inventory		Job 14	
$ 5,000*	(2) $2,000	$4,200*	
(1) 14,000		(2) 2,000	

Exercise

1. Enter the information contained in transaction 1 preceding onto the sample T-account model for Quality Publishing. Then make the appropriate entries for each of the following transactions in the space provided *and* on the T-accounts.
2. Direct materials were transferred to the managers responsible for producing jobs: job 14, $2,000; job 15, $400; job 16, $600; indirect materials, $3,000—all of which were used.

	Debit	Credit
Job 14 in progress—materials		
Job 15 in progress—materials		
Job 16 in progress—materials		
Overhead incurred—indirect materials		
Materials inventory		

(Also enter these transactions into the T-account model for Quality Publishing.)

3. Corporate payroll costs for April were $10,000. Initially, record these costs in the corporate payroll expense account:

	Debit	Credit
Corporate payroll expense		
Cash		

Specific portions of the corporate payroll are then applied to jobs directly. Of the $10,000, $2,800 was assigned to job 14, $2,600 to job 15, $1,400 to job 16, and $1,200 to indirect labor activities:

	Debit	Credit
Job 14—direct labor		
Job 15—direct labor		
Job 16—direct labor		
Overhead incurred—indirect labor		
Corporate payroll expense		

4. Beginning-of-the-month balances existed in both the accounts payable and accounts receivable accounts ($15,000 and $7,000, respectively). Receivables were collected and suppliers paid during April, thus eliminating these beginning balances:

	Debit	Credit
Cash		
Accounts receivable		
Accounts payable		
Cash		

5. Additional overhead costs of $2,800 were incurred as the jobs progressed through production stages:

	Debit	Credit
Overhead costs incurred		
Cash		

6. Overhead was assigned 100% of direct labor costs for each job (refer to data in transaction 3 for direct labor costs for each job):

	Debit	Credit
Job 14 in progress—overhead applied		
Job 15 in progress—overhead applied		
Job 16 in progress—overhead applied		
Overhead costs applied		

7. As job 14 was finished, the published books were subjected to a quality control inspection and found to meet standards; therefore, the order was transferred to finished jobs inventory until shipment could be arranged with the customer. Appropriate billings were prepared, and the order was shipped in late April, 1 week after its completion. Job 15 was similarly completed and transferred to finished goods inventory (total the costs for each project):

	Debit	Credit
Finished jobs inventory		
Job 14 in progress		
Job 15 in progress		

8. Upon completion, jobs were billed to customers and arrangements made for delivery. Since Quality Publishing is on an accrual basis, sales are recorded in the month of production and delivery. Thus finished goods are transferred to the cost-of-sales account when delivery is completed. Therefore, job 14 can now properly be reflected as a completed contract. A bill for $14,500 is prepared and sent to the customer:

	Debit	Credit
Accounts receivable		
Sales—job 14		
Cost of sales		
Finished goods inventory		

9. Total the entries in the T-accounts. How do overhead costs incurred and overhead

costs applied compare? _____

How do cost of sales and sales for the month of April compare? _____

_____

— — — — — — — — — — — — — — —

1. Given.

2.

	Debit	Credit
Job 14 in progress—materials	$2,000	
Job 15 in progress—materials	400	
Job 16 in progress—materials	600	
Overhead incurred—indirect materials	3,000	
Materials inventory		$6,000

3.

	Debit	Credit
Corporate payroll expense	$10,000	
Cash		$10,000
Job 14—direct labor	2,800	
Job 15—direct labor	2,600	
Job 16—direct labor	1,400	
Overhead incurred—indirect labor	1,200	
Corporate payroll expense		8,000

Note: After posting both entries, note that some corporate payroll costs remain unallocated. These administrative and selling expenses have no real bearing on the production process.

4.

	Debit	Credit
Cash	$15,000	
Accounts receivable		$15,000
Accounts payable	7,000	
Cash		7,000

5.

	Debit	Credit
Overhead costs incurred	2,800	
Cash		2,800

		Debit	Credit
6.			
	Job 14 in progress—overhead applied	$ 2,800	
	Job 15 in progress—overhead applied	2,600	
	Job 16 in progress—overhead applied	1,400	
	Overhead costs applied		$ 6,800
7.	Finished jobs inventory	27,200	
	Job 14 in progress		11,800
	Job 15 in progress		15,400
8.	Accounts receivable	14,500	
	Sales—job 14		14,500
	Cost of sales	11,800	
	Finished goods inventory		11,800

Compare your T-account model with the following:

Cash		Accounts Receivable		Accounts Payable	
$12,000*	(3) $10,000	$15,000*	(4) $15,000	(4) $7,000	$ 7,000*
(4) 15,000	(4) 7,000	(8) 14,500			(1) 14,000
	(5) 2,800				
$7,200		$14,500			$14,000

Materials Inventory		Jobs-in-Process Inventory	Finished Jobs Inventory	
$ 5,000*	(2) $6,000	Detailed information	(7) $27,200	(8) $11,800
(1) 14,000		from this account is		
		posted directly into		
$13,000		accounts for each		$15,400
		specialized job.		

Job 14		Job 15		Job 16	
$ 4,200*	(7) $11,800	$ 9,800*	(7) $15,400	$ 800*	
(2) 2,000		(2) 400		(2) 600	
(3) 2,800		(3) 2,600		(3) 1,400	
(6) 2,800		(6) 2,600		(6) 1,400	
$11,800		$15,400		$4,200	

Overhead Costs Incurred		Overhead Costs Applied		Corporate Payroll	
(2) $3,000			(6) $6,800	(3) $10,000	(3) $8,000
(3) 1,200					
(5) 2,800					
$7,000			$6,800		$2,000

*Asterisks indicate beginning balance in the account.

Cost of Sales			Sales	
(8) $11,800				(8) $14,500
$11,800				$14,500

9. Overhead costs incurred exceeded overhead costs applied by $200 (underapplied). Sales exceeded cost of sales by $1,700 for the month of April.

13.   Relating Costs to Financial Statements.   Once flows of costs are diagrammed as in the T-account model, their relevance to financial statements must be considered.

> Costs assigned to units sold during the period flow directly to the cost-of-goods-sold section in the income statement. Those assigned to units remaining in inventory flow into the current assets section of the balance sheet.

Example.   Company XYZ produces 10,000 units of its product at a cost of $2 per unit. Half of these units are sold immediately. The remaining portion is held in inventory for future sale:

XYZ Company
Income Statement
for the Period Ended XXXX

Sales revenues		$XXXX
Less: Cost of goods sold		
Materials	$XXXX	
Labor	XXXX	
Overhead	XXXX	
Total costs	$20,000	
Less: Ending inventory	10,000	
Cost of goods sold		$10,000
Gross profit		$ XXX
Other expenses		XXX
Net income		$ XXX

XYZ Company
Balance Sheet
for the Period Ended April XXXX

Assets		Liabilities and Equity	
Cash	$XXXX	Current liabilities	$XXXX
Accounts receivable	XXXX		
Inventory	$10,000	Long-term liabilities	XXXX
Total	$XXXX		
		Owner's equity	XXXX
Long-term assets	XXXX		
		Total liabilities and	
Total assets	$XXXX	owner's equity	$XXXX

This simplified illustration depicts the relationship between product costs in the income statement and the balance sheet. One key assumption is made: Underlying cost accounting procedures operate on the premise that all production costs appropriately attach to jobs or units that are produced. This assumption is sometimes called *absorption costing* because manufacturing costs are absorbed into units sold as well as those remaining as inventory for future sale.

Exercise

Using the data developed in the T-account model, consider the relevance of the flow of costs to Quality's financial statements for April.

Quality Publishing Company
Income Statement
for the Period Ended April XXXX

Sales revenues
Less: Cost of goods sold (jobs completed)
Plus/minus: Under/overapplied overhead
Adjusted cost of goods sold
Gross profit
Other expenses
Net income

Partial Balance Sheet

Cash
Accounts receivable
Inventories
  Materials
  Jobs in process
  Finished jobs
Accounts payable

Note: Only specific balance sheet accounts are evaluated as a part of this cost accounting exercise.

_ _ _ _ _ _ _ _ _ _ _ _ _ _

Income Statement

Sales		$14,500
Cost of sales		
(job 14)	$11,800	
Underapplied		
overhead	200	
Adjusted cost of sales		12,000
Gross profit		$ 2,500
Corporate payroll		2,000
Net income		$ 500

Balance Sheet

Cash		$ 7,200
Accounts receivable		14,500
Inventories		
Materials	$13,000	
Jobs in process	4,200 (job 16)	
Finished jobs	15,400 (job 15)	32,600
Accounts payable		14,000 (materials purchased)

14. A Comprehensive Job-Order Costing System – Application. As a review and a means of integrating the important elements of job-order costing, read and complete the following comprehensive problem.

Superior Construction specializes in the total development of housing subdivisions within nearby communities. As these suburban areas are constructed, as many as six different model homes are built. These can be modified to some extent according to the family's desires, requiring that each home be treated as a separate project from a cost-accounting viewpoint. For purposes of this analysis, six homes have been selected as a reference point. Thus six separate jobs (40 to 45) serve as the basis for the integrated system.

The company maintains a warehouse from which all materials are requisitioned. Labor costs for each construction crew average $8 per worker-hour. Overhead is applied at a rate of $6 per worker-hour, 75% of the direct labor costs. The following transactions occurred during the accounting period investigated.

Materials were issued from the central warehouse to each of the jobs in the following amounts:

Job 40	$ 14,000
41	16,000
42	24,000
43	20,000
44	12,000
45	14,000
	$100,000

Direct labor hours were charged to the jobs on a weekly basis, and overhead was assigned at the appropriate predetermined rate. Total hours during the period for each job were as follows:

Job 40	1,500 hours (crew time)
41	1,800 hours (crew time)
42	2,500 hours (crew time)
43	2,200 hours (crew time)
44	1,000 hours (crew time)
45	1,000 hours (crew time)

Jobs 40, 41, 42, and 43 were completed and the homes were accepted by the buyers. Each was carried in finished jobs inventory for 30 days while negotiations were being completed. Job 43 remains in finished goods at period-end while the sale is being closed, but the other three contracts are finalized. Jobs 44 and 45 will be sold in the first month after this accounting period has been completed.

These data represent all information needed to accumulate costs for each of the jobs in progress. In addition, after analyzing the flows of costs, the impact of these data on Superior's financial statements can be determined.

1. As the first step in accumulating relevant costs of Superior's six jobs in progress, make the appropriate entries for assigning direct materials, labor, and applied overhead costs. Certain of the account balances are necessarily given as a starting point for your recording efforts:

Account Classification	Debit	Credit

2. Post each of these entries on the applicable inventory accounts (T-account model).

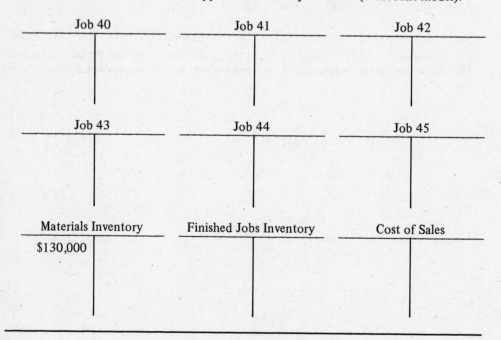

Corporate Payroll Costs	Overhead Costs Incurred	Overhead Costs Applied
$120,000	$50,000	

3. Record and post cost data (total costs assigned) for each of the jobs in progress.

Job Number	Total Costs Assigned

4. Four jobs were completed (40, 41, 42, and 43). Costs assigned to these jobs, $186,000, were transferred to finished jobs inventory. At period end only job 43 remains in this inventory, because jobs 40, 41, and 42 have been sold. Record and post these data to the appropriate accounts below and on the T-account model.

	Debit	Credit
Finished jobs inventory		
Job 40 in progress		
Job 41 in progress		
Job 42 in progress		
Cost of sales		
Finished jobs inventory (40, 41, 42)		

5. When financial statements are prepared for the accounting period, the balance sheet will contain the following data about inventories:

Materials
Jobs in progress   (job   )
Finished jobs   (job   )

6. The income statement reveals the following information relative to costs incurred during the accounting period:

Cost of sales
Corporate payroll
Overhead
  (over/under)applied

- - - - - - - - - - - - - -

1.

	Debit	Credit
Job 40 in process	$14,000	
Job 41 in process	16,000	
Job 42 in process	24,000	
Job 43 in process	20,000	
Job 44 in process	12,000	
Job 45 in process	14,000	
Materials inventory		$100,000

	Debit	Credit
Job 40 in process	$12,000	
Job 41 in process	14,400	
Job 42 in process	20,000	
Job 43 in process	17,600	
Job 44 in process	8,000	
Job 45 in process	8,000	
Corporate payroll costs		$ 80,000

	Debit	Credit
Job 40 in process	$ 9,000	
Job 41 in process	10,800	
Job 42 in process	15,000	
Job 43 in process	13,200	
Job 44 in process	6,000	
Job 45 in process	6,000	
Overhead costs applied		$ 60,000

2.

Job 40		Job 41		Job 42	
$14,000	$35,000	$16,000	$31,200	$24,000	$59,000
12,000		14,400		20,000	
9,000		10,800		15,000	
$35,000	$35,000	$41,200	$31,200	$59,000	$59,000

Job 43		Job 44		Job 45	
$20,000	$50,800	$12,000		$14,000	
17,600		8,000		8,000	
13,200		6,000		6,000	
50,800	$50,800	$26,000		$28,000	

Materials Inventory		Finished Jobs Inventory		Cost of Sales	
$130,000	$100,000	$176,000	$135,200	$135,200	
$ 30,000		$ 50,800		$135,200	

Corporate Payroll Costs		Overhead Costs Incurred		Overhead Costs Applied	
$120,000	$80,000	$50,000			$60,000

3. Job Number   Total Costs Assigned

40	$ 35,000
41	41,200
42	59,000
43	50,800
44	26,000
45	28,000
	$240,000

4.

	Debit	Credit
Finished jobs inventory	$186,000	
Job 40 in process		$ 35,000
Job 41 in process		41,200
Job 42 in process		59,000
Job 43 in process		50,800
Cost of sales	$135,200	
Finished jobs inventory		$135,200

5. Materials inventory	$ 30,000	
Jobs in process	54,000	(job 44–45)
Finished jobs	50,800	(job 43)

6. Cost of sales (jobs 40, 41, and 42)	$135,200
Corporate payroll (administrative and selling expenses)	40,000
Overapplied overhead	10,000

You may wish to review the questions at the beginning of this chapter before completing the Self-Test that follows.

CHAPTER 4 SELF-TEST

1. Matching — Terminology/Concepts

Match the following terms to the definitions.

1. Cost accounting	6. Job-order costing
2. Direct labor	7. Overhead applied
3. Direct materials	8. Overhead incurred
4. Documentation	9. Prime costs
5. Indirect overhead costs	10. Predetermined overhead rates

_____ (a) Production expenditures are traced directly to specific projects or customer orders as a basis for management planning and control decisions.

_____ (b) Indirect production costs are assigned to units of output (jobs, projects, etc.) on the basis of a predetermined overhead rate.

_____ (c) The relationship between estimated overhead costs and expected levels of production output; rates are used for assigning overhead to units of output during an accounting period.

_____ (d) Expenditures other than direct materials and direct labor that are incurred in producing units of output.

_____ (e) Indirect production costs that are actually expended during an accounting period.

2. Multiple Choice

Select the most appropriate choice for each of the following questions.

_____ (a) The XYZ Company purchased its materials on account from a supplier. Select the response that best captures the meaning of recorded debits and credits for the following entry.

	Debit	Credit
Jobs in process	$6,000	
Accounts payable		$6,000

1. The debit decreases the jobs-in-process inventory.
2. The debit increases the jobs-in-process inventory.
3. The credit decreases the accounts payable liability.
4. The credit increases the accounts payable liability.
5. Both 1 and 3 are valid statements.
6. Both 2 and 4 are valid statements.

_____ (b) Estimates of overhead costs for the coming year were $100,000. Direct labor was expected to be $50,000 for the same period. At year-end, both estimates were somewhat in error because actual overhead incurred was $120,000 and actual labor costs were $80,000. The overhead rate that should have been used to apply these costs to jobs in process was:
1. 80%.
2. 120%.
3. 160%.
4. 200%.
5. None of the above.

_____ (c) One company uses an overhead rate of $5 per direct labor-hour. Job X required 100 direct labor-hours during the period, while all other jobs used a total of an additional 900 hours. In total, the company incurred $4,000 in overhead for the period. Which of the following entries would you expect to find on this company's books?
1. A debit to overhead incurred for $5,000.
2. A credit to overhead applied for $5,000.
3. A credit to overhead incurred for $4,000.
4. A debit to overhead applied for $4,000.
5. None of the above.

_____ (d) In a recent accounting period, the selected company incurred $10,000 in overhead costs. Jobs in process, however, was assigned $12,000 based on the company's predetermined overhead rate. Select the most appropriate response.
1. This company would reflect underapplied overhead in the amount of $2,000.
2. Its costs of sales would be increased by a debit for $2,000 when the accounts are closed.
3. The company would reflect overapplied overhead in the amount of $2,000.
4. Cost of sales would be decreased by a credit for $2,000 when the accounts are closed.
5. Both 1 and 2.
6. Both 3 and 4.

_____ (e) The normal flow of costs in a job-order system would occur as follows:
1. Jobs in process to finished goods to cost of sales.
2. Jobs in process to cost of sales.
3. Finished goods to jobs in process.
4. None of the above.

3. Analyzing Cost Flows

The Ace Construction Company constructed three homes during the past 3 months. Job 1 has been completed and all contractual details are settled; thus the new owners are now in the process of occupying the property. Job 2 is completed, but the contract will not be finalized for a few more days. Job 3 is about 90% complete at this time. The following data are contained in the company records:

	Job 1	Job 2	Job 3
Direct materials	$10,000	$20,000	$20,000
Direct labor	20,000	30,000	40,000

Overhead is applied on a basis of 100% of direct labor costs. As a company policy, the price for each home is to be 150% of the costs assigned to the job. Using these data, respond to each of the following questions.

(a) Develop measures of total costs for each of the three jobs.

	Job 1	Job 2	Job 3
Direct materials			
Direct labor			
Overhead			
Total job costs			

(b) Review the information in the case and establish an appropriate measure for each of the following financial statement classifications.

Jobs-in-process inventory _____

Finished jobs inventory _____

Cost of sales _____

(c) Determine the company's project income to be reported for this quarter.

Revenues $_____

Cost of sales _____

Project income $_____

4. Supporting Documentation

Identify the document or documents that would generally be used in support of the flows of costs:

(a) Direct materials to jobs in process. _____

(b) Direct labor to jobs in process. _____

ANSWERS

1. Matching – Terminology/Concepts (5 pts)

(a) 6 (introduction, 1 pt)   (b) 7 (frame 10, 1 pt)   (c) 10 (frame 9, 1 pt)
(d) 5 (frame 7, 1 pt)   (e) 8 (frame 10, 1 pt)

2. Multiple Choice (5 pts)

(a) 6 (frame 2, 1 pt)   (b) 4 (frame 10, 1 pt)   (c) 2 (frame 10, 1 pt)
(d) 6 (frame 11, 1 pt)   (e) 1 (frame 12, 1 pt)

3. Analyzing Cost Flows (15 pts)

(a) Project costs (frame 12, 5 pts)

	Job 1	Job 2	Job 3
Direct materials	$10,000	$20,000	$ 20,000
Direct labor	20,000	30,000	40,000
Overhead[a]	20,000	30,000	40,000
Total project costs	$50,000	$80,000	$100,000

[a] 100% of direct labor costs.

(b) Financial statement classification (frame 13, 5 pts)

Jobs-in-process inventory	$100,000	Job 3
Finished jobs inventory	80,000	Job 2
Cost of sales	50,000	Job 1

(c) Project income (frame 13, 5 pts)

Revenues	$75,000	(150% of costs)
Cost of sales	50,000	
Project income	$25,000	

4. Supporting Documentation (6 pts)

(a) Materials requisitions, to obtain needed materials from inventory. Purchase orders, for buying goods from outsiders. Materials receiving slips, to indicate that purchased items have been received. (frame 3, 3 pts)

(b) Job time tickets, which reflect the number of hours assigned to each job. Personnel records, to indicate appropriate wage rates for each individual. Contract labor invoices, which are used as support when outside services of a specialized nature are required. (frame 6, 3 pts)

Total possible points: 31. You should have scored at least 25.

CHAPTER 5

Process Costing Systems

 Can you . . .

- Use process costing to trace manufacturing costs through operating departments to units produced?
- Determine equivalent units of production for partially completed units?
- Determine the average cost per unit produced?
- Value work-in-process inventories in terms of costs incurred during an accounting period?
- Analyze the effect of differing flows of costs on the overall cost-tracing process?
- Use FIFO costing?

These management accounting skills are the focus of this chapter.

Cost accounting systems provide management with information to evaluate performance in various segments of a company's operations. Although plans can be based entirely upon estimates, the availability of historical information such as costs incurred in a prior period improves management's ability to predict more accurately the expenses that are likely to be incurred. Data generated by cost systems are clearly an important management resource.

Carried further, these historical cost data can easily serve as a basis for control decisions. In this context, managers can react quickly to significant changes in cost patterns, making decisions to improve both current and future operations. At a minimum, a solid foundation for future planning decisions can be structured. The management planning and control processes are thus linked by using cost accounting information for decision making.

> **Process costing** is a system to assign production costs first to operating departments and then to units of output.

Process costing differs from job-order costing by the nature of the output produced. In job-order systems, the units of output are unique, specifically designed to satisfy a customer's stated needs. In process costing, on the other hand, output units are similar or identical.

Consider the process of manufacturing automobiles. A large number of the raw material components are common to all cars produced. The same is true for the majority of the skills provided by direct labor personnel. Indirect overhead is another common cost factor. Differences occur in the interiors, colors, and the various accessories added to each automobile. Nonetheless, the cars are considered to be a common output of the automobile manufacturing process because most costs are incurred for common components. The same can be said for such products as refrigerators, televisions, and most home appliances. Note the difference between these outputs and the production from a job-order system where each unit is unique.

Since manufacturing processes generate units of output that are basically the same, management's attention has traditionally been directed to achieving *efficiency*, that is, producing units for the minimum reasonable amount of costs while obtaining desirable quality levels. One approach to achieving efficiency focuses on combining similar types of labor skills or equipment into a departmental unit or *production department*, a specialized unit in a manufacturing operation. Costs are traced first to the department and then to the units of output it produces in a given accounting period. Simply stated, total production costs are traced through production departments to units of output. The resulting measure is an average cost per unit for the time period under consideration.

The first step in process accounting is to identify the departmental units in the production organization. Costs are then accumulated in the same classifications used in job-order costing: direct materials, direct labor, and overhead. The second step is to develop a measure of output for each department. This measure, termed *equivalent units of production*, explicitly recognizes that some units may be only partially complete at period-end. The third step is to determine the average cost per unit of output. Finally, costs are assigned both to units transferred out of the department (to other operations or to finished goods inventory) and to units remaining in the department's ending inventory. Each of these steps is examined in detail in this chapter. Of primary importance is the development of skill in tracing costs through production departments to units of output as a basis for both inventory valuation and financial statement preparation.

AVERAGE COSTING

The primary purpose of process cost accounting systems is to trace costs to common units of product. A first step is to describe the types of products under consideration and the kinds of costs incurred. Given this descriptive framework, attention is directed to measuring output during the period and assigning costs to the units produced.

> **Average costing** is a specialized costing method that combines beginning inventory costs with current-period production costs. This measure is then divided by production output to create a measure of average costs per unit.

The specific steps involved in average costing are illustrated in the following practical setting.

Vista Manufacturing specializes in producing an entire range of consumer products. Attention is now directed to a new product line of televisions. Research and development activities were recently completed, and an assembly department has been established for these production activities.

Raw materials are purchased almost entirely from other divisions in the company, so all necessary components are available immediately on request. The conversion process (converting raw materials into finished products) is largely labor-oriented. Thus this new department in Vista tends to view direct labor and overhead costs as inseparable; they are termed *conversion costs* and are applied to units produced in terms of actual costs incurred.

Materials are assumed to flow into production uniformly. Production in the department occurs on six assembly lines operating 8 hours per day, 5 days per week. Each line requires 60 persons and produces between 80 and 85 units per hour.

A metal frame is placed on the line, and each of the unit's personnel add material components (subassemblies, tubes, etc.) as the unit progresses through the line. Materials flow "uniformly"; that is, components are added in direct proportion to time expended in the conversion process. Thus, when the company uses 60 employees on a line, each would use 1/60 of the materials.

Production cost data for this department's first operating period were: $492,000 in direct materials, $196,000 in direct labor, and $132,000 in departmental overhead. The department completed and transferred to finished goods 80,000 units. There were 4,000 units in process at period-end.

1. Equivalent Units of Production—Materials Flowing Uniformly. The first step in tracing production costs to units of output is to develop a measure of departmental results during the given period. This measure represents how many units were completed and transferred to another department or finished goods as well as what production effort was expended on the department's ending inventory.

Ideally, all units started within a production department would be completed during the period. In practice, however, such an ideal is rarely found. Since we are attempting to develop an average production cost per unit, the basis for tracing costs must be units totally completed, that is, those passing through all phases of production. Therefore, management must estimate how complete each unit is in terms of a percent. For example, 1,000 units considered to be 50% complete are thought of as being equal to 500 completed units. In reality, of course, those units near the end of the assembly line may be 95% complete, whereas those located near the beginning of the line may be only 5% complete. The simplest description of the 50% average is as follows: had the workers put forth efforts to complete each of the 1,000 ending inventory units before any others were started, the efforts and costs would be sufficient to complete 500 units (50% × 1,000 units).

> **Equivalent units of product** is a measure of production output used to determine average cost per unit produced. It includes units completed and transferred as well as partially completed units, which are converted into terms of whole units by multiplying the number of units in the ending inventory by the conversion percentage.

Example. A schedule reflecting the equivalent units of product for Vista would be as follows:

	Equivalent Units of Product
Units completed and transferred	80,000
Units in ending inventory (4,000 units × 50%)	2,000
Equivalent units of production	82,000

If Vista assumes that the department's inventory is 50% complete at the end of the given period, the ending inventory of 4,000 units can be converted to 2,000 equivalent units of production. Other departments may operate on different conversion percentages.

Exercise

Using the same number of units completed and transferred and remaining in the ending inventory, what would Vista's equivalent units of product be if management assumed a conversion percentage of 75%? _____ Or 25%? _____

– – – – – – – – – – – – – – – –

83,000; 81,000.

2.   Conversion Costs. The second phase of process cost accounting requires that costs be traced to the equivalent units of production. In many manufacturing processes, labor and overhead are treated as a single cost factor.

> **Conversion costs** are the direct labor costs and manufacturing overhead costs required to convert raw materials into finished goods.

Example. If Company X spends 1 cent in materials, 2 cents in labor, and 2 cents in overhead to produce a pencil, conversion costs would be 4 cents. It takes 2 cents in labor and 2 cents in overhead to convert the 1 cent of raw materials into a finished pencil.

Exercise
Referring to the previously described production process, what are the individual and total conversion costs for Vista's new television department during its first operating

period? _____

– – – – – – – – – – – – – –

$196,000 in direct labor and $132,000 for departmental overhead, for a total of $328,000.

3.   Average Cost per Unit. The *average cost per unit* is a measure developed by dividing manufacturing expenses of a production department by the number of units it produces during an accounting period.

$$\text{average cost per unit} = \frac{\text{costs during period}}{\text{equivalent units of product}}$$

Example. Vista's average cost per unit appears in the following schedule:

	Materials	Conversion Costs	Total
Costs incurred during the period	$492,000	$328,000	$820,000
divided by			
Equivalent units of product	82,000	82,000	82,000
equals			
Average cost per unit	$6.00	$4.00	$10.00

Exercise
In another of Vista's departments, production expenses were $510,400 in direct materials, $214,200 in direct labor, and $129,000 in departmental overhead. This department completed and transferred 85,000 units and had 6,000 units (50% complete) in its ending inventory. Develop a schedule similar to the one in the preceding example to illustrate these data.

- - - - - - - - - - - - -

	Materials	Conversion Costs	Total
Costs incurred during the period divided by	$510,400	$343,200	$853,600
Equivalent units of product equals	88,000[a]	88,000	88,000
Average cost per unit	$5.80	$3.90	$9.70

[a] 85,000 units completed and transferred to finished goods plus 3,000 equivalent units of product (6,000 units 50% completed) in the ending inventory.

4.   Valuing Inventories. The value of finished goods is easily determined. The equivalent-unit concept also allows you to determine easily the value of ending inventory.

> Average costs per unit are applied *both* to units transferred to finished goods and to those remaining in the department's ending inventory.

Example. Vista's television department transferred 80,000 units to finished goods inventory during the period. Each unit absorbed $6.00 in materials and $4.00 in conversion costs. In total, therefore, the total costs traced to finished goods inventory were $80,000. The ending inventory of 4,000 units was assumed to be 50% completed at period-end or 2000 equivalent units in terms of efforts and costs expended. Thus these units would absorb $12,000 in materials costs (2,000 × $6.00 per unit) and $8,000 in conversion costs (2,000 × $4.00 per unit), for a total of $20,000.

Taken together, total production costs for the period have now been traced to units produced. Of the total $820,000 in production costs, $800,000 flowed into finished goods inventory and $20,000 remained in the assembly department's ending inventory.

Exercise

Using the data from the second department (exercise in frame 3), determine the value of finished goods inventory $ _____ and its ending inventory $ _____ . Note that these two measures account for all production costs incurred: $ _____ .

– – – – – – – – – – – – – – – –

Transferred to finished goods inventory: $824,500 (85,000 × $9.70); ending inventory: $29,100 (3,000 units × $9.70); total costs: $853,600.

5. Beginning Inventories. Tracing costs to units of production is somewhat complicated by the presence of a beginning inventory. Operating on the basic concept of equivalent units, however, the method can be expanded to accommodate this condition.

> When determining average cost per unit, the total cost includes *both* beginning inventory costs and current-period costs.

Example. In Vista's second month of operation of its television production, its beginning inventory was 4,000 units that were 50% complete. This beginning inventory was the *ending inventory* for the prior month. Recall that it was valued at $12,000 in materials and $8,000 in conversion costs, a total of $20,000. Therefore, total production costs for the second month are:

	Materials Costs	Conversion Costs	Total
Beginning inventory	$ 12,000	$ 8,000	$ 20,000
Current-period costs	524,800	379,200	904,000
Total costs	$536,800	$387,200	$924,000

Carried further, dividing these costs by equivalent units of production of 88,000 gives an average cost per unit of $6.10 in materials and $4.40 in conversion costs, or a total average cost per unit of $10.50. These costs are slightly different from those of the first month because in practice one would rarely expect costs per unit to remain constant from one month to another. Obviously, management must analyze these costs to determine the specific causes of cost changes; such control-type problems are treated in a succeeding chapter.

Exercise

At the end of the second month of operation, Vista's television department had an ending inventory of 6,000 units 50% completed. Convert this ending inventory into a beginning inventory for the third month of operation.

	Materials Cost	Conversion Costs	Total
Beginning inventory	$18,300	$13,200	$31,500
	(3,000 × $6.10)	(3,000 × $4.40)	(3,000 × $10.50)

6.   Equivalent Units of Production—Materials Flowing Nonuniformly. Process-costing activities revolve around certain basic concepts: equivalent units, average costs per units, and valuing inventories on the basis of actual production costs incurred. By changing the practical setting, additional dimensions of the process-costing method can be explored.

One modification in cost-tracing procedures occurs when all materials are entered at the beginning of the production process. In this instance, of course, the assumption that materials and conversion costs are applied uniformly is invalid. Instead, tracing stems from the premise that all units of production are 100% complete as to materials while only partially complete as to conversion costs. In addition, the assumption that inventories are 50% complete at period-end is likely to be modified to meet specific operating conditions. To illustrate these changes, a highly technical production process is used as an example.

Technology, Inc., was formed to introduce modern, innovative equipment into businesses. Extensive efforts are being expended to introduce a line of mini desk computers. The company's strategy is to develop a line of high-quality, low-priced computers that can be made available to the majority of office personnel. Technology has been innovative in its product lines, and its approach to the production process is also unique.

All computer subassemblies are tested thoroughly before being used in production. After testing, each unit is placed on a movable cart in a preassembly storage area. When the cart is completely filled with the various subassemblies and other components, all direct materials costs have been incurred. In other words, when a production cart is moved to the final assembly area, each desk computer is 100% complete as to materials.

To assemble its computers, Technology has adapted its production process to satisfy stringent quality standards. Each unit passes through a series of work stations occupied by two people. One person completes a particular phase of the production process; the second conducts all required quality tests. Each worker performs assembly operations for half the day and quality tests for the remainder of the day.

At the end of each accounting period, the status of inventory in the final assembly department is evaluated. Because work progresses for varying amounts of time, however, the stages of completion as to conversion costs are subject to change from period to period. Specific procedures have been developed to accomplish this measurement requirement.

For costing purposes, the company has a unique set of requirements. Direct materials costs are accumulated for each product and are assigned to the department as production begins. All assembly employees are highly skilled and are compensated on a weekly salary. Therefore, the charges to the department are relatively fixed from week to week. Finally, manufacturing overhead relates almost wholly to depreciation and maintenance of the quality testing equipment. Overhead is charged back to the department on the basis of total equipment hours used during a period. All three classifications of costs are treated separately as product-costing information is developed.

The following data are available to trace cost flows in the assembly operation of Technology, Inc.

	Beginning Inventory	Current Period	Total
Direct materials costs	$2,000	$22,000	$24,000
Direct labor costs	3,800	38,000	41,800
Manufacturing overhead	1,900	19,000	20,900
Total	$7,700	$79,000	$86,700

State of Completion

	Quantity	Materials	Conversion Costs
Units in beginning inventory	30	100%	40%
Units started during period	170	100%	
Units completed and transferred	180	100%	
Units in ending inventory	20	100%	50%

Note that each unit is completed as to materials but only partially completed as to conversion costs. This factor has a significant effect on the measure of production output during the period. Its implications become clear as equivalent units of product are determined for this operation.

> When materials and conversion costs do not flow uniformly into a process, separate equivalent units of production must be determined. Conversion percentages may also vary.

Example. Technology, Inc.'s data for equivalent units of production would be as follows:

Materials	Units	Percentage of Completion	Equivalent Units
Units completed and transferred	180	100%	180
Plus: Ending inventory	20	100%	20
Equivalent units (direct materials)			200

Conversion	Units	State of Completion	Equivalent Units
Units completed and transferred	180	100%	180
Plus: Ending inventory	20	50%	10
Equivalent units (conversion costs)			190

Note that equivalent units of production for direct materials costs differs from the equivalent units of production for conversion costs.

Exercise

What is the measure of direct materials equivalent units for the beginning inventory of Technology, Inc.? _____ What is the measure of conversion costs equivalent units for the beginning inventory? _____

– – – – – – – – – – – – – –

30 (30 X 100%); 12 (30 X 40%).

7.   Review–Average Costing

$$\text{Average cost per unit} = \frac{\text{beginning inventory costs + current costs (total costs)}}{\text{equivalent units of production}}$$

Assign average costs per unit to finished goods and ending inventories.

As a review of the concepts presented thus far, use the data provided about Technology, Inc., to trace cost flows as indicated:
1. Calculate the average direct materials cost per unit. _____
2. Calculate the average direct labor cost per unit. _____
3. Calculate the average manufacturing overhead cost per unit. _____

Complete the following schedules to assign costs to finished goods and ending inventories:

Cost Classification	Units Transferred	Cost per Unit	Total Cost
Direct materials	_____	_____	_____
Direct labor	_____	_____	_____
Manufacturing overhead	_____	_____	_____
Costs to finished goods			=======

Cost Classification	Quantity X	Completion Percentage =	Equivalent Units	X	Average Cost per Unit =	Total
Direct materials	_____ X	_____ =	_____ X		_____ =	_____
Direct labor	_____ X	_____ =	_____ X		_____ =	_____
Manufacturing overhead	_____ X	_____ =	_____ X		_____ =	_____
Costs in ending inventory						=======

- - - - - - - - - - - - - - -

1. $2,000 (beginning inventory) + $22,000 (current costs) = $24,000 (total costs) divided by 200 equivalent units = $120 average direct materials cost per unit.
2. $3,800 (beginning inventory) + $38,000 (current costs) = $41,800 (total costs) divided by 190 equivalent units = $220 average direct labor cost per unit.
3. $1,900 (beginning inventory) + $19,000 (current costs) = $20,900 (total costs) divided by 190 equivalent units = $110 average manufacturing overhead costs per unit.
4.

Cost Classification	Units Transferred	Cost per Unit	Total Cost
Direct materials	180	$120	$21,600
Direct labor	180	220	39,600
Manufacturing overhead	180	110	19,800
Costs to finished goods			$81,000

Cost Classification	Quantity X	Completion Percentage =	Equivalent Units	X	Average Cost per Unit =	Total
Direct materials	20 X	100% =	20 X		$120 =	$2,400
Direct labor	20 X	50% =	10 X		220 =	2,200
Manufacturing overhead	20 X	50% =	10 X		110 =	1,100
Costs in ending inventory						$5,700

As a final step, the separate measures of total costs—units transferred and units in ending inventory—are combined for comparison to total production costs in the original data. The total costs transferred to finished goods ($81,000) and the ending inventory valuation ($5,700) equal total production costs of $86,700. Thus all relevant costs have been assigned to production output.

FIRST IN/FIRST OUT (FIFO) COSTING

Each process costing system must be adapted to meet the specific needs of an organization. One major reason for adjusting procedures is the fact that the costs of resources can change frequently. When these conditions exist, a totally different approach to the tracing of costs is needed. A specialized method, called the *first in/first out (FIFO) costing technique*, is used.

> **First in/first out** or **FIFO costing** is designed to separate prior-period and current-period expenses when determining measures of average cost per unit. This method is particularly useful when significant changes in costs occur between accounting periods.

As the basis for this discussion, a furniture manufacturing process will be analyzed.

Executive Furnishings, Inc., is one of the oldest in the country in the business of making office furnishings for business executives. Its reputation for high-quality workmanship affords the opportunity for significant profits, but constantly changing prices for materials are a source of concern. These economic conditions caused the company to change its process-costing system from the simple-average approach to a FIFO approach.

Executive Furnishings offers a limited line of office furniture, with each product made of the highest-quality wood and all production work performed by skilled personnel. Thus the costs of producing any particular piece of furniture are quite high compared to normal industry standards. To keep prices in line with costs, management must be able to recognize immediately when the prices of wood increase. In the simple average costing system, however, new and old purchase prices were merged together. Thus the full impact of cost changes was sometimes overlooked.

After obtaining advice from outside consultants, the approach to costing was changed. A FIFO system was designed and implemented. In this system, the beginning inventory is kept separate from units that are started and completed during the period. Thus costs of materials used in a prior period are clearly differentiated from those incurred during the current period. The tracing process is more precise, considerably improving management's ability to monitor changes.

For purposes of analysis, focus is directed to the costing procedures applied as Executive Furnishings, Inc., produces a new line of executive desks. The market forecast suggests that 500 desks can be started in November, but the prices of wood are increasing due to shortages in supply. Alternative sources are not available, and thus management must adapt to this changing cost structure. Since the line has not been formally introduced, prices to distribution outlets can still be modified. Consequently, a precise tracing of production costs is critically important to achieving acceptable profits from this product line.

Materials and conversion costs are applied uniformly in this production process. The following operating data are available for analysis:

	Units	Percent Completion	Materials Costs	Conversion Costs	Total
Beginning inventory	80	50%	$ 7,200	$ 4,000	$11,200
Current-period costs			28,000	14,000	42,000
Total			$35,200	$18,000	$53,200
Units completed and transferred	150	100%			
Ending inventory	50	60%			

8. Equivalent Units of Production. Measures of equivalent units of production in a FIFO system are slightly different from those used in average costing systems. Since materials and conversion costs are applied uniformly, a single measure serves effectively in the tracing process.

First determine an **equivalent unit of production** by completing the following schedule:

	Quantity	Percent Completion	Equivalent Units
Units completed and transferred			
Plus: Ending inventory			
Subtotal			
Less: Beginning inventory			
Equivalent units of production			

Example. Executive Furnishings, Inc.'s schedule would appear as follows:

	Quantity	Percent Completion	Equivalent Units
Units completed and transferred	150	100%	150
Plus: Ending inventory	50	60%	30
Subtotal			180
Less: Beginning inventory	80	50%	40
Equivalent units of production			140

Note that this schedule for computing equivalent units includes the beginning inventory data because costs sometimes change dramatically from period to period. Consequently, costs included in the beginning inventory can differ markedly from those incurred currently. These two sets of costs must then be traced separately to units transferred to finished goods.

Exercise

In a given month, Vista's television production department completed and transferred 85,000 units. Beginning inventory had been 4,000 units (50% complete) and ending inventory was 6,000 units (50% complete). Determine equivalent units of production for this period using the FIFO system.

	Quantity	Percent Completion	Equivalent Units
Units completed and transferred	85,000	100%	85,000
Plus: Ending inventory	6,000	50%	3,000
Subtotal			88,000
Less: Beginning inventory	4,000	50%	2,000
Equivalent units of production			86,000

9.   Equivalent Units of Production—Alternative Approach.   A second approach to developing the equivalent unit measure may be helpful. This approach subtracts the beginning inventory units from the units completed and transferred and then adds the other efforts performed during the period.

Equivalent units of production can also be determined using the following schedule:

	Equivalent Units
Units completed and transferred	
Less: Beginning inventory units	
Equals units started and completed	
(current period)	
Plus: Other efforts	
Completion of the beginning inventory ($X\%$ of X units)	
Work on ending inventory ($X\%$ of X units)	
Equals production output (equivalent units)	

Example. In Executive Furnishings' case, of the 150 units completed and transferred to finished goods, 80 units had been started in the prior period. Thus only 70 of these units were started and completed for transfer during the period. In addition, efforts were expended to complete the beginning inventory, and further, to partially finish the ending inventory. Their schedule would appear as follows:

	Equivalent Units
Units completed and transferred	150
Less: Beginning inventory units	80
Units started and completed (current period)	70
Other efforts	
Finish beginning inventory (50% X 80 units)	40
Work on ending inventory (60% X 50 units)	30
Production output (equivalent units)	140

Exercise

Again, use the data from the preceding example (frame 8) to determine the equivalent units of production using the alternative method.

	Equivalent Units
Units completed and transferred	85,000
Less: Beginning inventory units	4,000
Equals units started and completed (current period)	81,000
Plus: Other efforts	
Finish beginning inventory (50% X 4,000 units)	2,000
Work on ending inventory (50% X 6,000 units)	3,000
Equals output (equivalent units)	86,000

Note that both approaches to measuring equivalent units of production again yield the same results. Clearly, however, added insights can be gained by studying in more detail the specific units to which efforts are applied. Of particular relevance is the fact that FIFO procedures concentrate specifically on the need to complete beginning inventory as a separate production step. The reason rests in the fact that these units contain costs from *two separate periods*. The first period's costs are attached to the 50% completion in the beginning inventory at the outset. Current-period costs, of course, are applied to all current production efforts.

10.   Current-Period Average Costs.   Although procedures used in measuring equivalent units are the same in most systems, development of cost information in a FIFO system is substantially different. Specifically, you must develop a measure of current-period average costs to use in valuing units produced.

In the FIFO approach, use only current-period costs in developing average costs per unit produced:

$$\textbf{current-period average costs} = \frac{\text{current materials costs} + \text{current conversion costs}}{\text{equivalent units}}$$

Example.   In Executive Furnishings' situation, the current-period costs are $200 per unit.

$$\frac{\$28,000 \text{ (current materials cost)}}{140 \text{ (equivalent units)}} = \$200 \text{ (current-period average cost)}$$

Conversion costs for the current period are similarly converted into a per unit cost measure. Costs incurred for direct labor and overhead were $14,000 for this period. Dividing this total by 140 equivalent units of production, the average cost per unit for conversion costs is $100 ($14,000 ÷ 140 equivalent units). These measures of per unit costs can be used in valuing both units transferred to finished goods and those remaining in the department's ending inventory.

Exercise. Assume that Vista's television production department incurred $559,000 in materials expenses and $387,000 in conversion costs during the particular month of operation being analyzed. These represent current-period costs. Using the equivalent units of production calculated in the last frame, what are the current-period average costs for

Vista's department in this instance? _____

_ _ _ _ _ _ _ _ _ _ _ _ _ _ _

Materials $6.50 per unit ($559,000 divided by 86,000); conversion costs $4.50 per unit ($387,000 divided by 86,000).

11.   Beginning Inventory Costs. The FIFO costing system is effective because beginning inventory costs are separated from current-period costs. One impact of this separation was observed as per unit costs were computed. Its effect will similarly be noted as cost-tracing procedures are completed.

Costs are first assigned to units transferred to finished goods inventory. This procedure in a FIFO system is divided into two parts. Units in the beginning inventory are assumed to be completed *first* because they were placed in the process first, the essence of the FIFO method.

> In a FIFO system, separate beginning inventory costs by using the costs from the prior month for the beginning inventory and adding the current costs in materials and conversion costs that are required to complete these beginning inventory units. This will separate the total beginning inventory costs.

Example. Executive Furnishings' beginning inventory represents 40 units in equivalent terms (80 X 50%). Production costs of $11,200 were incurred in the prior period as the beginning inventory was processed to its stated degree of completion. The remaining 40 units of equivalent production in the beginning inventory were completed during the current period. Current-period material costs of $200 per unit and current-period conversion costs of $100 per unit must then be traced to the unfinished portion of the beginning inventory as illustrated in the following schedule:

	Materials Costs	Conversion Costs	Total Costs
Beginning inventory (50% complete)	$ 7,200	$4,000	$11,200
Completion costs			
Materials (40 units at $200)	8,000		8,000
Conversion (40 units X $100)		4,000	4,000
Total costs	$15,200	$8,000	$23,200

Of critical importance to this measure is that the beginning inventory contains measures of costs incurred in two different periods, precisely the information management desires. For Executive Furnishings, materials costs last period were $7,200 for 40 equivalent units, an average of $180 per unit. This average cost is $20 *less* per unit than the current-period cost. Thus a significant raw materials price increase has apparently occurred. Management must recognize this cost change and take actions to control expenses.

Exercise

In the month being analyzed, Vista's television production department had a beginning inventory of 4,000 units that were 50% complete at the beginning of the period. This represented $14,000 in materials costs and $9,000 in conversion costs. Use these data and the information from frame 10 to separate out the total costs for Vista's beginning inventory to reach completion.

- - - - - - - - - - - - - - -

	Materials Costs	Conversion Costs	Total Costs
Beginning inventory (4,000 units 50% complete)	$14,000	$ 9,000	$23,000
Completion costs	13,000		13,000
Materials (2,000 units at $6.50)			
Conversion (2,000 units at $4.50)		9,000	9,000
Total costs	$27,000	$18,000	$45,000

Notice that the materials costs have decreased from one period to the next while labor costs have remained constant. (This occurred because a new electrical subassembly was introduced in the current period.)

12. Units Started and Completed Costs

> Next, trace costs to units started and completed during the period by subtracting the units in the beginning inventory from units completed and transferred.

Example. Executive Furnishings' beginning inventory upon completion accounted for 80 of the units transferred to finished goods and was valued at $23,200. The remaining 70 units (150 completed and transferred less 80 in beginning inventory) were started and completed wholly during this period. Consequently, these units absorb only current-period production costs, as illustrated in the following schedule:

Units Started and Completed (This Period)	Quantity	Current-Period Cost	Total Cost
Materials cost	70	$200	$14,000
Conversion cost	70	100	7,000
Total cost	70	$300	$21,000

Exercise

Vista's television department completed and transferred 85,000 units at the end of the second period. Materials costs were $6.50 per unit, conversion costs $4.50 per unit. What were the total costs for units *started and completed* during the second month of operations?

Units Started and Completed (This Period)	Quantity[a]	Current-Period Cost	Total Cost
Materials cost	81,000	$ 6.50	$526,500
Conversion cost	81,000	4.50	364,500
Total cost	81,000	$11.00	$891,000

[a] 85,000 units completed and transferred *minus* 4,000 units in the beginning inventory.

13. Total Costs of Units Completed and Transferred

> Combine costs traced to the beginning inventory with those assigned to units *started* and completed during the period to obtain the total cost of units transferred to finished goods.

Example. Executive Furnishings' incurred $23,200 in expenses to complete its beginning inventory and an additional $21,000 to start and complete units during the period for a total cost of $44,200.

Exercise

Determine the total costs for units completed and transferred by Vista's television production department during the second month of operation.

- - - - - - - - - - - - - - - -

$936,000 ($45,000 in beginning inventory costs and $891,000 in costs for units started and completed during the period).

14.   Valuing Ending Inventories.   The final phase of the cost-tracing process, valuing ending inventories, is identical in all costing systems.

> In a FIFO system, use *only* current-period average costs to value the ending inventory.

Example.   Executive's ending inventory would be valued as follows:

Ending Inventory	Quantity	X	Completion Percentage	=	Equivalent Units	X	Current Cost	=	Total Cost
Materials cost	50	X	60%	=	30	X	$200	=	$6,000
Conversion cost	50	X	60%	=	30	X	$100	=	3,000
Total cost									$9,000

As a final point, note that the costs assigned to units transferred out, $44,200, when combined with the ending inventory valuation of $9,000, is equal to the total production costs of $53,200. Had there been an error in the cost-tracing process, these cost figures would not have been in balance.

Exercise

Develop a schedule reflecting Vista's television department's ending inventory for the second month of operation.

- - - - - - - - - - - - - - -

Ending Inventory	Quantity	X	Completion Percentage	=	Equivalent Units	X	Current Cost	=	Total Cost
Materials cost	6,000	X	50%	=	3,000	X	$6.50	=	$19,500
Conversion cost	6,000	X	50%	=	3,000	X	$4.50	=	13,500
Total cost									$33,000

Again, note that the ending inventory valuation of $33,000 combined with the $936,000 transferred to finished goods inventory equals the $969,000 total production costs, indicating that tracing of costs has been accurate.

15. Review—FIFO

> To **trace costs** using the first in/first out (FIFO) method:
> 1. Determine an equivalent unit of production (frames 7 and 8).
> 2. Determine current-period average costs (frame 9).
> 3. Determine costs to complete the beginning inventory (frame 10).
> 4. Determine costs of units *started* and completed (frame 11).
> 5. Combine costs of beginning inventory and units started and completed (frame 12).
> 6. Value the ending inventory (frame 13).
> 7. Verify the accuracy of cost tracing by adding costs of goods transferred (step 5) and value of ending inventory (step 6). The total should be the same as total production costs for the period.

As a final review of FIFO costing, use the following data for Specialty Products, Inc. Trace all costs incurred during the period using the FIFO method.

Specialty Products, Inc., has developed a miniature pocket calculator and sales are expanding rapidly. The sales manager has asked for a thorough analysis of the production costs of the product. Specialty's production operates on a FIFO costing system, and all materials are added at the beginning of the period. The following data are provided by the accounting department for a given month.

Units completed and transferred	15,000
Beginning inventory	(5,000 units/20% complete)
Ending inventory	(10,000 units/40% complete)

Costs	Materials	Conversion
Beginning inventory	$ 25,000	$ 3,000
Current period	100,000	54,000

(a) What is the measure of equivalent units for conversion? _____
Materials? _____
(b) What is the measure of current-period average cost for conversion? _____
Materials? _____
(c) What is the valuation of the beginning inventory after it is completed?

_____
(d) What is the measure of total costs transferred to finished goods? _____
(e) What is the valuation of the ending inventory? _____
Note: Have you now accounted for all production costs?

— — — — — — — — — — — — — —

(a)

	Equivalent Units of Production	
	Materials	Conversion
Transferred out	15,000	15,000
Ending inventory	10,000 (100%)	4,000 (10,000 X 40%)
Subtotal	25,000	19,000
Beginning inventory	5,000 (100%)	1,000 (5,000 X 20%)
Equivalent units	20,000	18,000

(b)

Materials	Conversion
$\dfrac{\$100,000}{20,000} = \$5/\text{unit}$	$\dfrac{\$54,000}{18,000} = \$3/\text{unit}$

(c)

	Materials	Conversion	Total
Beginning inventory	$25,000	$ 3,000	$28,000
Cost to complete			
Materials	—0—		—0—
Conversion[a]		12,000	12,000
Total	$25,000	$15,000	$40,000

[a] The beginning inventory was 20% complete; during this period, the remaining 80% (4,000 units) must be completed at a current cost of $3 per unit.

(d) 15,000 units were transferred out; of these, 5,000 units were in the beginning inventory and the remaining 10,000 units were started and completed during this period.

Transferred out

Beginning inventory	$ 40,000
Current period (10,000 X $8)	80,000
Total costs	$120,000

(e) Ending inventory valuation:

Materials	(10,000 × $5)	$50,000
Conversion	(4,000 × $3)	12,000
Total		$62,000

Total costs

Transferred out	$120,000
Ending inventory	62,000
Total	$182,000

You may want to review the questions at the beginning of this chapter before completing the Self-Test that follows.

CHAPTER 5 SELF-TEST

1. Matching – Terminology/Concepts

Match the following terms to the definitions.

1. Actual costs	9. Efficiency
2. Average cost per unit	10. Equivalent units of product
3. Average costing	11. FIFO costing
4. Conversion costs	12. Historical costs
5. Cost accounting	13. Job-order costing
6. Departmental overhead	14. Process costing
7. Direct labor costs	15. Production department
8. Direct materials costs	

_____ (a) A measure developed by dividing manufacturing expenses of a production department by the number of units it produces during an accounting period.

_____ (b) A system designed to trace or assign production costs to major projects or programs.

_____ (c) Procedures designed to trace manufacturing costs through production departments into units of output; specialized measurement procedures are used to ensure that consistent valuations of inventory can be achieved.

_____ (d) Specialized units in a manufacturing operation; costs are traced initially to each department and then to goods produced within this unit when process costing is applied.

_____ (e) A term describing the combination of direct labor costs and manufacturing overhead costs.

_____ (f) Procedures designed to separate prior-period and current-period expenses when determining measures of average cost per unit.

_____ (g) Costs other than direct material and direct labor incurred within a specific operating unit and ultimately traced to units produced.

_____ (h) A measure of production output that is used as the basis for determining average cost per unit produced. Partially completed units are converted into terms of whole units.

_____ (i) A system to assign production costs first to operating departments and then to units of output.

_____ (j) A specialized costing method in which beginning inventory costs are combined with current-period production costs and then divided by production output.

2. Equivalent Units of Product

(a) The Lunar Company operates a series of manufacturing departments as its products are produced. In one department, materials and conversion costs (direct labor and overhead) flow uniformly. Its beginning inventory was 1,000 units that were 40% completed in the prior month. Carried further, 12,000 units were completed and transferred to finished goods. The ending inventory of 3,000 units were 60% complete at month-end. Compute the equivalent units for this product.

(b) Another of Lunar's departments differs from the earlier one in that materials are entered wholly at the beginning of the process. Thus equivalent units are 100% complete as to materials at all times. Conversion costs are applied uniformly through-out the period. This department completed and transferred 5,000 units during the month. Its ending inventories of 2,000 units were 50% complete as to conversion costs. The beginning inventory of 3,000 units had been 80% complete as to conver-sion costs. Compute equivalent units of product for materials _____; for conversion costs _____ .

3. Average Costing versus FIFO

The management of Lunar Company is considering the possibility of adopting a FIFO costing system rather than the average-costing procedures now used. For purposes of this analysis, assume that materials and conversion costs flow uniformly throughout the month. The following data were provided. Equivalent units of product for the period were 5,000 units under both average costing and FIFO costing.

	Materials	Conversion Costs
Beginning inventory	$ 10,000	$ 20,000
Current-month costs	140,000	80,000
Total	$150,000	$100,000

(a) Compute the average cost per equivalent unit using *average costing.* _____
(b) Compute the average cost per equivalent unit using *FIFO costing.* _____

4. Average Costing

Another of Lunar's departments transferred 10,000 units to finished goods inventory in a specified month. Its ending inventory of 4,000 units was 75% completed as to materials and 60% completed as to conversion costs. Average materials costs for the period were $6.00 per unit. Average labor costs were $4.00 per unit.

(a) Determine the costs transferred to the finished goods inventory. _____
(b) Determine the costs assigned to this month's ending inventory. _____

5. FIFO Costing

As an experiment, the Lunar Company decided to apply the FIFO costing method in one department. The following data were developed as the basis for assigning one month's costs:

	Materials	Conversion	Total
Beginning inventory	$ 60,000	$ 80,000	$140,000
Current-period costs	180,000	210,000	390,000
Total	$240,000	$290,000	$530,000

In addition, a schedule for equivalent units of product was developed for the cost tracing process:

	Materials	Conversion
Completed and transferred	30,000 units	30,000 units
Less: Beginning inventory	20,000 units	20,000 units
Started, completed, and transferred	10,000 units	10,000 units
Ending inventory (10,000 units)	8,000 (80%)	5,000 (50%)
Beginning inventory (20,000 units)	12,000 (60%)	6,000 (33⅓%)
Equivalent units	30,000 units	21,000 units

(a) Calculate the cost of units transferred to finished goods. _____

(b) Determine the cost valuations for ending work-in-process inventory. _____

ANSWERS

1. Matching – Terminology/Concepts (see Glossary, 10 pts)

(a) 2	(b) 13	(c) 5	(d) 15
(e) 4	(f) 11	(g) 6	(h) 10
(i) 14	(j) 3		

2. Equivalent Units of Production

(a) 13,400 equivalent units [12,000 + (60% × 3,000) – (40% × 1,000)]   (frames 1 and 8, 3 pts).

(b) Materials 4,000 units (5,000 + 2,000 – 3,000); conversion costs 3,600 [5,000 + (50% × 1,000 units) – (80% × 3,000 units)]   (frame 5, 3 pts).

3. Average Costing versus FIFO

(a) $50 ($250,000 ÷ 5,000 units) (frame 3, 5 pts).

(b) $44 ($220,000 ÷ 5,000 units) (frames 7–14, 5 pts).

4. Average Costing

(a) $100,000 (10,000 units × $10) (frame 4, 5 pts).

(b) 27,600 (4,000 × 75% × $6) + (4,000 × 60% × $4) (frame 13, 5 pts).

5. FIFO Costing

(a) Costs to finished goods (frames 7–14, 7 pts)

	Materials	Conversion	Total
Beginning costs	$ 60,000	$ 80,000	$140,000
Costs to complete			
Materials (12,000 × $6)	72,000		72,000
Conversion (6,000 × $10)		60,000	60,000
Total	$132,000	$140,000	$272,000
Other units	60,000	100,000	160,000
Cost of beginning inventory	$192,000	$240,000	$432,000

(b) Ending work-in-process inventory (frame 13, 5 pts)

Materials (8,000 × $6)	$48,000
Conversion (5,000 × $10)	50,000
Total	$98,000

Note: The total of (a) and (b) ($530,000) accounts for all production costs incurred in the beginning inventory as well as those incurred during the current period.

Total possible points: 48. You should have scored at least 38.

CHAPTER 6

Standard Costing Systems

 Can you . . .

- Explain what standard costs and variances are?
- Determine and record in a proper format materials cost variances? Materials usage variances?
- Determine and record in a proper format direct labor rate variances? Efficiency variances?
- Determine and record in a proper format variable overhead spending variances? Efficiency variances?
- Apply standard costing to fixed manufacturing overhead variances, including the determination and recording of budget variances, volume variances, a planned idle capacity variance, and marketing variances?
- Summarize favorable and unfavorable variances in a management control report to show their effects on projected gross profit?

After working through the materials in this chapter, you should be competent to do all of the preceding cost accounting procedures.

The availability of cost information is crucial to achieving success in any organization. Objectives can be stated either in terms of profitable growth in the private sector or providing quality services in the public sector. In both cases, responsible managers must be continuously aware of the cost implications of their decisions. Cost accounting systems provide the basis for systematically accumulating information for planning and control purposes.

Standard costing procedures complement both job-order and process systems. The emphasis changes, however, from accumulating cost information to using these data for planning and control purposes. Viewed from this perspective, standard costing is a bridge between information about an organization's past activities and future-oriented decisions made by responsible personnel.

> **Standard costs** are estimated future costs that are developed as a basis for planning and control purposes.

Standards are preestablished cost targets that serve as guidelines for evaluating operating performance as well as goals toward which actions can be directed. These same measures can be used as control tools when actual results are compared to the target levels to determine variances.

> A **variance** is the difference between costs actually incurred and those expected when relevant standards or budgets are used.

The entire chapter is devoted to an examination of standard costs and variances. Of utmost importance is that when significant differences between actual and planned performance levels are detected, the control process must be initiated. Causes of problems are identified and corrective actions can then be taken to improve overall performance.

Procedures used in setting standards vary from organization to organization, depending on management's philosophy about goals and objectives. Three basic types of standards can be readily identified:

—*Historical standards*—target costs are based almost wholly on past results of comparable operations.

—*Reasonably attainable standards*—target costs are established at levels of performance expected to be achieved in the coming period.

—*Ideal standards*—target costs can be achieved only if almost perfect production conditions are encountered. These represent the best results that could occur.

In the first approach, standards are based on average costs of prior periods determined from information obtained directly from cost accounting records. If significant changes in material, labor, or overhead costs are expected, adjustments are made.

A second approach to developing a standard cost is to evaluate the likelihood of improvements in functions to be performed. Realistic estimates allow efforts to be directed toward achieving "reasonably attainable" standards. Underlying this particular strategy is the theory that employees are more likely to be positively motivated when goals are realistic. These positive attitudes should then contribute to increased effectiveness and efficiency throughout the particular operating environment.

The third approach to setting standards focuses on developing performance measures attainable only under "ideal" circumstances. Implicit in such targets is the premise that maximum output levels are always desired. Given this view, attention is directed to achieving near perfection. Ideal standards are often based on engineering specifications with adjustments for machine breakdowns or other production hindrances built into the targets. Variations between actual performances and these ideal standards are monitored through the management control process.

Although all three approaches to developing standards occur in practice, materials in this chapter are based on the assumption that the system revolves around "reasonably attainable" standards, the second approach. Attention is directed specifically to using standard costs for direct materials, direct labor, variable factory overhead, and fixed factory overhead as a basis for planning and control decisions.

The use of standard costing is most prevalent in manufacturing industries because of their need for large volumes of output and efficient production methods. Therefore, manufacturing operations are selected as the basis for discussions of standard costing, although the basic concepts are also applicable on a much broader scale. The various dimensions of standard costing will be demonstrated as the cost accounting methods of Hospitality Uniforms, Inc., are analyzed.

Hospitality Uniforms, Inc., specializes in producing and marketing uniforms for personnel working in the hospitality service industries. Its major clientele include leading hotel and restaurant organizations throughout the world. Long-term contracts are signed to ensure reasonable service to customers and a relatively stable demand for Hospitality's products. As a general rule, a client decides to change its employees' uniforms well in advance of the planned changeover date. Usually, sufficient quantities of sample uniforms are purchased to allow a testing of the product's acceptability to both employees and customers.

An order of 2,000 uniforms has been received from a major client. Management expects to complete production in approximately 4 weeks. Since this particular uniform is not substantially different from those used previously by the customer, production problems should be minimal. Equally important, standards developed for previous production activities need to be modified only slightly. The assumption of "reasonable attainability" seems quite valid in this case. Following is a summary of the relevant standard costing information for this uniform, Model 437.

Standard Costs
Uniform Model 437

Direct materials	3 yards at $3 per yard	$ 9.00
Direct labor	½ hour at $6 per hour	3.00
(includes fringe-benefit costs of $1 per hour)		
Variable manufacturing overhead	½ hour at $6 per hour	3.00
Fixed manufacturing overhead	$5 per uniform	5.00
Total		$20.00

Two points should be noted as these cost data are used for planning and control purposes. First, the direct labor costs relate to two different production activities, cutting and sewing. The cost per unit (uniform) measure includes fringe benefit expenses and represents the average wage rates paid to personnel involved in these operations. Second, variable overhead per hour is separated from the fixed overhead cost component in this company. Variable manufacturing overhead costs are applied to products on a basis of direct labor hours per unit. Fixed overhead, on the other hand, is applied on a per unit basis because the company's overall production capacity is evaluated in terms of this output measure.

Hospitality's uniforms in this contract sell for $25. Thus, since only nominal amounts of nonproduction costs are incurred, a profit of approximately $5 per unit is anticipated. As cost increases occur, reevaluations of pricing on each uniform model are required. Standard cost data serve as the basis for these evaluations. Direct materials costs, direct labor requirements, and the need for specialized equipment are thus subjected to thorough analysis before accepting a new contract. The uses of standards in this manner demonstrate their value as a planning tool. Control, on the other hand, occurs by comparing actual performances to expected operating results—that is, variances.

STANDARD COSTING FOR DIRECT MATERIALS

Standard cost data serve effectively in a planning context because the information can serve as a basis for assessing the profit impact of specific events and decisions. Equally important, however, are the uses of these data for control purposes. As the first step in controlling product costs, standards provide a basis for determining whether prices paid for direct materials are comparable to those anticipated when the target measures were established. Two variances are considered in standard costing for direct materials: materials cost variance and materials usage variance. These measures, in turn, serve as a basis for control action. Relevant data in a standard costing system are also entered into the accounting records. Finally, standard costs are combined with variances to provide information in the income statement format.

1.   **Materials Price Variances.**   The first step in standard costing focuses on the analysis of prices paid for materials when they are purchased from suppliers. A standard (expected price) is set and the actual costs are compared to this standard.

> **Materials price variances** are the differences between prices actually paid for production materials and those that should have been paid at standard. Prices greater than expected are called **unfavorable variances**; those less than expected are called **favorable variances**. This variance measure is applied to amounts of materials actually purchased and is recorded at the time the purchases are made.

Example.   Hospitality Uniforms, Inc., set a standard of $3.00 per yard for raw materials. A review of the purchasing department's cost information reveals that 6,600 yards of material was purchased for the order of 2,000 uniforms. The price due the supplier was $21,450. (An invoice documented the purchase and all appropriate receiving documents were prepared as the materials were received.) Dividing the price paid by the number of yards resulted in a price of $3.25 per yard being paid. This is more than the standard; therefore, the material's price variance is unfavorable. The actual variance is $1,650 (25¢ × 6,600 yards). This difference indicates that purchasing personnel spent more for materials than management intended.

Exercise

Assume that the same customer who placed the order for 2,000 uniforms places another order for 500 more uniforms of Model 437. Using the same standards, what is the material price variance if Hospitality Uniforms, Inc., purchases 1,700 yards of material for $5,950? _____ What is the material price variance if it purchases 1,700 yards for $5,015? _____

— — — — — — — — — — — — — —

The first purchase would be an unfavorable variance of $850. ($5,950 divided by 1,700 yards equals $3.50/yard. This is 50 cents per yard more than the $3.00 standard. Multiplying 1,700 yards by 50 cents equals $850 variance.) In the second purchase, however, a favorable variance of $85 occurs. ($5,015 ÷ 1,700 yards = $2.95/yard. The 5 cents difference times 1,700 yards equals $85.)

2.   Recording Materials Price Variances.   The total cost of the material price variation can be quite significant in terms of evaluating the financial performance of either individual functions or complete product lines. In either case, the variance must be formally recorded in the records. Standard costing systems contain specific procedures for these purposes.

The entry to record these cost data includes (1) assignment of the materials costs to the raw materials inventory, (2) a measure of the variance, and (3) the payment (or the liability) to the supplier.

The first element in the entry requires that the direct materials be assigned to an appropriate raw materials inventory account. In a standard costing system, the inventories are maintained at *standard cost* valuations rather than actual costs incurred. The reason for this adjustment rests on the premise that standards reflect costs that "should have been" incurred. Differences between the actual costs and standard costs are thus traced to the particular decisions rather than to inventories per se. Recording this variance information ensures that such data are formally included in the company's financial records. Equally important, however, is the need for continuous reviews of variance data to identify the probable causes of differences between standards and actual results. If variances are caused by faulty procedures or decisions, corrective actions can be taken. Sometimes, however, such differences are caused by conditions beyond the manager's control, for example unexpected price raises in cost of materials. Future plans should then explicitly consider these changes in conditions. Standards must be adjusted where appropriate if the "reasonably attainable" assumption is to remain valid.

To record materials cost variances for planning and control purposes:
1. Assign costs to raw materials inventory using *standard* valuations.
2. Enter a debit for unfavorable variances, a credit for favorable variances.
3. Enter a credit to accounts payable or cash using *actual* costs incurred.

Example. Hospitality Uniforms' entry for recording materials purchase price variance would be as follows:

	Debit	Credit
Raw materials inventory (standard costs)	$19,800	
Materials purchase price variance	1,650	
Accounts payable (actual costs)		$21,450

Raw materials costs were obtained by multiplying the actual quantity of materials purchased (6,600 yards) by the *standard* cost per yard ($3.00). The second part of the entry reflects the total amount of the materials price variance. Each of the 6,600 yards of material purchased was priced at $0.25 more than standard; therefore, the total variance is $1,650 (6,600 yards × $0.25 variance per yard). Since this is an unfavorable variance, it is recorded as a *debit.* The final portion of the entry reflects a credit to accounts payable since Hospitality purchases all materials on credit. Had they paid cash, it would have been credited to cash. The amount of the entry is the total purchase price, reflecting costs *actually* paid. Perhaps most important in developing this standard costing variance, however, is that the variance measure is created at the *point of purchase.* This occurs because the variation relates specifically to the material quantities purchased rather than the times when they are used in production.

Exercise

Use the data from the two hypothetical purchases of materials for the order of 500 uniforms to complete journal entries for each, reflecting materials cost variances:

1.

2.

- - - - - - - - - - - - - - - -

1.

	Debit	Credit
Raw materials inventory (1,700 yards × $3.00)	$5,100	
Materials purchase price variance (1,700 × $0.50)	850	
Accounts payable (actual costs incurred)		$5,950

2.

	Debit	Credit
Raw materials inventory	5,100	
Materials purchase price variance (1,700 × $0.05)		85
Accounts payable		5,015

Note that in the second purchase, the variance is entered as a credit since costs incurred were less than expected (favorable variance).

3. Materials Usage Variances. The second stage in accounting for direct materials in a standard costing system is to monitor resource usage in the production process. By comparing actual usage during a given period to what should have occurred at standard, a measure of variation can be determined. Again, this measure serves as a basis for control action. Favorable variances occur when less materials are used than the standard requires; unfavorable variances represent an excessive use of materials.

> **Materials usage variances** are the differences between quantities of materials actually used and amounts that should have been used when standards are applied. The variance measure is applied to materials transferred from raw materials inventory and is recorded as this usage occurs.

Example. Hospitality Uniforms' production department requested from inventory and actually used 6,300 yards to produce 2,000 uniforms. Each uniform should have required 3 yards at standard, or a total of 6,000 yards. The difference between standard usage (6,000 yards) and actual usage (6,300 yards) is multiplied by the standard rate ($3.00 per yard) to provide the appropriate measure of the materials usage variance: $900 (300 yards over standard X $3.00 per yard). This is an unfavorable variance.

Exercise
1. What would the material usage variance be if the production department requested 1,400 yards of material to produce the second order of 500 uniforms? _____
2. What would it be if they requested 1,500 yards? _____
3. 1,600 yards? _____

— — — — — — — — — — — — — —

1. $300 favorable variance. (500 uniforms X 3 yards = 1,500 yards at standard; actual usage was 100 yards less, multiplied by $3.00 per yard.)
2. No variance.
3. $300 unfavorable variance. (100 yards over standard X $3.00 per yard.)

4. Recording Materials Usage Variances. The first step in assigning these direct materials costs is to make a charge to the production department. For cost purposes, production areas are treated as work-in-process inventory accounts. Again, the inventory is transferred at its standard cost valuation because materials flowing into it from the raw materials inventories were valued at standard cost. (Recall that the materials price variance was identified and recorded at the point of purchase.)

> **To record materials usage variances** for planning and control:
> 1. Debit the work-in-process inventory using *standard* measures.
> 2. Debit unfavorable variances; credit favorable variances.
> 3. Credit the raw materials inventory.

Example. Hospitality Uniforms' entry for materials usage variance for the order of 2,000 uniforms would be as follows:

	Debit	Credit
Work-in-process inventory	$18,000	
Materials usage variance	900	
Raw materials inventory		$18,900

The production department is assessed a charge of $18,000 (6,000 yards at $3.00 per yard). Note that costs assigned to work-in-process inventory are based on the standard cost of $3.00 per yard. The charge to work in process is a debit because this inventory account is being increased. The measure involved is the quantity of materials that *should* have been used (6,000 yards) at the standard rate ($3.00 per yard). The materials usage variance of $900 is unfavorable and is recorded as a debit to portray costs in excess of standard amounts intended. (The opposite entry, a credit, would occur had the variance been favorable, that is, had actual costs been less than standard costs.) The third element in the entry reflects the release of materials from raw materials inventory. This transfer of costs is supported by a materials requisition form that identifies the assignment of 6,300 yards of material to the production area. Each yard is assigned the *standard* cost rate, $3.00, thereby reducing the raw materials inventory by a total of $18,900, which has been transferred to the work-in-process inventory.

Exercise

Make the appropriate entries to reflect the materials usage variances calculated for the order of 500 uniforms (preceding frame).

1.

2.

3.

Remember that inventories are always valued at standard costs.

- - - - - - - - - - - - - -

1.	Debit	Credit
Work-in-process inventory (1,500 × $3.00) (what *should* occur—standards)	$4,500	
Materials usage variance (favorable)		$ 300
Raw materials inventory (1,400 × $3.00)		4,200
2. Work-in-process inventory (remains the same)	4,500	
Materials usage variance (none)	−0−	−0−
Raw materials inventory (1,500 × $3.00)		4,500
3. Work-in-process inventory	4,500	
Materials usage variance (unfavorable)	300	
Raw materials inventory (1,600 × $3.00)		4,800

STANDARD COSTING FOR DIRECT LABOR

After direct material variances are analyzed, specific elements of the conversion process, direct labor and variable overhead, are analyzed. Direct labor costs include both the wages and fringe benefits paid to production personnel. The cost of production efforts must take into account both the *rate* paid to employees and the number of hours worked, or their *efficiency*.

In the case of Hospitality Uniforms, Inc., the standard direct labor cost for both cutting and sewing functions is $6.00 per hour. Of this amount, $5 is the average wage rate; the remaining 20%, or $1 per hour, is incurred for fringe benefits. During the production period, 2,000 uniforms were produced to satisfy the relevant customer order. Each uniform should require ½ hour at a standard cost rate of $6.00 per hour. Records reveal that the department actually worked 900 hours at a total cost of $5,850. These data provide the basis for completing the standard direct labor cost variances and recording these data in the company's financial records.

5. Direct Labor Rate Variances. The first variance to be measured in analyzing direct labor costs is rate variance, that is, the difference between the rate that should be paid according to the standard and the wage rate actually paid to production workers. Payroll records clearly document the amounts paid to each employee. Any unfavorable labor rate variance may be caused by using too high a proportion of workers who are earning wages greater than the expected costs. The responsible department manager must determine the cause for unfavorable variance and implement appropriate corrective action to avoid similar future variations.

> **Direct labor rate variances** are the differences between direct labor costs per hour and standard cost per hour. The measure is applied to actual hours used during a given accounting period.

Example. In the case of Hospitality Uniforms, wages actually paid were $5,850. Dividing this amount by the number of hours worked, 900 hours, results in an average rate actually paid of $6.50 per hour. Since this variance is $0.50 greater than the standard, the measure is unfavorable. The direct labor rate variance is computed by multiplying the actual hours worked (900) by the variation between standard and actual rate ($0.50 per hour). Therefore, this variance is determined to be an unfavorable variance of $450 for the production period being evaluated.

Exercise
1. Determine the direct labor rate variance if the department actually worked 1000 hours at a total cost of $5,850. _____
2. Determine the direct labor rate variance if the department worked 1,100 hours at a total cost of $6,325. _____

— — — — — — — — — — — — — — —

1. $150 favorable variance. ($5,850 ÷ 1,000 = $5.85 per hour, $0.15 less than expected, times 1,000 hours worked.)
2. $275 favorable variance. ($6,325 ÷ 1,100 = $5.75 per hour, $0.25 less than expected, times 1,100 hours worked.)

6. Direct Labor Efficiency Variances. The second component of the direct labor variance is the efficiency variance, which reflects differences between the number of hours expected at the standard production rate and the number of hours actually worked. Again, payroll records clearly indicate the number of hours worked by each employee.

> **Direct labor efficiency variances** are the differences be-
> tween labor-hours actually used relative to hours that
> should have been used based on standards developed. The
> financial measure is the standard rate per hour applied to
> hours actually worked during the period.

Example. Hospitality Uniforms has established a standard of ½ hour per uniform, so for 2,000 uniforms, it was anticipated that 1,000 hours would be required. Since operating data reveal that only 900 hours were worked, this variance of 100 hours is favorable. Its measure in terms of costs is the difference between actual and standard hours times the standard rate of $6.00 per hour. Therefore, the direct labor efficiency variance is $600.

Exercise
1. Determine the direct labor efficiency variance if the department actually worked 1,000 hours at a total cost of $5,850. _____
2. Determine the direct labor efficiency variance if the department worked 1,100 hours at a total cost of $6,325. _____

— — — — — — — — — — — — — — —

1. No variance.
2. $600 *unfavorable* variance. (100 hours over standard X $6.00 per hour.)

7. Recording Direct Labor Variances. Direct labor costs are charged to the work-in-process inventory. Recall that inventory accounts in a standard costing system are valued at standard measures. The direct labor rate and efficiency variances are then credited or debited, depending on whether they are favorable or unfavorable. Finally, the total amount of production payroll for the period is credited, representing an increased liability for the accrued payroll account.

> **To record direct labor variances** for planning and control:
> 1. Debit the work-in-process inventory (using standard measures).
> 2. Enter a debit for unfavorable rate variances, a credit for favorable.
> 3. Enter a debit for unfavorable efficiency variances, a credit for favorable.
> 4. Enter a credit for the accrued payroll account.

Example. The entry for Hospitality Uniforms' direct labor costs would be as follows:

	Debit	Credit
Work-in-process inventory (direct labor)	6,000	
Direct labor rate variance	450	
Direct labor efficiency variance		600
Accrued payroll		5,850

Since inventory accounts are valued at standard measures, costs assigned in this case reflect 1,000 hours of standard production activity at the standard rate of $6.00 per hour. This amount is debited to the work-in-process inventory because this asset account is increased by these costs. The direct labor *rate* variance of $450 is a debit because it is unfavorable. The second variance, direct labor *efficiency*, of $600 is a credit because it is favorable. The final element in the entry reflects the total amount of production payroll for the period, $5,850 (900 hours at an actual rate of $6.50 per hour).*

Exercise

1. Using the variances determined in the two preceding exercises, record the variances if the department actually worked 1,000 hours at a total cost of $5,850.

2. Do the same for the situation in which the department worked 1,100 hours at a total cost of $6,325.

- - - - - - - - - - - - - -

1.	Debit	Credit
Work-in-process inventory (direct labor)	$6,000	
Direct labor rate variance		$ 150
Direct labor efficiency variance	—0—	—0—
Accrued payroll (actual costs)		5,850

*Note: Keep in mind that workers who are paid above standard may also produce more (be more efficient) than expected—an important management consideration. In this instance, of course, both the rate and efficiency variances would be favorable, a credit entry, and the standard amount applied to the work-in-process inventory would exceed actual labor costs incurred.

2.

	Debit	Credit
Work-in-process inventory (direct labor)	$6,000	
Direct labor efficiency variance	600	
Direct labor rate variance		$ 275
Accrued payroll		6,325

STANDARD COSTING FOR VARIABLE OVERHEAD

Variable overhead costs are indirect costs because they are not easily traceable to a product being produced. Costs classified as variable are assumed to change in direct proportion to production volume (C/V/P). Overhead is applied on the basis of a pre-determined rate (standard), for example estimated overhead divided by estimated activity in terms of units, direct labor-hours, machine-hours, or some other variable. At period-end this applied rate must be compared to costs actually incurred to determine variances. When overhead is applied on a direct labor-hour basis, the measures of variances for variable overhead parallel those recorded in the direct labor section. Standard costing for variable overhead, like that for direct labor, is measured in terms of both spending and efficiency.

In the case of Hospitality Uniforms, Inc., overhead was applied at the rate of ½ hour @ $6.00 per hour. A review of production data shows that the production department incurred $5,175 in variable overhead costs for the production period, during which 900 direct labor-hours were worked. These data provide the information needed to determine variable overhead variances.

8. **Variable Overhead Spending Variances.** The analysis of variable overhead costs begins by measuring the spending variance and identifies differences in average cost per hour relative to the standard rate.

> The **variable overhead spending variance** is the difference between actual variable overhead costs incurred per hour and those that should have been incurred at standard. This difference in cost per hour is applied to each hour actually worked during the period.

Example. Hospitality Uniforms incurred an average variable overhead rate of $5.75 per hour ($5,175 divided by 900 hours). Compared to the standard rate of $6.00 per hour, this is a spending variance of $0.25 per hour. This factor is then multiplied by the direct labor-hours worked (900) to determine the total variance of $225. Since the actual cost per hour is less than the related standard, the variable overhead spending variance is favorable.

Exercise

1. Determine the variable overhead spending variance if the production department incurred $6,090 in variable overhead costs during a production period in which 1,050 direct labor-hours were worked to produce the 2,000 uniforms.

2. Determine the variable overhead spending variance if $5,917 in variable overhead costs were incurred during a period in which 970 direct labor-hours were worked.

— — — — — — — — — — — — — —

1. $210 favorable variance. ($6,090 ÷ 1,050 hours = $5.80 per hour, $0.20 less than standard cost X 1,050 hours = $210 less than expected.)
2. $97 unfavorable variance. ($5,917 ÷ 970 hours = $6.10 per hour, $0.10 more than standard cost X 970 hours = $97 more than expected.)

Again, the manager must discern the reasons for any differences. In some cases, the standard may need to be revised. Often, however, minor changes in operating procedures cause such variances. Nevertheless, the existence of a variance clearly indicates that certain differences exist between expectations and actual performance. Until the causes for these differences are known, plans for future activities cannot be effectively formulated.

9. Variable Overhead Efficiency Variances. The second variance in the analysis of variable overhead costs is the efficiency variance. Its structure, too, is similar to the direct labor efficiency variance.

> **Variable overhead efficiency variances** are the differences between hours used and those that should have been used according to standards. The financial measure is stated in terms of the standard variable overhead rate.

Example. Since Hospitality Uniforms, Inc., requires 2,000 uniforms to fill their customer's order, the production department could have used 1,000 hours during the period. Instead, the necessary activities were accomplished in only 900 hours. The difference between actual hours worked and allowable hours at standard, 100 hours, is the key measure of efficiency. Multiplied by the standard rate per hour ($6.00), the total efficiency variance is $600. The measure is reflected as a credit entry because the variance is favorable.

Exercise
1. Determine the variable overhead efficiency rate if 1,050 direct labor-hours are worked and $6,090 in variable overhead costs are incurred.

2. Determine the variable overhead efficiency rate if 970 direct labor-hours are worked and $5,917 in variable overhead costs are incurred.

- - - - - - - - - - - - - -

1. $300 unfavorable variance. (50 hours more than expected X $6.00 per hour.)
2. $180 favorable variance. (30 hours less than expected X $6.00 per hour.)

10.   Recording Variable Overhead Variances.   When the analyses of standard costing variances are complete, relevant data are formally recorded in the financial records. First, the actual variable overhead costs incurred are entered into a control account as a debit and into various accounts as credits. This reflects the fact that variable overhead expenditures require credits in most cases to cash, accounts payable, or other expense accounts. When the credit can be to another expense account, this can reflect the transfer of a cost from one department to another.

Next costs are assigned to the work-in-process inventory account, using standard cost per hour and allowable standard hours as the basis as a debit representing an increase to this asset account. The variable factory overhead applied account is credited.

Finally, variances are recorded at the end of the production period, when the control (incurred) and applied overhead accounts are closed. Variable factory overhead applied is debited; variances are debited or credited as appropriate, and variable factory overhead incurred is credited.

> **To record variable overhead variances:**
> 1. Debit the overhead incurred to the variable manufacturing overhead control account. Credit various accounts such as cash or accounts payable.
> 2. Debit standard cost and allowable hours to work-in-process inventory—variable overhead. Credit variable factory overhead applied.
> 3. Close the control and applied overhead accounts at period-end by debiting variable factory overhead applied, debiting unfavorable overhead variances, crediting favorable overhead variances, and crediting variable factory overhead incurred.

Example. The records of Hospitality Uniforms would show the following:

	Debit	Credit
1. Variable manufacturing overhead control (actually incurred)	$5,175	
Various accounts (cash, accounts payable, accumulated, depreciation, etc.)		$5,175
2. Work-in-process inventory—variable overhead (1,000 hours at $6.00—by standards)	$6,000	
Variable factory overhead applied		$6,000
3. Variable factory overhead applied (close account)	$6,000	
Variable overhead spending variance		225
Variable overhead efficiency variance		600
Variable factory overhead incurred (close control account)		5,175

Exercise

1. Using the variances determined in the two preceding exercises, on a separate sheet of paper, make the appropriate entries to record variable overhead costs of $6,090 incurred with 1,050 direct labor-hours worked.
2. Do the same for a period in which overhead costs incurred were $5,917 with 970 direct labor-hours worked.

- - - - - - - - - - - - - - -

	Exercise 1		Exercise 2	
	Debit	Credit	Debit	Credit
Variable manufacturing overhead control	$6,090		$5,917	
Various accounts		$6,090		$5,917
Work-in-process inventory—variable overhead	6,000		6,000	
Variable factory overhead applied		6,000		6,000
Variable factory overhead applied	6,000		6,000	
Variable overhead spending variance		210	97	
Variable overhead efficiency variance	300			180
Variable factory overhead incurred		6,090		5,917

FIXED MANUFACTURING OVERHEAD VARIANCES

Four separate cost classifications are found in many manufacturing systems: direct materials, direct labor, variable overhead, and fixed overhead. Fixed manufacturing costs are different from the other costs, however, because they are *not* responsive to volume changes. For this reason, analytical procedures for fixed manufacturing overhead costs are one of the most complex of the commonly used cost accounting techniques.

Preceding discussions have focused on the production of one customer order in Hospitality Uniforms, Inc. The study of fixed manufacturing overhead will be more effective if the company's total production activities are now considered.

Hospitality Uniforms, Inc., was most successful in its early years. Consequently, 5 years ago the Board of Directors committed resources to purchase land to construct a total operating complex designed specifically for producing a wide range of uniforms. Since many different tasks and functions must be performed, the total operation is separated into smaller operating departments. A particular manager is responsible for productivity within each specialized operating unit.

The production complex was designed to provide an annual capacity of 100,000 uniforms. This level of output, termed *practical capacity*, is used as the basis for planning fixed costs. The measure recognizes that occasional problems in production such as machine breakdowns will occur. Nevertheless, this activity level is considered reasonably attainable.

Hospitality Uniforms, Inc., expects to incur $500,000 in fixed costs during the production period now being considered. In terms of standard costing, therefore, each uniform is expected to bear its proportionate share of fixed manufacturing overhead costs, $5.00 per unit. Standard cost variance analysis is applied when differences occur between expected costs and those actually incurred. The following data appear in this company's records for this production period.

Cost information

Budgeted fixed overhead costs at capacity	$500,000
Actual fixed overhead costs incurred	$480,000

Production information

Practical capacity	100,000 uniforms
Planned production (based on the sales forecast)	80,000 uniforms
Actual production (based on orders recorded)	70,000 uniforms

11. Fixed Variance Overhead Budget Variances. The first variance to be measured in analyzing fixed manufacturing overhead is the budget variance. Favorable variances occur when production exceeds practical capacity as the result of overtime or extra shifts. Unfavorable variances, the usual occurrence, reflect that actual production is less than could occur if the total practical capacity were used.

> **Fixed overhead budget variances** are the differences between fixed overhead costs actually incurred and those budgeted at practical capacity.

Example. Hospitality Uniforms, Inc., budgeted at practical capacity, $500,000 (100,000 uniforms × $5.00 per uniform). Only $480,000 in fixed overhead costs were actually incurred. The difference between the two figures, $20,000, is a favorable variance because costs actually incurred were less than budgeted.

Exercise

What would the fixed variance overhead budget variance be if the company had incurred $550,000 in fixed overhead expenses during the period? _____

– – – – – – – – – – – – – – – –

A $50,000 unfavorable variance would occur.

Variance analysis provides financial measures useful for control purposes. These data, however, are only the starting point for such efforts. Managers must first determine whether the variance commands their immediate attention. If differences are significant, the likely causes of the problem must be detected and corrected. However, because fixed costs are non-volume-related, a large variance in this area was possibly caused by a management decision. Such variances are frequently anticipated by management. Thus analysis efforts generally focus on large, unexpected variances.

12.   Fixed Overhead Volume Variances.   A second measure to compute when analyzing fixed manufacturing overhead costs is the volume variance. Specifically, this measure reflects costs associated with the ability to use a company's total production capacity in any given period. It reflects the difference between practical production capacity and actual production capacity and is the combination of two other variances. The first is the *fixed overhead expected idle capacity variance*, which reflects the *expected* volume variance from what could practically be produced. The second variance is the *fixed overhead marketing variance*, which allows management to analyze the difference between sales forecasts and actual sales in a given period.

Fixed overhead volume variance combines the effects of:
—**Fixed overhead idle capacity variance**, which is the difference between units at practical capacity and the planned production to satisfy the sales forecast. The financial measure is presented in terms of fixed overhead cost per unit.
—**Fixed overhead marketing variance**, which is the difference between units in the sales forecast and those actually produced and sold. Its financial measure is also stated in terms of fixed overhead cost per unit.

Example. Hospitality Uniforms' volume variance was 30,000 units. It had the practical capacity to produce 100,000 units, but only produced 70,000 during the given period. Considered in terms of standard costs, each uniform is expected to absorb $5.00 in fixed manufacturing overhead. Therefore, the volume variance of 30,000 units cost $150,000 during this period, a measure reflecting underapplied fixed overhead. An unfavorable variance of $150,000 would be cause for alarm for most managers *if* they did not consider the two variances that combine to produce total volume variance. In Hospitality Uniforms' case, $100,000 of this loss was anticipated. The expected idle capacity variance was 20,000 uniforms at $5.00 per unit. (100,000 practical capacity minus 80,000 planned production = 20,000 expected idle capacity variance.) What remains, $50,000, is the unexpected marketing variance. Management planned to produce and sell 80,000 uniforms, but only 70,000 were actually ordered, an unfavorable variance of 10,000 uniforms at $5.00 per unit.

Exercise

Describe the total volume variance and its components if the company actually produced 90,000 uniforms during the period. (Use the same standards.)

_____

Total volume variance would be an unfavorable variance of 10,000 units, costing $50,000 at standard. Expected idle capacity variance would be constant—20,000 units at $5.00 per unit; anticipated loss: $100,000. Marketing variance would be a favorable variance of 10,000 units, offsetting fixed costs of $50,000. Combining these two variances, 20,000 units unfavorable (idle capacity) minus 10,000 units favorable (marketing) variance, leaves a total volume variance of 10,000 units as an unfavorable variance. Although the net variance of $50,000 is unfavorable, it is less than was anticipated by management in the original overall plan.

13. Recording Fixed Overhead Variances. The final step is to record these variance data using procedures similar to those used in recording variable overhead. The factory overhead control account is used to record overhead costs actually incurred, and as in previous cases, applied overhead costs flow to the work-in-process inventory account. Variances are recorded when the overhead control and applied accounts are closed at the end of the period.

> **To record fixed overhead variances:**
> 1. Debit the fixed manufacturing overhead control account with overhead actually incurred. The offsetting credit is to various accounts, such as accounts payable, cash, and so on.
> 2. Debit the work-in-process inventory—fixed overhead account using standard cost times the number of units actually produced. Credit the fixed overhead applied account for the same amount to record overhead costs assigned to units produced.
> 3. Debit the fixed manufacturing overhead applied account, debit and/or credit the fixed overhead variances as appropriate, and credit the fixed manufacturing overhead control account to record variances.

Example. The records reflecting Hospitality Uniforms' fixed overhead costs would be as follows:

	Debit	Credit
Fixed manufacturing overhead control (actual)	$480,000	
Various accounts		$480,000
Work-in-process inventory—fixed overhead	350,000	
(70,000 uniforms at $5.00)		
Fixed overhead applied		350,000
Fixed manufacturing overhead applied	350,000	
Total volume variance		
Fixed overhead idle capacity variance	100,000	
Fixed overhead marketing variance	50,000	
Fixed overhead budget variance		20,000
Fixed manufacturing overhead control		480,000

Note that the budget variance compares overhead actually incurred to the amount budgeted for the period. Since these costs are fixed, the budgeted amount does not change, even though the volume produced is different from the original plan.

Exercise

Record the flow of fixed overhead costs and variances incurred had actual production been 90,000 units. Actual fixed overhead costs for this level of activity were $515,000; all other factors remain constant. (Use your own paper.)

	Debit	Credit
Fixed manufacturing overhead control (actual)	$515,000	
Various accounts		$515,000
Work-in-process inventory—fixed overhead	450,000	
Fixed overhead applied		450,000
Fixed overhead applied	450,000	
Fixed overhead budget variance	15,000	
Fixed overhead idle capacity variance	100,000	
Fixed overhead marketing variance		50,000
Fixed overhead control		515,000

Fixed overhead applied is based on the 90,000 units produced for sale at the standard cost rate of $5/unit in fixed overhead costs. The budget variance results when the actual fixed overhead incurred ($515,000) is compared to the budget ($500,000). The fixed overhead idle capacity variance did not change from the preceding data because planned production (80,000 units) was less than practical capacity (100,000 units). The marketing variance becomes favorable because actual orders received (90,000 units) exceed the planned sales (80,000 units).

A COMPREHENSIVE STANDARD COSTING PROBLEM

Standard costing systems provide management with a powerful tool to plan for and control costs. A thorough knowledge of this technique is vital to overall effectiveness in most profit-oriented environments and in many not-for-profit sectors. As a review of standard costing, consider data from another manufacturing company. You should be able to analyze each of the four major cost classifications: direct materials, direct labor, variable overhead, and fixed overhead; to record variances in each; and to incorporate the data into the appropriate sections of an income statement.

Leisure Products produces fiberglass tables and chairs for use on houseboats and other water crafts. This product line is manufactured in one plant and then shipped directly to retail outlets throughout the country. The following standard costs have been established for one line of deck chairs.

Deck Chair Model 13

Cost Classifications	Standard	Product Cost
Direct materials (fiberglass)	6 pounds at $2.50	$15
Direct labor	½ hour at $6.00	3
Variable overhead	¼ machine-hour at $20.00	5
Fixed overhead	$7.00 per unit	7
Total standard cost		$30

These chairs are sold to retail outlets for $40.00. No inventories are maintained by Leisure Products. In general, orders are filled and shipped within 30 days after they have been received. Below is a listing of the actual manufacturing costs incurred for these products during a particular period, and other relevant operating information for Model 13 of the deck chair product line.

Operating Data—Model 13

Plant production capacity	5,000 chairs per year
Sales forecast	4,200 chairs
Units produced and sold	4,400 chairs
Materials purchased	30,000 pounds at $2.40
Materials used	25,000 pounds
Direct labor costs	2,400 hours at $5.50
Variable overhead incurred	$21,600 (1,200 hours at $18)
Fixed overhead budgeted at capacity	$35,000
Fixed overhead incurred	$30,000

The fixed overhead budget was based on the plant's practical capacity of 5,000 units per year at $7.00 per unit. Variable overhead is applied to products based on machine-hour basis; each unit requires 15 minutes, a cost of $5.00 per unit.

14.   Applying Standard Costing Techniques. Using the preceding data, make the following determinations:

1. Direct materials costs

   (a) Direct materials price variance (frame 1) _____

   (b) Direct materials usage variance (frame 3) _____

2. Direct labor costs

   (a) Direct labor rate variance (frame 5) _____

   (b) Direct labor efficiency variance (frame 6) _____

3. Variable manufacturing overhead costs

   (a) Variable overhead spending variance (frame 8) _____

   (b) Variable overhead efficiency variance (frame 9) _____

4. Fixed manufacturing overhead costs

   (a) Fixed overhead budget variance (frame 11) _____

   (b) Total fixed overhead volume variance (frame 12) _____

      (1) Fixed overhead idle capacity variance _____

      (2) Fixed overhead marketing variance _____

- - - - - - - - - - - - - - - -

1. (a) $3,000 favorable (standard cost of $2.50 per pound – actual price paid of $2.40 = $0.10 per pound X quantity purchased, 30,000 lb).

   (b) $3,500 favorable (standard is 4,400 chairs X 6 lb per chair, or 26,400 lb; only 25,000 lb was used, for a difference of 1,400 lb multiplied by $2.50 standard cost per pound).

2. (a) $1,200 favorable (standard rate of $6.00 per hour – actual average hourly rate of $5.50 = $0.50 less than the standard X 2,400 hours actually worked = $1,200).

   (b) $1,200 unfavorable (standard is 2,200 hours—4,400 units produced at ½ hour per unit. Actually used: 2,400 hours, or 200 hours more than allowed X $6.00 per hour = $1,200).

3. (a) $2,400 favorable (standard of $20 per hour – $18 actual cost per machine hour = $2.00 per hour X 1,200 actual hours = $2,400).

   (b) $2,000 unfavorable [1,200 actual machine hours – 1,100 standard hours (4400 units X ¼ hour) = 100 hours X standard rate of $20.00 per hour = $2,000].

4. (a) $5,000 favorable [standard is $35,000 (practical capacity at 5,000 X $7.00 per unit) – $30,000 actual fixed overhead = $5,000 less than budgeted].

   (b) $4,200 unfavorable (5,000 units practical capacity – 4,400 units produced and sold = 600 units X $7.00 standard cost per unit = $4,200).

   (1) $5,600 unfavorable (5,000 practical capacity – 4,200 units forecast = 800 units X $7.00 per unit = $5,600).

   (2) $1,400 favorable (4,400 units produced – 4,200 units forecast = 200 units more than expected X $7.00 per unit = $1,400).

15.   Recording Standard Costing Data.   The second step in the standard costing process requires that all relevant data be recorded in the financial records. In the spaces below, record the entries that should be made by Leisure Products Company's management accountants.

1. Direct materials purchases (frame 2)

2. Direct materials usage (frame 4)

3. Direct labor costs (frame 7)

4. Variable overhead costs (frame 10)

5. Fixed overhead costs (frame 12)

- - - - - - - - - - - - - - - -

	Debit	Credit
1. Raw materials inventory	$75,000	
Materials price variance		$ 3,000
Accounts payable		72,000
2. Work-in-process inventory	$66,000	
Materials usage variance		$ 3,500
Raw materials inventory		62,500

	Debit	Credit
3. Work-in-process inventory	$13,200	
Direct labor efficiency variance	1,200	
Direct labor rate variance		$ 1,200
Accrued payroll		13,200
4. (a) Variable overhead control	$21,600	
Various accounts		$21,600
(b) Work-in-process inventory	22,000	
Variable overhead applied		22,000
(c) Variable overhead applied	22,000	
Variable overhead—efficiency variance	2,000	
Variable overhead spending variance		2,400
Variable overhead control		21,600
5. (a) Fixed overhead control	$30,000	
Various accounts		$30,000
(b) Work-in-process inventory	30,800	
Fixed overhead applied		30,800
(c) Fixed overhead applied	30,800	
Fixed overhead—idle capacity variance	5,600	
Fixed overhead—budget variance		5,000
Fixed overhead—marketing variance		1,400
Fixed overhead control		30,000

16. Management Control Reports. Once standard costing data are obtained, they can be cast into the form of a management control report to be used in planning and control decisions.

> A **management control report** summarizes the variances revealed through standard costing and the effect on the gross profit.

Example. Information contained on a management control report for Hospitality Uniforms, Inc., might be as follows:

Management Control Report
Uniform Production Department
for the Production Period Ended XXXX

Sales (70,000 units at $25)	$1,750,000
Standard cost of sales (70,000 units at $20)	1,400,000
Estimated standard gross profit	350,000
Add: Favorable manufacturing variances	20,000
Subtotal	370,000
Less: Unfavorable manufacturing variances	100,000
Adjusted gross profit	$ 270,000

Exercise

Using the information derived in frames 14 and 15, complete the following management control report for Leisure Products Company Product—Model 13, Deck Chairs.

Management Control Report
Product—Model 13 (Deck Chairs)
for the Production Period Ended XXXX

Sales (_____ units at $ _____) $ _____

Standard cost of sales (_____ units at $ _____)   _____

Estimated standard gross profit $ _____

Add: *Favorable manufacturing variances*

  _____   _____

  _____   _____

  _____   _____

  _____   _____

  _____   _____

  _____   _____

  Total favorable variances   _____

Less: *Unfavorable manufacturing variances*

  _____   _____

  _____   _____

  _____   _____

  _____   _____

  _____   _____

  Total unfavorable variance   _____

Adjusted gross profit $ _____

Management Control Report
Product—Model 13 (Deck Chairs)
for the Production Period Ended XXXX

Sales (4,400 units at $40 each)		$176,000
Standard cost of sales (4,400 units at $30)		132,000
Estimated standard gross profit		$ 44,000
Add: *Favorable manufacturing variances*		
Materials price variance	$3,000	
Materials usage variance	3,500	
Labor rate variance	1,200	
Variable overhead—spending variance	2,400	
Fixed overhead—budget variance	5,000	
Fixed overhead—marketing variance	1,400	
Total favorable variances		16,500
Subtotal		$ 60,500
Less: *Unfavorable manufacturing variances*		
Labor efficiency variance	1,200	
Variable overhead—efficiency variance	2,000	
Fixed overhead—idle capacity variance	5,600	
Total unfavorable variances		(8,800)
Adjusted gross profit		$ 51,700

Note that the net effect of favorable manufacturing variances reduces costs assigned to products at standard. Conversely, unfavorable variances increase the costs. Taken together, management can quickly observe the effects of standard costing variances on expected gross profit levels. Consequently, planning and control decisions can be improved substantially when this management accounting technique is applied in a timely manner.

CHAPTER 6 SELF-TEST

1. Matching — Terminology/Concepts

Match the following terms to the definitions.

1. Fixed overhead budget variance
2. Fixed overhead idle capacity
3. Fixed overhead marketing variance
4. Fixed overhead volume variance
5. Labor efficiency variance
6. Labor rate variance
7. Materials price variance

8. Materials usage variance
9. Overhead applied
10. Overhead incurred
11. Standard costs
12. Variable overhead efficiency variance
13. Variable overhead spending variance
14. Variances

_____ (a) Difference between units in the sales forecast and those actually produced and sold.

_____ (b) Difference between prices actually paid for production materials and those that should have been paid at standard — recorded at point of purchase.

_____ (c) Difference between hours used and those that should have been used, given the standard involved for machine usage.

_____ (d) Difference betweeen labor-hours actually used relative to hours that should have been used. Financial measure is the standard rate per hour.

_____ (e) Estimates, future costs that are developed as a basis for planning and control.

_____ (f) Costs assigned to units actually produced during a period that are based on a predetermined overhead rate.

_____ (g) Difference between units at practical capacity and the planned production to satisfy the sales forecast.

_____ (h) The difference between fixed overhead costs actually incurred and those anticipated at practical capacity.

_____ (i) Costs actually incurred for all production activities not directly identifiable with units produced.

_____ (j) The combined effects of the planned idle capacity variance and the marketing variance.

2. Variance Analysis

The Apollo Company has just completed 1 month's operations. The following data are provided for your analysis.

	Standard Cost/Unit
Direct materials (1 lb at $6.00/lb)	$6.00
Direct labor (½ hr at $4.00/hr)	2.00
Variable overhead (50% of direct labor costs)	1.00
Cost per unit	$9.00

Actual operating data for Apollo during the period are as follows:

Production	1,000 units using 11,000 lb raw material
Raw materials purchase	1,200 lb at $5.80/lb
Labor costs	450 hr at $4.40/hr
Variable overhead	450 hr at $2.20/hr

Compute standard costing variances and indicate whether each is favorable or unfavorable for the following:

(a) Materials price variance (at point of purchase) _____

(b) Materials usage variance _____

(c) Labor rate variance _____

(d) Labor efficiency variance _____

(e) Variable overhead spending variance _____

(f) Variable overhead efficiency variance _____

3. Recording Variances

(a) Apollo, in a succeeding month, purchased 2,000 pounds of material on account at a price of $6.50 per pound. Its standard has remained at $6.00 per pound. Record this purchase in the proper format.

(b) The manufacturing department used all 2,000 pounds of material in the production of 1,800 units. The standard remains at 1 pound of materials per unit of product. Record this usage entry.

(c) Apollo's production of 1,800 units required 850 hours of labor at an average cost of $4.50 per hour. The standards remain the same even though labor costs are obviously increasing. Record this transaction.

(d) Variable overhead cost for the 1,800 units produced was $2,125 (850 hours at $2.50). The standards have not changed. Record the transaction.

4. Other Variances

Apollo has a total practical capacity of 10,000 units per year. In a recent year of operations, its budgeted fixed manufacturing cost was $80,000 ($8.00 per unit). The sales forecast was 8,000 units, but unfortunately, only 7,500 units were produced and sold. Actual fixed overhead for the year was $72,000. Compute the following and indicate whether each is favorable or unfavorable.

(a) Fixed overhead budget variance _____

(b) Fixed overhead volume variance _____

(c) Planned idle capacity variance _____

(d) Marketing variance _____

ANSWERS

1. Matching – Terminology/Concepts

(a)	3 (frame 12, 1 pt)	(b)	7 (frame 1, 1 pt)
(c)	12 (frame 9, 1 pt)	(d)	5 (frame 6, 1 pt)
(e)	11 (introduction, 1 pt)	(f)	9 (frame 12, 1 pt)
(g)	2 (frame 12, 1 pt)	(h)	1 (frame 11, 1 pt)
(i)	10 (frame 12, 1 pt)	(j)	4 (frame 12, 1 pt)

2. Variance Analysis

(a) $240 (F): 1,200 lb ($6.00 – $5.80) (frame 1, 2 pts)
(b) $600 (U): $6.00 (1,000 lb – 1,100 lb) (frame 3, 2 pts)
(c) $180 (U): 450 hours ($4.00 – $4.40) (frame 5, 2 pts)
(d) $200 (F): $4.00 (500 hours – 450 hours) (frame 6, 2 pts)
(e) $90 (U): 450 hours ($2.00 – $2.20) (frame 8, 2 pts)
(f) $100 (F): $2.00 (500 hours – 450 hours) (frame 9, 2 pts)

3. Recording Variances

		Debit	Credit
(a)	Raw materials inventory	$12,000	
	Materials price variance	1,000	
	Accounts payable		$13,000 (frame 2, 3 pts)
(b)	Work-in-process inventory	$10,800	
	Materials usage variance	1,200	
	Raw materials inventory		$12,000 (frame 4, 3 pts)
(c)	Work-in-process inventory	$ 3,600	
	Labor rate variance	425	
	Labor efficiency variance		$ 200
	Accrued payroll		3,825 (frame 7, 3 pts)
(d)	Variable overhead applied	$ 1,800	
	Variable overhead spending variance	425	
	Variable overhead efficiency variance		$ 100
	Variable overhead incurred		2,125 (frame 10, 3 pts)

4. Other Variances

(a) $8,000 (F): ($80,000 – $72,000) (frame 11, 3 pts)
(b) $20,000 (U): $8 (10,000 units – 7,500 units) (frame 12, 3 pts)
(c) $16,000 (U): $8 (10,000 units – 8,000 units) (frame 12, 3 pts)
(d) $4,000 (U): $8 (8,000 units – 7,500 units) (frame 12, 3 pts)

Total possible points: 46. You should have scored at least 37.

SECTION THREE

Specialized Decision Making

Data derived from cost/volume/profit analysis, profit planning, cash budgeting, cost accounting, and standard costing are indispensible to effective planning and control. Such data can reveal problem areas while there is still time to correct the problems. Other management accounting techniques can help pinpoint specific reasons for the occurrence of problems revealed and can be used to make specialized decisions, the focus of this section.

Fundamental to making specialized decisions is the establishment of a responsibility accounting system with well-defined responsibility centers and objective measures to evaluate and control each center's performance (Chapter 7).

Using data accumulated within a responsibility accounting system, your ability to assess critical factors in specialized decision areas will be greatly improved. Four specific types of decisions are especially important: special order pricing, making or buying units for use in production, processing products to their completion rather than selling them in intermediate markets, and evaluating whether business segments or departments should be continued or dropped (Chapter 8).

Finally, after all current financial needs have been evaluated, management accounting techniques can be used to prepare capital budgets to assess the desirability of long-range resource commitments. Decisions related to the capital budget are more effective when they incorporate specialized measures, such as return on investment, the payback period, and measures using discounted cash flows (Chapter 9).

Clearly, management accounting is useful to assess past performance, current status, and future plans.

CHAPTER 7

Responsibility Accounting Systems

Can you . . .

- Explain what responsibility accounting is?
- Identify various responsibility centers within an organization?
- Determine and analyze return on investment? Product line income? Rate of growth in sales?
- Complete an analysis of the contribution margin, including contribution margin effect variance, quantity effect variance, and marketing mix effect variance?
- Develop a flexible budget?
- Develop flexible performance criteria?

Before beginning the study of responsibility accounting systems, you may want to review the first two chapters of this book, especially the discussions of contribution margin (pp. 16–17) and return on investment (pp. 38–40).

Responsibility accounting practices compare achievements to performance goals. These comparisons are the bases for tailoring data to specified decision-making requirements and for evaluating performance at various levels of authority in an organization. An effective responsibility accounting system determines the extent to which managers exert influence over operating results. These results, in turn, are measured in different ways as the nature of a manager's responsibility changes.

When responsibility accounting systems are used, an organization is first divided into responsibility centers to monitor activities. Specific criteria are established to serve as guidelines for executing practical control procedures.

> A **responsibility accounting system** separates an organization into responsibility centers so that financial data can be tailored to managers' decision-making requirements and performance can be objectively evaluated.

Implicit in this "center" concept is that each manager has sufficient authority to achieve established goals. Thus responsible individuals can be held accountable for achievements within the framework of a financial plan. Reports provide comparative data, actual results relative to planned targets, to monitor performance, as illustrated by the following portrayal of planned and actual performance data:

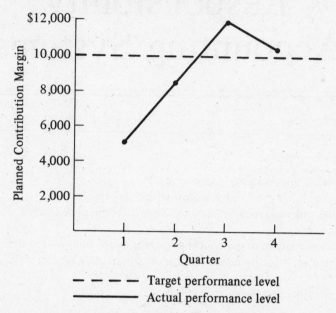

— — — — Target performance level
———————— Actual performance level

Responsibility accounting systems emphasize *controllability*, with control viewed as the ability to influence directly any results achieved. Influence is exercised when managers are given the authority to act. For example, a manager in a large organization is responsible for executing the marketing program for a new product. A subordinate suggests spending a substantial sum for a specific type of promotion. After much deliberation, the manager decides to commit only a portion of the requested funds, holding the remainder until measures of the program's initial effectiveness can be developed. Control has thus been exerted by the manager's ability to influence both the amount and the timing of this expenditure.

RESPONSIBILITY CENTERS

The initial step in establishing a responsibility accounting system is to establish clearly defined responsibility centers.

> A **responsibility center** is a unit in an organization distinguishable by the scope of a manager's decision-making authority. Evaluations of performance are based on either return on investment, profits, revenues, or costs.

Usually, the larger the organization, the greater the number of responsibility centers.

A system of responsibility accounting revolves around two fundamental principles. First, data must be tailored to a manager's decision-making needs. The manager, in turn, must have the authority to act and to be accountable for results achieved. The effectiveness of control reports rests on the relevance and understandability of information provided. *Relevance* means that reported data are, in fact, appropriate to decisions that must be made. *Understandability* implies that those involved have sufficient knowledge about the information to react effectively.

Second, problem areas must be pinpointed so that improvements can be made. Reports must thus be complemented by efforts to assess critical cause/effect relationships responsibly.

In structuring practical control reports, each level of management must be addressed in terms of their particular responsibilities. One purpose of these information flows is to facilitate periodic performance evaluations. A comprehensive report is provided in the following case as a frame of reference for our discussion of responsibility accounting.

International Elegance, Inc., is a highly specialized importer of fashionable accessories for women of all ages. The company's success is based on its expertise in two product lines. The first and oldest, line A, is perfumes and cosmetics. A more recent addition, line B, scarves and jewelry, is now equally successful as a complementary line of products. The "Elegance" efforts are well known throughout the industry, and many observers attribute this reputation to innovative management.

The company, originally created by a brother and sister, is now operated by an entire family. Earlier, before financial success was achieved, many experiments in developing management information were conducted. Ultimately, those involved adapted a responsibility accounting system as the framework for performance evaluations. An example of this hypothetical company's periodic reports provides a basis for evaluation. The general framework serves as a starting point for explaining the kinds of information reported. Analytic procedures are described in succeeding sections.

The company's performance objectives include a desired 15% return on investment, that each product should constitute at least 25% of sales, that an annual growth of 5% increase in sales be achieved, and that product costs should not exceed 65% of revenues earned. Expense allowances are established at 25% of total earned contribution margin.

International Elegance, Inc., has adopted the calendar month as its time frame for reporting operating results. The president and other top executives receive weekly summaries of all financial information, but other managers receive only data that relate to their specific segments of responsibility.

International Elegance, Inc.
Responsibility Accounting Report
for the Period Ended 19XX

	Perfumes and Cosmetics	Scarves and Jewelry	Monthly Total	Year to Date
Revenues	$60,000	$40,000	$100,000	$1,500,000
Costs of goods sold	42,000	18,000	60,000	900,000
Contribution margin	$18,000	$22,000	$ 40,000	$ 600,000
Direct product line marketing expenses	3,000	7,000	10,000	200,000
Product line income	$15,000	$15,000	$ 30,000	$ 400,000
Indirect marketing and administration costs			15,000	200,000
Net income before taxes			$ 15,000	$ 200,000
Taxes (40%)			6,000	80,000
Net income after taxes			$ 9,000	$ 120,000

Total assets reflected on the balance sheet are $1,200,000. Included in this measure are two assets not currently contributing to profits. Land was purchased at a cost of $150,000 for use as a future site, and goodwill from a prior-year purchase of a smaller company in the industry is carried at a book value of $50,000. Net income after tax in the most recent year of operations was $120,000.

Using the preceding data, the performance of International Elegance can be evaluated.

1.   **The Investment Center—Return on Assets.**   At the highest level, management is accountable for performance over a broad range of activities. Since decisions at this responsibility level affect both the investment base (total resources) and profitability (returns generated), top management is viewed as an investment center. Usually, it is the company's president who is ultimately responsible for performance throughout the total organization. Therefore, this executive needs a measure of results encompassing all significant financial effects of actions. Frequently, the measure used is return on assets, a measure which, you recall, combines the working asset base with the measure of net income after tax. In a publicly held company a measure based on equity might be more appropriate. Return, in either sense, reflects the relationship of net income after taxes to a selected investment base.

Two other performance measures frequently used at this level of responsibility are the product line income, with each product expected to generate a net income of a pre- specified percent of sales revenues, and rate of growth of sales. Financial plans for a given period are compared with actual results to determine not only level of performance, but any problems that may exist.

> In an **investment center** managers are responsible for the total results achieved. Performance measures are stated in terms of return on investment, in working assets, product line income relative to sales, and rate of growth in sales.

Example. As the president of Elegance, Inc., assesses the company's performance during the period just completed, his first step is to measure return on assets. For this purpose he includes only those assets that "work" to directly affect profits. Therefore, both land carried at $150,000 and goodwill, in the amount of $50,000, are subtracted from total assets on the balance sheet. The asset base is thus measured at $1,000,000.

This adjustment is made based on the belief that only certain company resources contribute directly to profits. Land held for future expansion, goodwill, and other intangible assets are generally viewed as nonworking assets for two reasons. First, they are not readily sold and, thus, cannot be effectively valued in terms of realizable value. Second, costs associated with intangibles are not directly traceable to measures of future profitability. Although no absolute guidelines regarding treatment of intangible assets prevail in this industry, this company's practice is considered acceptable.

The return on assets for Elegance's most recent year is determined by dividing the appropriate net income measure of $120,000 by working assets valued at $1,000,000. The ratio is determined to be 12%. Compared to the 15% return Elegance had hoped to earn, or a net income of $150,000, Elegance has fallen short of its goal by $30,000. This represents approximately 20% ($30,000 divided by $150,000) of the budgeted measure and is clearly significant.

The president considers three separate types of control information as he evaluates each 4-week period. First, the net income after tax is compared to the target measure expected to be earned through that date. At the end of the third period, for example, the company should have earned $30,000 ($3/12 \times $120,000). Actual earnings at that date were only $25,000. Thus the difference between actual and target earnings is $5,000, or 16.7% of the target ($5,000 \div $30,000). Such a variance may indicate serious problems.

A second key measure is the product line income. Each product is expected to generate a net income representing at least 25% of sales. The perfume/cosmetic line did yield this 25% ($15,000 \div $60,000), but the second line, scarves and jewelry, generated product line income of 37.5% ($15,000 \div $40,000), a measure greater than the desired target.

The third performance measure of interest to the president is the rate of growth in sales. Evaluation of progress here requires that current performance be compared to that of prior periods. Total sales for product line B during the first 3 months of last year were $200,000. During the same period in the current year, its sales were only $180,000, a decline of $20,000, or 10% ($20,000 \div $200,000) of the target level.

Exercise

A sporting goods company, Superstar, Inc., has three major lines of products: baseball, football, and basketball equipment. Each segment represents a separate division that is responsible totally for its own asset base. Divisional financial goals are set as follows:

return on investment in working assets should be at least 12%; each product line should generate an income of at least 15% of sales; and sales should grow at the rate of approximately 15% per year.

The basketball division has an asset base of $2,000,000. All its assets contributed last year to a net income after tax result of $250,000. Within the division, the Uniforms Department generated a product line income of $150,000 on a sales base of $750,000. Its sales had increased from $600,000 in the preceding year.

(a) What is the Baseball Division's return on investment in working assets? _____ Does this performance level satisfy the goal? _____

(b) What is the Uniform Department's performance in terms of product line income relative to sales? _____ Does this measure satisfy the established goal? _____

(c) What is the Uniform Department's rate of growth in sales during the past year? _____ Does this growth satisfy the performance criterion? _____

(a) 12.5% ($250,000 ÷ $2,000,000); yes, this return exceeds the 12% standard.
(b) 20% ($150,000 ÷ $450,000); yes, the performance is greater than the 15% target.
(c) 25% ($150,000 ÷ $600,000); yes, the growth rate exceeds the goal of 15% annually. Note that the increase in sales is compared to the base year when the growth rate is developed; only in this way can a valid measure of the rate of growth be established.

2. Profit Centers—Product Line Profit. The next level of responsibility is viewed as a profit center. Managers are usually vice-presidents who can influence profits through their decisions affecting revenues and costs, but their authority is restricted with respect to significant changes in the investment base. This limitation in authority is the core of a responsibility accounting system, because managers are not held accountable for factors over which they have no control. Each executive in a profit center is totally accountable for performance in a well-defined segment of the overall operation.

Several key control issues must be addressed in evaluating profit centers. Note first that product line profit is *not* the same as net income after taxes. The difference in a responsibility accounting context rests in the fact that the vice-presidents have no authority to influence indirect marketing and administrative costs. Decision-making authority with respect to these costs is restricted to the president. In addition, taxes are not viewed as controllable. Using these authority limits, each responsible executive's ability to influence product line results is defined clearly by the measure of product line profits.

Product line profits are measured by first determining revenues of the product and subtracting from it the cost of goods sold. Such costs are variable because they change in direct proportion to sales volume. The difference between revenues and variable cost of sales is the contribution margin. This contribution margin is clearly the responsibility of the specified vice-president because this individual can influence both the product line prices and the costs of purchases. Consequently, the vice-president's total accountability for these activities reflects the essence of the responsibility accounting concept.

Next direct marketing expenses are subtracted from this contribution margin to determine the *product line income.* Again, the product line vice-president or the manager responsible for the profit center has full authority to control the level of the direct marketing expenditures.

> In **profit centers**, managers' authority focuses on decisions relating to both revenues earned and costs incurred. The performance measure is often termed **product line profit**, that is, the contribution margin for a defined product or group of products less costs directly assignable to the segment. It excludes costs that are arbitrarily allocated to the products and over which no control can be asserted.

Example. In Elegance, the profit centers are defined as product lines A and B. Profit responsibilities are assigned to two vice-presidents, each totally accountable for performance in a well-defined segment of the operation. In the case of product line A, revenues of $60,000 clearly relate to the two products involved. The cost of goods sold, $42,000, reflects the purchase price of the imported goods as well as all related delivery costs borne by the company. Contribution margin is $18,000 for product line A. When direct product line expenses are subtracted ($3,000), the product line income is $15,000, representing 25% of product line revenues ($15,000 ÷ $60,000). If this measure had been below the president's target of 25%, immediate analysis of the causes for this variance could be mandatory.

Exercise
Evaluate the efforts of the vice-president of product line B for the same period.

- - - - - - - - - - - - - -

Product line B profit is 37.5% ($15,000 ÷ $40,000), 12.5% greater than expected.

3. Revenue Centers—Increase in Sales. In many organizations, regional sales managers are responsible for generating revenues. Each executive is responsible for a group of salespeople who operate within a defined sales area. The performance criterion for judging progress in these revenue centers is growth. Quite simply, a sales target is defined in terms of increasing prior year revenues. Reports are provided to monitor progress toward the set target with information always available for any given month relative to the same month in the prior year. Similarly, data are provided yearly. Thus managers at this level can easily establish benchmarks for evaluating a subordinate's performance for any particular period.

> In a **revenue center**, a manager's responsibility is defined in terms of the ability to influence revenues through decisions. The performance measure is an anticipated growth in total revenues for the particular product the manager is responsible for.

Example. Elegance's product line A generated total revenues of $720,000 in the prior year. The target for the current year is to achieve an increase of 5% in total sales. Consequently, in dollar terms, the sales manager is expected to generate an increase of $36,000 for the year, or $3,000 per month.

Exercise

Product line B generated $600,000 in revenues during the prior year. Elegance expects that growth of 8% is attainable in the coming year. This measure can be converted into a specific monthly sales increase target in terms of dollars. What would the dollar target for monthly sales increases be in this case? _____

_ _ _ _ _ _ _ _ _ _ _ _ _ _ _

$4,000 ($600,000 × 8% × $\frac{1}{12}$).

4. Cost Centers. Cost centers include segments in an organization where only certain classifications of costs can be controlled. Focus is usually on controlling cost of goods sold, with a purchasing manager in each line accountable for maintaining product costs within specified percentage levels. Significant differences from the prespecified percent of revenues earned are analyzed and explained.

In addition, cost responsibility often rests with individual salespersons. Their performance can be evaluated by two criteria: (1) contribution margin generated, and (2) costs of servicing customers in relation to this contribution margin. In a sense, therefore, each salesperson can be viewed as both a contribution margin center and a cost center. Considering the salesperson's performance in a practical context, the amount of contribution margin earned is controllable. By concentrating on products with the highest contributions, performance gains can be accomplished. For example, if product 1 has a contribution margin rate of 80% while product 2 generates only 60%, the salesperson who sells only product 1 will have substantially higher performance than one who sells only product 2. For this reason, company policy often dictates that minimum levels of sales in all product lines be established each quarter. These vary, of course, from region to region. Bonuses are frequently paid to those who exceed the quota, so an incentive to generate contribution margin has a continuous effect.

Sales personnel are evaluated carefully, however, in a cost center context. They are limited to the extent to which they can incur selling costs, usually established as a percentage of contribution margin earned. Circumstances cause the expense allowance ratio to vary among sales personnel, of course, but in general, the policy provides an excellent tool for controlling expenses.

> In a **cost center**, managers have authority to influence only
> costs incurred for specific products.

Example.   Two different levels of responsibility exist in International Elegance's
cost centers. The first focuses on controlling cost of goods sold. Each of the four basic
products is considered a separate cost center with a purchasing manager accountable for
each line. The manager responsible for perfumes operates on the guideline that product
costs should not exceed 65% of revenues earned. Consequently, in a period where sales
revenues from perfumes are $10,000, the purchasing cost should not exceed $6,500,
which is 65% of total revenues.

The final level of cost responsibility is seen to rest with individual salespersons, each of
whom is evaluated by contribution margin generated and costs of servicing customers.
Expense allowances are established at 25% of total earned contribution margin. For
example, a salesperson who is operating toward a quarterly target of $10,000 in contribu-
tion margin is limited to selling expenses during the quarter of $2,500.

Exercise

Referring again to Superstar, Inc., the manager of the Uniforms Department attempts
to limit his product costs to 70% of sales. His sales personnel are allowed to expend a
maximum of 15% of the sales dollars they generate in order to promote the business.

(a) If sales in a particular period are $50,000, what are the expected product costs?

_____

(b) What kind of report would you desire to assist you to control these costs if you were
the manager? _____ How often should it be prepared?

_____

— — — — — — — — — — — — — — — —

(a) $35,000 (70% X $50,000).
(b) The report should compare the budgeted target in costs with those that were actually
incurred. Reports might be issued as often as the manager desires, but clearly, a summary of information is needed at least at the end of each accounting period.

CONTRIBUTION MARGIN ANALYSIS

A responsibility accounting system uses analytical procedures to identify causes of
differences between planned contribution margin and amounts actually earned during the
period. *Contribution margin analysis* assesses three possible sources of problems:
(1) declines in contribution margin per unit, (2) quantities sold, or (3) product mix (the
proportion of each product relative to its planned significance in the profit plan).

In the case of International Elegance, Inc., top management has evaluated performance
reports during the first quarter of the given year and has become concerned with results
achieved in the perfume line of products. Two new products were expected to generate
significant contribution margin throughout the year. These two products are so similar in

nature that a customer would not buy both at the same time, an important distinction when product mix variances are analyzed. Management assumes that product 1, the more elegant in fragrance, will be selected by customers most often. In cases where desired results are not achieved, the interchangeable nature of these products requires use of a specialized variance analysis technique to identify causes of problems that occur.

Elegance's responsibility reports have presented information to all levels of management. Efforts must now be directed to analyzing causes of the problem and implementing corrective actions. The following data were included in Elegance's quarterly responsibility accounting reports.

Profit Plan
Selected New Products
for the Quarter Ended 19XX

	Product 1			Product 2			Total Product Line Performance		
	Units	Average Price	Total	Units	Average Price	Total	Units	Average Price	Total
Sales	1,200	$20	$24,000	800	$10	$8,000	2,000	$16	$32,000
Variable costs	1,200	10	12,000	800	5	4,000	2,000	8	16,000
Contribution margin	1,200	$10	$12,000	800	$ 5	$4,000	2,000	$ 8	$16,000

Actual Profit Performance
Selected New Products
for the Quarter Ended 19XX

	Units	Average Price	Total	Units	Average Price	Total	Units	Average Price	Total
Sales	1,000	$18.00	$18,000	600	$10	$6,000	1,600	$15	$24,000
Variable costs	1,000	10.80	10,800	600	6	3,600	1,600	9	14,400
Contribution margin	1,000	$ 7.20	$ 7,200	600	$ 4	$2,400	1,600	$ 6	$ 9,600

Several problems with the performance of these new products are readily observable simply from reviewing these data. First, and most apparent, neither product achieved its desired sales level. Second, contribution margins are below planned levels in each instance. Finally, the profit plan was based on an expectation of product 1 comprising 60% of total new product sales, with the remaining 40% expected for product 2. The final data reflect that product 1 generated 62.5% (1,000 units ÷ 1,600 total units) of these total sales data; product 2 accounted for only 37.5% of new product sales during the period.

Most important in this overall analysis is that the new product contribution margin performance was $64,000 *less* than expected. Management is concerned and wants to determine the specific causes of failure to achieve planned targets. Contribution margin analysis is particularly useful in measuring the effects of changes in the contribution margin, quantities, and product mix.

5. Contribution Margin Effect Variance. The first step in analyzing the contribution margin is to look at the difference between planned contribution margin and what was actually achieved.

> **Contribution margin effect variance** is the portion of differences in total product line contribution margins caused by variations between planned and actual contribution margins for units actually sold. It is calculated by multiplying the number of units sold by the difference between planned and actual contribution margins.

Example. Elegance, Inc., expected product 1 to earn a contribution margin per unit of $10 (sales price per unit of $20 less variable cost per unit of $10). Reports for the quarter reveal that the actual contribution per unit was $7.20. This $2.80 difference between planned and actual results is multiplied by the 1,000 units actually sold. The total of $2,800 is the contribution margin effect, a negative variance caused by failure to achieve the planned contribution margin per unit.

Management is informed about the effects of these declines in contribution margin per unit through a schedule such as the following:

**Effects of Changes in
Contribution Margin per Unit[a]**

	Units Sold	Difference in Contribution Margin per Unit	Variance
Product 1	1,000	($2.80)	($2,800)
Product 2	_____	( )	( )
Contribution margin effects—total variance			(____)

[a]( ) represents an unfavorable variance (i.e., actual results failed to meet the planned expectations).

Exercise

Determine the contribution margin effect variance for product 2. _____ Then complete the schedule in the preceding example.

- - - - - - - - - - - - - -

$600. Actual contribution margin per unit for product 2 is $1.00 less than the expected target ($5.00 in contribution margin per plan relative to the $4.00 actually earned). Multiplying this per unit difference by the number of product 2 units actually sold, a variance of $600 is measured (600 units × $1.00 in average difference per unit). The schedule would be as follows:

Product	Units Sold	Difference in Contribution Margin per Unit	Variance
1	1000	($2.80)	($2,800)
2	600	(1.00)	(600)

Contribution margin effects—total
variance   ($3,400)

Note: The premise underlying this report is that the manager responsible for new product activities can influence both unit prices and product costs involved. In Elegance, Inc., the product line vice-president has this responsibility.

6.   **Quantity Effect Variance.** The next step in contribution margin analysis is to determine the effects of quantity changes. First, compute differences between planned and actual quantities of units sold. Then multiply these differences by the average contribution margin. The *average contribution margin* is calculated by dividing the total planned contribution margin by the total planned volume in units. This average measure of contribution margin per unit is used with products that are considered to be interchangeable.

> **Quantity effect variance** is the portion of differences in total contribution margin for a product or group of products caused by variations between planned quantities of units sold and actual quantities sold within the period. The financial measure used is the average planned contribution margin for all products included in the plan. To calculate this variance measure, multiply the average contribution margin by the differences between planned and actual quantities of units sold.

Example. Elegance, Inc., reports show that product 1 actual sales quantities are 200 units less than expected. The total plan called for a total volume of 2,000 units and a total contribution margin of $16,000, for a planned average contribution margin of $8 per unit ($16,000 ÷ 2,000). Since product 1 sales were 200 units less than the plan, the quantity effects variance for this line is $1,600 (200 units × $8 average contribution margin).

As with contribution margin effects, a schedule of these variances is prepared for management.

**Effects of Changes in
Quantities of New Product Sales[a]**

Product	Differences (Planned vs. Actual) Quantities Sold	Average Overall Contribution Margin per Unit	Variance
1	200	$8	($1,600)
2	_____	_____	_____
Total quantity effects variance			═══════

[a]( ) represents an unfavorable variance.

Exercise

Determine the quantity effect variance for product 2. _____ Then complete the schedule in the preceding example.

— — — — — — — — — — — — —

$1,600. Product 2 sales were also 200 units below the planned expectations. This is multiplied by the average contribution margin ($8) to obtain the $1,600 unfavorable quantity effects variance for product 2. The schedule would be:

Product	Differences (Planned vs. Actual) Quantities Sold	Average Overall Contribution Margin per Unit	Variance
1	(200 units)	$8	($1,600)
2	(200 units)	8	(1,600)
Total quantity effects variance			$3,200

Note: These reports are usually sent to regional sales executives because they are responsible for generating product sales targets and are accountable for correcting problems affecting new product efforts.

7. **Marketing-Mix Effect Variance.** When two or more products are considered interchangeable, a mix analysis is conducted to measure interactions between these products. To determine marketing-mix variance, first determine differences between actual quantities sold during the period and target quantities included on the profit plan. Then multiply these differences by the variance between planned contribution margin per unit for the specific product relative to the average contribution for the products combined.

> **Marketing-mix effect variance** is the portion of differences in total contribution margin for a group of products that is caused by combined variations between (1) planned and actual quantities of products sold, and (2) differences between actual product contribution margin yielded and the average expected for all products in the plan. To calculate the measure of this variance, determine differences between actual quantities sold and target and multiply this difference by the variance between planned contribution margin and *average* contribution margin.

Example. Since products 1 and 2 of Elegance, Inc., fit the description of interchangeable products, mix analysis is appropriate. Product 1 is slightly more fragrant, elegant, and expensive. Therefore, some customers choose first to experiment with product 2. Such interactions frequently occur. Consequently, when actual performance differs from the plan, analysis of variances focuses on the difference in contribution margin attributable to this marketing mix variance.

The quantity effects variance data indicated that actual sales for product 1 were 200 units less than anticipated. The plan assumed that product 1 would generate a contribution margin of $10 per unit. This is a difference of $2 per unit from the *average* contribution margin expected for the two products combined ($8 per unit). This variation in contribution margin measures is directly attributable to the effects of product mix interaction. Multiplying the difference in planned and actual quantities for product 1, 200 units, by the difference in contribution margin per unit due to mix, $2, a total variance of $400 is measured. This variance is unfavorable because both the quantities and contribution margin differences are caused by performance results below those assumed in the profit plan.

As before, a management report is prepared as a basis for evaluating product mix effects:

**Effects of Changes in
Product Mix of New Product Sales[a]**

Product	Differences (Planned vs. Actual) Quantities Sold	Differences—Planned Contribution Margin vs. Average Overall Contribution Margin	Variance
1	(200)	($2.00)	($400)
2	( )		
Marketing-mix variance			

[a]( ) represents an unfavorable variance.

Exercise

Determine the marketing-mix effect variance for product 2 and enter the relevant information into the schedule in the preceding exercise. _____

— — — — — — — — — — — — — —

$600. The difference between expected product 2 sales, 800 units, and the quantity actually sold, 600 units, is 200 units multiplied by the difference in contribution margin, $3 per unit ($5 per unit of product 2 in the plan relative to $8 in planned average contribution margin for combined new product activity). The completed schedule would be as follows:

Product 1	(200 units)	($2.00)	($400)
Product 2	(200 units)	$3.00	600
Marketing-mix variance			$200

Notice that the mix effect variance for product 2 is *favorable* because *fewer* lower-priced product 2 units were sold than had been expected. The plan anticipated that product 2 sales would comprise 40% of total volume (800 units of product 2 relative to 2,000 units in total—products 1 and 2 combined). Actual sales of product 2 declined, however, to only 37.5% of the total volume (600 units of product 2 relative to 1,600 units in total), a significant decline because it reduces the overall impact of unfavorable results.

Since mix variance data are influenced only by an individual with authority over both products, at International Elegance responsibility for marketing-mix results rests solely with the marketing vice-president.

8.   Combine the preceding variance information into a summary report for top management review so that all involved personnel are kept informed both of progress relative to plans and potential problems that may be emerging.

New Product Lines
Contribution Margin Analysis
for the Quarter Ended 19XX

Measure	Variance
Contribution margin effects	
Product 1 _____	
Product 2 _____	_____
Quantity effects	
Product 1 _____	
Product 2 _____	_____
Marketing-mix effects	
Product 1 _____	
Product 2 _____	_____
Total contribution margin variance	_____

— — — — — — — — — — — — —

Contribution margin effects

Product 1	($2,800)	
Product 2	(600)	($3,400)

Quantity effects

Product 1	($1,600)	
Product 2	(1,600)	($3,200)

Marketing-mix effects

Product 1	($ 400)	
Product 2	(600)	$ 200
Total contribution margin variance		($6,400)

Note that the profit plan estimated contribution margin at a level of $16,000 for the combined results of both products. Actual results achieved were only $9,600, an unfavorable variance of $6,400, which is analyzed in detail in the preceding summary report.

FLEXIBLE BUDGETING

The *flexible budgeting* technique is an important tool in developing accurate forecasts.

International Elegance, Inc., has detected problems in its new product lines. Performance in terms of contribution margin has been analyzed and top management has decided to take action. A key manager has been assigned full responsibility for implementing the new program. Selected staff personnel are now assigned to this project.

Extensive marketing research studies have been conducted and reveal that improved profitability in this venture can be obtained most effectively by attracting additional retail outlets to market the new product lines. Therefore, the plan specifies the objectives of adding 80 outlets during the coming 3 years. Top management hopes that sales volume from each outlet will generate an average of at least $1,000 in contribution margin per year. Realizing that growth occurs gradually, the responsible manager has projected that contribution margin in total should increase by $40,000 to $50,000 the first year. In the remaining 2 years of the plan, an added $25,000 to $30,000 should be generated in each year. Since current outlets are expected to produce a contribution of $80,000 annually, this program should double Elegance's current volume in 3 years.

Commissions of 5% on increased contribution margin are to be paid to regional sales personnel. Similarly, advertising costs are projected at 5% of the increased contribution margin. Other variable marketing costs should approximate 10% of the added contribution margin dollars. Salaries for personnel time committed to the project are estimated to be $12,000 per year and are treated as fixed costs. In addition, charges for corporate services are to be assigned to this program at the rate of $12,000 per year.

9.   Developing a Flexible Budget.   The first step in developing a flexible budget is to establish a range of expected revenues and costs. The schedule begins with a measure of expected contribution margin because revenues and variable costs of goods sold are merged in with other financial data. Variable costs are stated in terms of percentages of the contribution margin since they change in direct proportion to volume changes. Fixed cost projections do *not* change even though volume may increase.

> **A flexible budget** focuses on revising variable cost budgets
> as volume changes occur. It establishes budgets for a range
> of permissible activity levels.

Example. Using the data provided for International Elegance, during the first year a minimum sales increase of $40,000 is expected, a maximum of $50,000. Actual sales will probably fall between these two extremes; therefore, their flexible budget for the first year would be as follows:

Projected contribution margin (outlets)	$40,000	$45,000	$50,000
Projected variable costs			
Sales incentives (5%)	2,000	2,250	2,500
Advertising (5%)	2,000	2,250	2,500
Other marketing activities (10%)	4,000	4,500	5,000
Total variable costs (20%)	$ 8,000	$ 9,000	$10,000
Projected fixed costs			
Salaries	12,000	12,000	12,000
Corporate services	12,000	12,000	12,000
Total fixed costs	$24,000	$24,000	$24,000
Projected net income	$ 8,000	$12,000	$16,000

Exercise

Assuming that fixed costs do not increase, what would be the results achieved if this manager fully executes his 3-year plan? In other words, Elegance can project its net income to be $ _____ in the third year if contribution from outlets increases to $110,000.

$64,000. Contribution margin may increase by as much as $110,000. Since the variable cost percentage is assumed to remain at 20%, total expenditures for these efforts should be $22,000. Fixed costs would remain at $24,000.

10. Evaluating Performance Using Flexible Budgets. Flexible budgeting is a primary performance evaluation technique. Flexibility in this procedure derives from the fact that the budget is adjusted to reflect relationships between the level of volume achieved and costs that should have been incurred at that volume.

> **Flexible budgets** are established at the beginning of a plan-
> ning period and then used as a basis for performance
> evaluations as progress occurs.

Example. If actual contribution margin for Elegance during the first year were $42,000, a flexible budget for this amount could be determined and compared with actual costs incurred in each category to ascertain favorable and unfavorable variances.

International Elegance, Inc.
Flexible Budget—New Products
for the Year Ended December 31, 19XX[a]

Contribution margin: $42,000	Budgeted Performance	Actual Performance	Variance
Variable costs			
Incentives (5%)	$ 2,100	$ 2,400	($ 300)
Advertising (5%)	2,100	2,100	−0−
Other marketing activities (10%)	4,200	4,500	(300)
Total variable costs (20%)	$ 8,400	$ 9,000	($ 600)
Fixed costs			
Salaries	12,000	16,000	($4,000)
Corporate service	12,000	13,000	(1,000)
Total fixed costs	$24,000	$29,000	($5,000)
Net income	$ 9,600	$ 4,000	($5,600)

[a]( ) indicates unfavorable variance.

This analysis indicates that profits were less than the target level by $5,600. The reason is that both variable and fixed expenses were more than expected. Generally, the manager is likely to be wholly accountable for differences between planned and actual variable costs. When fixed costs are considered, however, specific management decisions may lead to variations. Consequently, extensive investigations are often required when such differences arise. The decisions underlying unfavorable variances must be assessed. The only variance in the preceding analysis for which this manager was not responsible was the $1,000 additional charge for corporate services. This was entirely uncontrollable by the profit manager. The responsibility rests with a higher level of management and should be explained by the executive responsible for the increase in costs charged to this program.

Exercise

Use you own paper to develop a flexible budget to reflect International Elegance's progress during the second year of the plan based on an actual contribution margin of $60,000 earned and the following expenses: incentives, $3,100; advertising, $3,100; other marketing expenses, $5,000; salaries, $13,000; and corporate services, $12,000.

_ _ _ _ _ _ _ _ _ _ _ _ _ _ _ _

International Elegance, Inc.
Flexible Budget—New Products
for the Year Ended December 31, 19XX[a]

Contribution margin: $60,000	Budgeted Performance	Actual Performance	Variance
Variable costs			
Incentives (5%)	$ 3,000	$ 3,100	($ 100)
Advertising (5%)	3,000	3,100	(100)
Other marketing activities (10%)	6,000	5,000	1,000
Total variable costs (20%)	$12,000	$11,200	$ 800
Fixed costs			
Salaries	12,000	13,000	($1,000)
Corporate service	12,000	12,000	– 0 –
Total fixed costs	$24,000	$25,000	($1,000)
Net income	$24,000	$23,800	($ 200)

[a]( ) indicates unfavorable variance.

CONTROLLABILITY

A responsibility accounting system achieves control because data are traced directly to key decisions. In fact, control in a responsibility accounting system means the ability to influence actions or results through decisions. For example, a manager can control costs by influencing either their timing or amounts by making specific decisions. Thus an individual executive who is authorized to obtain and/or use a particular resource should be held accountable for costs involved. Only data about results that the manager's decisions can specifically influence should be sent to the manager. In other words, control reports should contain only information that managers can use to improve results for which they are clearly accountable. Sometimes, however, top management wants some managers, or maybe even all managers, to be kept aware of certain costs. These may then be included in the relevant control reports provided that the underlying reason is made known and clearly understood by all who are affected. Otherwise, the information provided is totally inappropriate for control purposes.

Using the preceding guidelines, two dimensions of controllability remain to be discussed. First, control limits must be set *before* actions are to be taken as a basis for judging which variances are significant. In this way, analytical efforts can be focused on the most important problems. Second, degrees of flexibility must be incorporated into the performance evaluation system to ensure recognition of varying levels of achievement.

11.   Establishing Control Limits.   An important dimension of controllability is to identify significant problem areas. This includes not only the analysis of variances, but also defining the kinds and amounts of variations from budgets or plans that signify key problems. Deviations from planned fixed costs generally require review because most variations in these costs are caused by specific management decisions. Cost changes may prove to be an important consideration when future plans are developed.

Variances in variable costs must be considered separately. As a starting point, establish policies before plans are implemented to clearly identify the kinds and amounts of variations that must be investigated. The causes of these variances must be analyzed and findings then reported to the responsible manager so that corrective action can be taken.

> **Control limits** can be stated in terms of dollars or percentages. If either the dollar or percentage limits are exceeded, the situation is reviewed.

Example. A departmental manager is responsible for controlling the costs of maintaining accurate inventory records. His budget allows the expenditure of $200 in costs during June. Actual costs for the month were $250. Company policy states that cost variances of more than $25 per month or 10% of the given budget must be investigated.

In this case the manager exceeded both the dollar amount (by $50) and the percentage amount (the variance represents 20% of the budgeted amount). An investigation in this particular case revealed that the added costs were incurred to hire part-time high school students to reorganize a storage area. The job was much larger than expected because most of the shelving had to be replaced. In the final analysis, the variance proved to be a necessary cost to ensure that proper inventory controls could be maintained in future periods. As always, common sense must be used by top-level management when analyzing the reasonableness of an unfavorable variance.

Exercise

The Uniform Department's manager received the following report about three categories of expense.

Expenses	Monthly Budget	Actual
Advertising	$150	$165
Travel	100	95
Telephone	50	60
Total	$300	$320

Company policy dictates that any variance from budget in excess of 8% must be explained. Which expense variations must this manager explain to his superiors?

- - - - - - - - - - - - - - -

Both advertising and telephone variances must be explained. Actual advertising expenses exceed the budget by 10% ($15 ÷ $150); the telephone expense variance is 20% ($10 ÷ $50). Note that the difference, whether positive or negative, is compared to the budgeted measure to determine the percentage.

12.   Promoting Excellence. The purposes of responsibility accounting systems and related control procedures are varied and depend largely on management's philosophy. Unfortunately, the need to limit expenditures sometimes overrides the desirability of promoting excellence. However, systems can be designed to promote both increases in profits and a desire to accomplish goals with a degree of excellence. The key to achieving this latter dimension often rests in designing flexible performance evaluation criteria. In many situations undue emphasis is placed on unfavorable variances from budgeted levels. Thus, where costs exceed limits, immediate actions are indicated. Equally important, however, is the need to recognize and reward outstanding performance. Facilitating excellence should be a primary objective of any system.

> Recognize and reward excellence by identifying a range of performance expectations before a plan is executed.

Example. Achieving a target level of revenues or costs might be "acceptable." Exceeding the target by 2% could be "above average," while performance at a level of 5% better than the target might be "outstanding."

Exercise

How might these same flexible levels of performance be established for performance

falling short of expectations?   _____

— — — — — — — — — — — — — —

Performance levels less than 2% might be identified as "below average" and those below 5% as "inferior."

Before final judgments are made, however, identify and analyze all relevant factors. Use flexible performance standards with care. For example, results may appear to be quite positive from a budget perspective, yet may indicate inferior quality. And some significantly unfavorable variances are beyond the control of those involved. Evaluation measures that lead to reasonable judgments and realistic future targets are mandatory for long-range effectiveness.

You may want to review the questions at the beginning of this chapter before completing the Self-Test that follows.

CHAPTER 7 SELF-TEST

1. Matching – Terminology/Concepts

Match the following terms to the definitions.

1. Contribution margin effect variance	7. Profit center
2. Cost center	8. Quantity effect variance
3. Flexible budget	9. Responsibility accounting
4. Investment center	10. Responsibility center
5. Marketing-mix effect variance	11. Return on assets
6. Product line profit	12. Revenue center

_____ (a) Focuses on the need to revise variable cost projections as volume changes occur by establishing a range of permissible activity levels at the beginning of a planning period which are used to evaluate performance as progress occurs.

_____ (b) Contribution margin for a defined product or group of products less costs directly assignable to the segment.

_____ (c) The portion of differences in total contribution margin for a product or group of products caused by variations between planned quantities of units sold and actual quantities that are sold within the period. The financial measure used is the average planned contribution margin for all products included in the profit plan.

_____ (d) The portion of differences in total contribution margin for a group of products caused by combined variations between planned and actual quantities of products sold and differences between actual product contribution margin yielded and the average expected for all products in the plan.

_____ (e) A responsibility center where a manager's authority focuses on decisions relating to both revenues earned and costs incurred.

_____ (f) The portion of differences in total product line contribution margins carried by variations between planned and actual contribution margins for units actually sold.

_____ (g) Units in an organization distinguishable by the scope of a manager's decision-making authority.

_____ (h) The broadest of the responsibility centers in which managers are responsible for results achieved in all areas.

_____ (i) Performance measure that relates net income after taxes to assets committed to a particular responsibility center in an organization.

_____ (j) The separation of an organization into centers so that financial data can be tailored more closely to a manager's decision-making requirements.

2. Contribution Margin Analysis

The X Company produces and sells two major product lines assumed to be interchangeable. Below are data relative to planned and actual contribution margins during a recently completed operating period.

Planned Performance

	Product 1			Product 2			Total Product Line Performance		
	Units	Average Price	Total	Units	Average Price	Total	Units	Average Price	Total
Contribution margin	1,500	$3	$4,500	500	$7	$3,500	2,000	$4	$8,000

Actual Performance

	Units	Average Price	Total	Units	Average Price	Total	Units	Average Price	Total
Contribution margin	2,000	$4	$8,000	800	$7.50	$6,000	2,800	$5	$14,000

Compute the following variances for each product as a basis for a management control report:

(a) Contribution margin effects

(b) Quantity effects variance

(c) Marketing-mix variance

3. Flexible Budgeting

The X Company establishes its flexible budget for three levels of potential annual revenues: $800,000, $900,000, and $1,000,000. Variable costs of goods sold are projected at 40% of revenues. Other general variable expenses for general operations should be 10% of the projected contribution margin. Fixed costs for general operations are estimated at $20,000 per month. The only additional factor to consider in the coming year is the implementation of a new compensation plan for certain sales representatives who are to receive a total of $120,000 in annual salaries plus 6% commission on revenues earned during the year. Develop flexible budgets for each of the possible revenue levels.

4. Controllability

(a) What two common types of limits are imposed to maintain control?

(b) Explain what a range of performance expectations is and what advantages it offers to management.

ANSWERS

1. Matching – Terminology/Concepts

(a) 3 (frame 9, 1 pt)	(b) 6 (frame 2, 1 pt)
(c) 8 (frame 6, 1 pt)	(d) 5 (frame 7, 1 pt)
(e) 7 (frame 2, 1 pt)	(f) 1 (frame 5, 1 pt)
(g) 10 (introduction, 1 pt)	(h) 4 (frame 1, 1 pt)
(i) 11 (frame 1, 1 pt)	(j) 9 (introduction, 1 pt)

2. Contribution Margin Analysis

(a) Contribution margin effects ($2,400–favorable)
Product 1 2,000 units × $1.00 = $2,000 favorable
Product 2   800 units × $0.50 = $400   favorable   (frame 5, 6 pts)

(b) Quantity effects ($3,200–favorable)
Product 1 500 units × $4.00 = $2,000 favorable
Product 2 300 units × $4.00 = $1,200 favorable   (frame 6, 6 pts)

(c) Marketing-mix variance ($400–favorable)
Product 1 500 units × $1.00 = $500 unfavorable
Product 2 300 units × $3.00 = $900 favorable   (frame 7, 6 pts)

Total variance is $6,000–favorable.

3. Flexible Budgeting

Sales revenues	$800,000	$900,000	$1,000,000
Variable costs of sales	320,000	360,000	400,000
Contribution margin	$480,000	$540,000	$ 600,000
General expenses			
10% of contribution margin	$ 48,000	$ 54,000	$ 60,000
Commission – 10% of revenues	80,000	90,000	100,000
Total variable expenses	$128,000	$144,000	$ 160,000
Contribution to overhead	$352,000	$396,000	$ 440,000
Fixed expenses – operations	240,000	240,000	240,000
– salaries (sales reps)	120,000	120,000	120,000
Total fixed costs	$360,000	$360,000	$ 360,000
Project net income or loss	($ 8,000)	$ 36,000	$ 80,000

(frames 9 and 10, 6 pts)

4. Controllability

(a) Control limits can be stated in terms of dollars or percentages not to be exceeded.
(frame 11, 1 pt)

(b) A range of performance expectations establishes clearly what is expected and what is clearly above or below expected results. It allows management to recognize and reward excellence. (frame 12, 1 pt)

Total possible points: 36. You should have scored at least 29.

CHAPTER 8

Short-Range Operating Decisions

Can you . . .

- Select and use relevant information to decide whether to make or buy a component part?
- Select and use relevant information to decide whether to process an item to completion or to sell it unfinished?
- Select and use relevant information to decide whether to continue a specific department's activities?
- Select and use relevant information to decide whether to produce special orders to sell to retailers under other than your brand name?

These specialized short-range operating decisions are the focus of this chapter.

Management accounting provides financial data for use in decision making. To be useful, this information must be clearly presented and easily understood by decision makers. Equally important is the need to monitor flows of information to ensure that the data are relevant, appropriate to decisions that must be made. Data are relevant only if they are received in a timely manner and have direct influence on managers' actions as they select a particular course of action.

> **Relevant data** are measures that are likely to change in the future as the result of a current operational decision. Usually, these data include revenues, variable costs, and all traceable costs that are identifiable specifically with the alternative in question.

This chapter assesses the impact of relevant data that relate to current operating decisions. Chapter 9 discusses capital budgeting techniques as relevant data are related to long-range commitments of capital resources. In both cases, data that are relevant to a decision, whether short- or long-range, are those that will change in the future because of actions taken by managers. Specifically, the following questions must be asked and answered satisfactorily:

—What financial factors are relevant?
—What is the net effect on profit?
—What other considerations are relevant?

Short-range operating decisions can be discussed by reviewing a selected number of common decisions likely to occur in the business world: a make-or-buy decision, a decision on whether to process a product to completion, a decision on whether to continue a department's activities in future periods, and a decision as to whether to sell products to outside retailers under a different brand name. Taken together, these four decisions provide a useful frame of reference for applying the relevance concept in a practical setting. In each case, attention is directed first to identifying the relevant data and then to presenting the information in an understandable format for use by managers in making decisions. Both the data and their ultimate use are essential management accounting contributions toward improving long-range profitability for any organization.

One company can serve as the basis for the discussion of short-range operating decisions, as all four decisions need to be made in a company such as Shamrock, Inc.

Shamrock, Inc., is an integrated company specializing in the production and sale of furniture for indoor and outdoor relaxation. At the center of its activities is a complete line of patio furniture. The entire product line is constructed of the highest-quality wood, and much of the production process requires the skills of master craftsmen. The company is well managed, and its executives are constantly alert for possible changes to improve profits. Managers at every level are given full authority to experiment with new ideas, but each effort is formally evaluated at the end of its first 12 months in operation so that only ventures promising long-range profits are continued.

Early in its history, Shamrock's owner decided to open selected retail outlets to work more closely with his customers. Although limited to only 40 small outlets in a small geographic region, the quality of Shamrock's products are recognized on a much broader scale.

MAKE-OR-BUY DECISIONS

As the name suggests, make-or-buy decisions involve deciding whether a component part can be made for less cost than would be incurred if it were purchased from an outside vendor, as well as other factors such as available capacity and vendor reliability.

An enterprising production manager at Shamrock was disturbed about inefficiencies in producing the leg assemblies for patio tables. In keeping with top management's philosophy, he was assigned responsibility for improving production. After consulting with the company's engineers and receiving little satisfaction, he contacted outside suppliers. One supplier agreed to supply 5,000 leg assemblies to Shamrock's specifications for $8.00 per unit, including all transportation charges.

Standard costs for the patio tables under consideration are as follows:

Standard Costs
Patio Tables

Materials—tabletops	$18.00	
—leg assemblies	5.50	
Labor (½ hour at $4.50 per hour)	2.25	
Variable overhead (100% direct labor)	2.25	
Fixed overhead[a]	7.00	$35.00 total

[a]Fixed overhead is based on a predetermined rate for a productive level of 5,000 units per year and a total fixed manufacturing overhead budget of $35,000 that relates wholly to the leased machinery used in the process.

These data provide the relevant information for a make-or-buy decision.

1. Financial Considerations in Make-or-Buy Decisions. Financial data relevant in a make-or-buy decision include the standard costs for producing a component as compared to the product cost if the buy alternative is selected.

> **Decision Rule:** When the total costs of a product can be decreased by purchasing subassemblies from another source, the "buy" alternative should be accepted. Relevant costs include increases in materials costs compared to decreases in labor, variable and fixed overhead costs, and the net change.

Example. The responsible production manager at Shamrock, a management accountant, and an industrial engineer met and determined that 10 minutes' labor time was spent assembling the table's legs. If these costs were eliminated, a savings of $0.75 per unit would result [(10 ÷ 60) × $4.50]. Since variable overhead is applied on the basis of 100% direct labor costs, another $0.75 per unit would be saved in variable overhead. In addition, the lease cost of the machine used in this process is estimated at $2.00 per unit of the fixed cost involved. Using these data, the manager made the following make-or-buy cost analysis. Note that the materials costs of the leg assemblies are somewhat higher than costs now incurred.

Patio Tables
Make-or-Buy Cost Analysis[a]

	Make	Buy	Difference
Materials	$23.50	$26.00	$2.50
Labor	2.25	1.50	(0.75)
Variable overhead	2.25	1.50	(0.75)
Fixed overhead	7.00	5.00	(2.00)
Total cost	$35.00	$34.00	($1.00)

[a]( ) represents reduction in costs.

Clearly, the cost differences are relevant to the decision. As currently produced, the patio table has a cost of $35.00. If the leg assemblies are purchased, the product's total cost would be $34.00, a *reduction* of $1.00 per unit. Based on financial data available, the decision would be to *buy* the preassembled component part.

Exercise

Superstar, Inc., the sporting goods company, is currently studying one of its product lines in the basketball equipment division. The product, a junior-sized basketball goal, currently has a total product cost of $50 per unit. A precut backboard is purchased from a supplier at $30 each. Upon analysis, the responsible manager learns that the wood— appropriately sized, but unfinished—can be purchased for only $22. However, paint will cost $0.50 per unit, labor cost for planing and painting will cost $2.50 per unit, and variable overhead for leased equipment will be $2 per unit.

(a) What are the relevant cost data to be used as a basis for the decision?

(b) Using only financial data as a basis for your decision, should the backboards be "bought" or "made" in this situation?

— — — — — — — — — — — — — —

(a) The relevant costs are those associated with the materials component of the backboard product. Relevant data include the current buy price, the costs of unfinished wood, paint, labor time, and the lease cost of the machine.

(b) Buy —materials costs $30/unit
    Make —materials $22.00/unit
        paint   0.50/unit
        labor   2.50/unit
        variable overhead   2.00/unit
    Total $27/unit
    Savings —make vs. buy $3/unit to make

2.   Nonfinancial Considerations in Make-or-Buy Decisions. Effective decision making uses *all* relevant information; it is not limited to financial data. Often many nonfinancial questions must be satisfactorily answered, or the short-range cost reduction benefits may be insufficient to warrant accepting a buy alternative.

> **A buy decision** must consider all relevant nonfinancial data as well, such as the reputation of the vendor, its capacity, and the internal effect of a buy decision.

Example. From a financial perspective, Shamrock's production manager would make a buy decision for the preassembled table legs. Before making a final decision, however, the manager would obtain relevant data to satisfactorily answer the following questions:
1. Is the proposed vendor reputable in terms of "quality" workmanship?
2. Does this source have the capacity to meet Shamrock's requirements on time?
3. Would the use of outside suppliers pose internal problems such as employee layoffs or a decrease in pride of workmanship?

Exercise
What other factors must the Superstar, Inc., manager consider as he evaluates the make-or-buy decision with respect to backboards?

- - - - - - - - - - - - - -

The manager must consider the reliability of the supplies of unfinished backboards, the company's capacity to do the planing and painting, and finally, whether the overall quality of the end product will be as good as that now provided to customers.

ADDITIONAL PROCESSING DECISIONS

Additional processing decisions focus on the profitability of continuing manufacturing activities for a specific product rather than selling it in a semifinished (unfinished) condition. Decision makers must consider not only the profitability of such additional processing, but also the underlying assumptions that are made.

Shamrock's production division is considering adding a new, less expensive, unfinished product line. Since only a few retail managers accept the idea as feasible, the president has asked for a financial evaluation of the proposal.

The company's less expensive product line is currently manufactured in batches of 1,000 units to achieve production efficiency. These unfinished products are packaged for shipment to retail outlets. Marketing research indicates that the availability of such unfinished units has little effect on the sales of major product lines, perhaps because Shamrock's weatherproof, staining process used in its major product lines is far superior to any other in the marketplace. This well-known, highly publicized fact has a significant impact on the whole industry, and Shamrock's share of the market continues to expand.

Their unfinished product is totally new in the industry. The question is whether the unfinished products should be finished before sale to customers. The product is sufficiently different from the major line that the two would not compete in any way. Thus, if the contribution margin on the new product can be improved by completing this additional process, the president is inclined to move in this direction.

Personnel are assigned to develop relevant information about this additional processing decision. As a basis for thier analysis, the following data are prepared:

	Unit Costs[a]
Materials costs	$40.00
Labor costs (2 hr at $5.00/hr)	10.00
Variable overhead (100% direct labor)	10.00
Fixed overhead ($20,000/1,000 units)	20.00
Total costs	$80.00

[a]Production in batches of 1,000 units.

The unfinished models sell in the retail outlets for $150 per set (table and 4 chairs).

After additional study, cost information was developed on the additional processing required to finish each unit with the weatherproofing stain. Materials costs are estimated at $10 per unit, labor costs at $3 per unit. The company has sufficient capacity to process at least 12 batches per year, far more than current demand, so additional fixed costs are not expected. Market research suggests that 6,000 of the finished models could be sold annually at $175 per unit, a volume closely approximating the number of unfinished models currently sold. Additional annual advertising costs would be $12,000. These expenditures are important to ensure that consumers become aware of the change in Shamrock's marketing strategy.

3. Financial Considerations in Additional Processing Decisions. The first step in determining the financial feasibility of undertaking additional processing is to analyze the anticipated revenue to be generated and compare this amount with the additional costs involved in further processing.

> **Decision Rule:** If the increase in revenues from additional processing exceeds the increases in costs incurred, added profits will be generated and the decision to process further should be made.

Example. Shamrock anticipates that 6,000 units of their less expensive product can be sold. If sold unfinished, sales would be $900,000 (6,000 units × $150). If these same units were carried through the additional finishing process, revenues would be $1,050,000 (6,000 units × $175). This difference in revenues of $150,000 is then compared to the relevant costs involved in this decision.

Relevant costs, those expected to change in the future because of the decision made, include additional materials costs of $60,000 ($10 per unit × 6,000 units), $18,000 additional labor costs ($3 per unit × 6,000 units), an additional $18,000 in variable overhead, and, finally, the additional advertising cost of $12,000 annually. The relevant data are summarized for analysis as follows:

Additional Processing Decision
Relevant Revenue/Cost Information
(6,000 units)

Revenues		$150,000
Less: Variable costs		
Materials	$60,000	
Labor	18,000	
Variable overhead	18,000	96,000
Contribution margin		$ 54,000
Less: Other costs		
Fixed overhead	−0−	
Advertising	12,000	12,000
Projected net income		$ 42,000

In this case, additional revenues of $25 per unit are clearly relevant also. Since this exceeds the increase of $16 per unit in variable costs, additional contribution margin of $9 per unit can be generated. Since 6,000 units are expected to be sold, the total increase of $54,000 in contribution margin is greater than the relevant advertising costs of $12,000 per year. Given these factors, profits are likely to increase if the additional processing functions are performed.

Exercise

As this Shamrock project was nearing the startup date, another significant factor became apparent. Because of expanded sales in other products, a shortage of storage space was occurring. As a result, warehouse space must now be leased for both raw materials and finished goods of the new product. Storage costs are expected to be $2,500 per month. Are these costs relevant to the decision? _____ Should the decision be changed? _____

– – – – – – – – – – – – – – – –

The warehousing costs of $30,000 are clearly relevant because the alternative cannot be executed unless these costs are borne. Thus the cost element changes because of the management decision.

Shamrock's profits on this venture should now approximate $6,000, and for this reason the alternative still appears to be favorable from a profitability viewpoint.

4.   Examining Assumptions Made in Additional Processing Decisions. Even if financial data available indicate that profits will increase by undertaking additional processing of a product, management must consider other qualitative factors, particularly the assumptions underlying the anticipated increase in profits.

> When making additional processing decisions, also determine:
> —Whether anticipated volume and price are realistic.
> —Whether capacity is readily available, so that fixed overhead costs do not increase.

Example.   In the case of Shamrock, one key assumption is that the sales of their less expensive products in a finished state will approximate 6,000 units per year. Of most importance to the validity of this forecast, however, is the assumption that customers will be willing to pay the added amount for these products. Given Shamrock's reputation for weatherproof staining, this assumption seems valid.

Additionally, the analysts assumed that Shamrock has sufficient capacity to process the needed units without incurring added fixed costs. Only those costs that change because of the decision should be considered. Since excess capacity is involved, current fixed costs should remain constant and, therefore, are *not* relevant to this decision.

Exercise

Shamrock's advertising agency has continued to evaluate this project even though their initial bid has been accepted. One of their more recent suggestions is concerned with an added promotional dimension. The new element would cost $6,000, but an added 2,000 units in volume may occur.

(a) Is this a relevant cost? _____

(b) What factors must the responsible manager evaluate as this possible decision is considered? _____

— — — — — — — — — — — — — — —

The added advertising expenditure of $6,000 becomes relevant only if the manager decides on this course of action. The added 2,000 units would generate $18,000 in contribution margin, an amount clearly sufficient to offset the additional costs. Conversely, the projected net income is now only $6,000, owing to the increased storage costs (exercise in frame 3). The uncertainty with respect to achieving the added volume is the critical factor, and thus the management's judgment is ultimately the deciding factor. Keep in mind that if the decision is made, the added revenues and variable costs, as well as the increased advertising expenditure, all become relevant data.

DEPARTMENTAL CONTINUANCE/DISCONTINUANCE DECISIONS

Managers are often faced with deciding whether to keep a specific department in operation or not, a decision equally important as manufacturing decisions and equally reliant upon relevant financial information. The decision is rarely as simple as whether the specific department is showing a change in net income; the focus must be on the entire organization's profit. Few departments can be evaluated as though they were separate and distinct from all other activities.

One of Shamrock's managers decided to develop a unit to specialize in selling and installing fireplaces. Although the markup on such products is quite attractive, the installation has posed some problems. In keeping with Shamrock's management philosophy, managers are encouraged to experiment with new marketing ventures. Policy dictates that all new activities be formally reviewed after 12 months. This evaluation is now being conducted for the fireplace department in question.

A set of financial statements has been developed to review this retail outlet's annual performance. To focus directly on fireplace sale and installation activities, a separate column for its activities is provided in the report. The data are designed in part to allow management to determine whether this department should be continued. Implicit in the decision is that its continuation could lead other retail outlets to add similar departments.

Shamrock, Inc.
Retail Outlet 13
A Summary of Operating Profits
for the Year Ended December 31, 19XX

	Dept. A Patio	Dept. B Family Room	Dept. C Fireplaces	Total
Sales revenues	$500,000	$300,000	$200,000	$1,000,000
Cost of merchandise	300,000	200,000	100,000	600,000
Contribution margin	$200,000	$100,000	$100,000	$ 400,000
Other expenses				
Salaries and wages	$ 30,000	$ 30,000	$ 20,000	$ 80,000
Advertising	10,000	10,000	20,000	40,000
Other direct expenses	20,000	5,000	35,000	60,000
General administrative expenses	60,000	30,000	30,000	120,000
Corporate services	30,000	15,000	15,000	60,000
Total expenses	$150,000	$ 90,000	$120,000	$ 360,000
Net income (loss)	$ 50,000	$ 10,000	($ 20,000)	$ 40,000

The financial statement data are useful as this decision is reached. Costs of merchandise are variable costs to the retail outlets. Direct expenses for the fireplace department relate specifically to the installation costs incurred. Finally, both general administrative expenses and those relating to corporate services are fixed, allocated to departments on the basis of contribution margin. In other words, Department C contributed 25% of the total margin earned ($100,000 ÷ $400,000); thus a corresponding proportion of these fixed costs were assigned to this department.

5. Profitability of the Individual Department. Determining whether to continue or discontinue a department begins with an analysis of the department's performance. Ultimately, however, its performance as it relates to the entire organization's profitability is the critical factor.

> **Decision Rule:** If a department's contribution margin is greater than necessary direct costs, its activities are making a positive contribution toward profitability and should be continued.

Example. To the person unfamiliar with management accounting techniques, it would appear obvious that Shamrock's fireplace department should be discontinued, as it shows a net loss of $20,000.

If Department C is discontinued, the first relevant data to consider are the revenues and costs of merchandise. Revenues will be reduced by $200,000, while the related merchandise costs will decrease by $100,000. Total contribution margin for the retail outlet would then be $300,000, assuming that all other departmental activities continue at the same level.

Certain other costs are also relevant because they, too, would be eliminated if this department's operations are discontinued. Fireplace salaries and wages of $20,000 would be eliminated, as would the $20,000 in advertising and $35,000 in other direct expenses (installation costs). In total, these three cost classifications comprise a total reduction of $75,000 for the total organization. They are *not* greater than the contribution margin they provide, however. According to the decision rule, management will not generally eliminate a department that is contributing to the coverage of overall overhead.

Exercise

Assume that Shamrock's management desires to use the decision rule that departments making contributions to the offsetting of corporate overhead costs should not be dropped. Would Department C be discontinued according to this rule? _____ Explain your conclusion.

No. Using this rule, Department C generates a contribution margin of $100,000 and has direct expenses of only $75,000. The remaining $25,000 can serve as a contribution toward offsetting overall corporate expenses of $180,000 (general administrative and corporate services expenses).

6. Allocated Costs and Overall Profits. It is critically important to analyze the implications of the allocated costs on overall performance of a specific department and the entire organization. Because of their special nature, allocated costs must generally be considered separately. To fully evaluate whether a department should be continued or not, it is often helpful to prepare a financial statement that reflects operating results without the effect of the department in question.

> **Departmental continuance/discontinuance decisions** focus on *overall* profits. Allocated costs, those expenses arbitrarily assigned on other than a cause/effect basis, are generally redistributed because they are noncontrollable. Thus they must be treated separately when evaluating performance in a responsibility center.

Example. The remaining costs for the Fireplace Department of Shamrock, Inc., are general administration and corporate services, allocated costs. The first question that management asks is whether these costs would be avoided in the future if Department C were discontinued. Top management observation indicates that these costs would *not* change, even if the Fireplace Department were discontinued.

To consider this implication, the outlet's financial statements are restated to reflect operating results without the effect of Department C.

Shamrock, Inc.
Retail Outlet No. 13
Projected Profits—Two Departments
for the Year Ended December 31, 19XX

	Dept. A Patios	Dept. B Family Room	Total
Sales	$500,000	$300,000	$800,000
Cost of merchandise	300,000	200,000	500,000
Contribution margin	$200,000	$100,000	$300,000
Other expenses			
Salaries	$ 30,000	$ 30,000	$ 60,000
Advertising	10,000	10,000	20,000
Other direct expenses	20,000	5,000	25,000
General administrative	80,000	40,000	120,000[a]
Corporate services	40,000	20,000	60,000[a]
Total expenses	$180,000	$105,000	$285,000
Net income (loss)	$ 20,000	($ 5,000)	$ 15,000

[a] Costs allocated in proportion to contribution margin.

First, note that the total allocated costs did *not* change. Second, the management policy of assigning costs to departments based on their respective proportion of total contribution margin was applied. In this latter regard, Department A contributed two-thirds of the total contribution margin for this proportion of the allocated costs. The same procedures apply to Department B.

As an initial reference point in the evaluation of the Shamrock outlet, notice that its total profits would decline by $25,000 if Department C were discontinued. This is because the contribution margin from fireplaces, $100,000, exceeds the direct departmental costs that were incurred, as noted earlier. This excess in contribution margin relative to the three departmental total expenses, $25,000, is the difference in overall profit.

Also notice that if Department C is discontinued, Departments A and B have to absorb more administrative and corporate service costs—so much so, in fact, that Department B shows a loss of $5,000. This result may cause management to consider discontinuing Department B. Department A would then be left with all the allocated costs and would also show a loss.

However, decision makers at this point would find it worthwhile to subject both classifications of allocated costs to extensive analysis. Perhaps some of the costs could be avoided if only two departments were serviced. Were this the case, some expenses *would* become relevant to the decision. Whether management should reanalyze these costs depends on the particular situation. Nevertheless, the focus must continue to be directed to identifying *relevant* financial factors when such decisions are required.

Exercise

If Departments B and C were eliminated, how would the general administrative and corporate services expenses be allocated? What would the effect be in terms of Department A?

— — — — — — — — — — — — — —

If Shamrock continues to allocate units on the basis of contribution margin percentages, Department A would absorb two-thirds of these costs ($120,000) and Department B one-third ($60,000). Then B would reflect a loss and it too would be a cause for concern. If B were also dropped, Department A would absorb the total allocated costs of $180,000, leaving it with a loss of $40,000. For reasons such as these, the decision rule concerning a department's overall contribution to overhead is clearly most appropriate when long-range profitability is the primary objective.

SPECIAL ORDER DECISIONS

Companies are sometimes approached with a large order at lower-than-normal costs and asked to produce their product under a different brand name. Such special order decisions are actions by management to accept an offer by a customer to buy goods at less than the normal price. The underlying criterion, again, is overall profitability, which can occur if revenues are greater than variable costs in a situation where fixed costs will not increase.

The president of Shamrock, Inc., has maintained an interest in expanding the markets his company serves. One patio product line has been particularly appealing to many large hotel chains, some of whom have expressed a desire to purchase large quantities of this chair to use on balconies provided with many of their rooms.

Sensing that a marketing opportunity might exist, the president appointed a manager to investigate this interest. The research was merely exploratory because the project's overall financial implications must be studied by the New Business Development Committee before contracts can be signed.

When the responsible manager requested production cost information for these chairs, the following data were provided:

Cost Classification	Per Chair
Materials	$16
Labor	4
Variable overhead	4
Fixed overhead	4
Total cost	$28

In addition, those involved in production planning informed the manager of other important factors. Fixed overhead costs for these chairs are significantly affected by the fact that specialized equipment is used in production. The capacity for production of the relatively new machinery has been established at 6,000 units per year maximum. Current production is 4,000 units per year, and no change in demand for available product line is expected. Thus both current and new product demands should be easily satisfied throughout the 5 years contained in Shamrock's long-range plan.

The president established three guidelines for the manager's activities. First, any accepted contract must improve Shamrock's overall profitability. Second, specialized sales agreements must not affect current customers; that is, companies purchasing these patio chairs must not compete directly with Shamrock's operating retail outlets. Finally, these contracts should not commit the company beyond the 5-year plan. With these guidelines as a reference, the manager initiated his research efforts.

The search for patio chair customers produced almost immediate results. One large hotel chain expressed interest in purchasing 3,000 chairs per year for the next 4 years. The manager, elated with the opportunity for success, asked for their formal order.

As the bid was being prepared, the hotel's purchasing manager investigated other interested chair manufacturers. The prices quoted ranged from $22 to $27 per unit. Aware of Shamrock's superior quality, he sent a bid for purchasing the chairs at a price not to exceed $27 per unit, their normal business practice. The offer was brought to the advisory committee's attention, but they were reluctant to consider a price below the product's standard cost per unit of $28. A special cost study was initiated to determine relevant costs involved in this order.

The relevant data relate to the potential contribution margin that can be generated. This hotel was willing to pay a maximum of $27 per unit. Since the contract calls for 3,000 units per year, a total of $81,000 can be earned annually.

7. Feasibility of Special Orders. When making decisions regarding special orders, management must consider whether the contribution margin results in a profit, given the variable and traceable costs that are identifiable specifically with the alternative in question.

> **Decision Rule:** If revenues result in a contribution margin that exceeds traceable costs identifiable specifically with the alternative, the special order should be accepted. The availability of usable capacity is a key factor to consider in special orders.

Example. Shamrock, Inc., can earn $81,000 annually by accepting the special order contract. Variable costs for these units are $24 ($16 in materials; $4 in labor; $4 in variable overhead), for total annual variable costs of $72,000 (3,000 units X $24 per unit). The annual contribution margin would therefore be $9,000. With a 4-year contract, Shamrock's management would expect to earn $36,000 in contribution margin from this special sales contract, certainly an appealing proposition.

Continuing the analysis, however, the manager and his advisory committee studied available information about production capacity. Current production is 4,000 units, so the available capacity for this order is 2,000 units, clearly insufficient for the 4-year contract requiring 3,000 units per year.

Thus Shamrock's production capacity is limited by its production equipment. After contacting many equipment manufacturers, the committee has determined that necessary resources can be purchased at a total cost of $50,000. This cost is relevant because the outlay is required if the decision to accept the hotel's 4-year order is accepted. To combine added cost to the order's projected contribution margin, the following schedule was completed:

Shamrock, Inc.
Special Order—Patio Chairs for Hotel Chain
for 4-Year Period Ended December 31, 19XX

Projected revenues (300 units X 4 years X $27)	$324,000
Less: Projected variable costs (12,000 units X $24)	288,000
Projected contribution margin	$ 36,000
Other costs (machinery)	50,000
Projected net income (loss)	($ 14,000)

It would appear that this special order should be rejected. As a basis for making the final decision, two separate considerations must be evaluated. First, have all elements relevant to the decision been studied? Second, were the president's guidelines followed as the informational basis for the decision was developed?

In establishing general rules for decisions, the basic guideline is that only relevant data be considered. Thus any measure of revenues or costs that is likely to change because of the decision should be included in the analysis. At the first level, the appropriate change in revenues is clearly relevant. So are the variable costs, those that change in response to volume changes. In this case the change in contribution margin is also relevant, as it serves as the frame of reference encompassing both revenues and variable costs.

Next the manager directs attention to the question of whether nonvariable costs are relevant to the decision. Again, any costs directly traceable to the order affect the decision. In this instance, costs associated with purchasing the needed equipment are relevant because current production capacity is not sufficient to meet the order. The costs of equipment are relevant because the investment in assets will change as a result of this decision. In the final analysis, of course, all these costs are controllable at this time because they can be influenced by the decision to accept or reject the order. Each of the key dimensions of management accounting data—variability, traceability, and controllability—is involved when the concept of relevancy is considered.

Considering the president's guidelines, this order must be rejected because its acceptance would result in a loss of $14,000 over the 4-year period.

Exercise.

Shamrock's manager for new business development learned a great deal about the concept of relevancy from his hotel order experience. Using this added perspective as a foundation, he pursued even more aggressively other opportunities that presented themselves. At the forefront was a possible contract with a locally owned motel organization. Although much smaller than the hotel chain, their growth potential appeared significant. Thus this organization, too, was interested in Shamrock's line of patio chairs.

The motel's requirement for the coming year was 1,000 units. They have formally offered to pay $25 per unit for the chairs. The possibilities for future contracts of a similar nature are excellent, but this motel's management is currently unwilling to commit to longer than 1 year. Shamrock's production capacity, of course, remains 6,000 units per year for this product line, and regular demand and standard prices established are expected to continue.

(a) What data are relevant for the manager to consider in making his decision?

(b) What is the net effect on profits if the offer is accepted?

(c) What other considerations are important to this decision?

(a) Revenues generated, standard costs, contribution margin, and capacity are all relevant factors. Revenues from this order should be $25,000 annually ($1,000 units at $25 per unit). These revenues are relevant because they will change as the result of the decision made. Contribution margin, measured by subtracting variable costs from revenues, is expected to be $1 per unit, or $1,000 for this contract. Since these contracts are effective on a year-to-year basis, management in both organizations must be aware that future cost increases may necessitate a different set of financial arrangements. Nevertheless, the fact that an increase in contribution margin should result certainly dictates that this possible contract be thoroughly considered.

Capacity is sufficient. Shamrock's capacity for this product line is 6,000 units per year, with 4,000 units committed to the company's retail outlets and their clientele. The remaining capacity of 2,000 units per year is available for use in special orders. Since the motel's request is for 1,000 units per year, their order can be satisfied within Shamrock's current production capacity.

(b) The motel's offer is expected to generate a net income of $1,000 during the 1-year contract, as indicated by the following report:

Shamrock, Inc.
Special Order—Patio Chairs for Motel Chain
for the Year Ended December 31, 19XX

Project revenues	$25,000
Less: Projected variable costs	24,000
Projected contribution margin	$ 1,000
Other costs	—0—
Projected net income	$ 1,000

(c) A key consideration is the set of guidelines established by the president. The first, profitability, has already been met. Regarding the second issue, the effect on normal retail volume of selling patio chairs to this motel, those responsible for the decision can visualize no marketing conflicts between Shamrock's retail outlets and the motel organization. Since this contract does not extend beyond the 5-year plan, it satisfies all criteria and can be accepted.

You may want to review the questions presented at the beginning of this chapter before completing the Self-Test that follows.

CHAPTER 8 SELF-TEST

1. Matching – Terminology/Concepts

Match the following terms to the definitions.

1. Additional processing decisions
2. Allocated costs
3. Controllability
4. Departmental discontinuance decision
5. Make-or-buy decision

6. Relevant data
7. Special order decisions
8. Special decisions
9. Traceable data
10. Variability

_____ (a) Actions by management to accept an offer by a customer to buy goods at less than the normal price and using a different brand name.

_____ (b) The concept that refers to costs that change in total in direct proportion to changes in levels of activity. Since these costs are generally assumed to be constant per unit of output, they often change in direct response to decisions affecting volume.

_____ (c) Concept that refers to the need for managers to influence financial factors within the scope of their authority.

_____ (d) Measures that are directly affected by a decision and are likely to change in the future as the result of that decision.

_____ (e) Expenses arbitrarily assigned on other than a cause/effect basis. Generally, such costs are noncontrollable and must be treated separately when evaluating performance in a responsibility center.

2. Make-or-Buy Decision

The AA Company manufactures complex electrical assemblies for use in hospital equipment. One important product is now being redesigned; thus the total production process is being analyzed to determine if cost savings are possible. The following costs are now being incurred for their product:

Direct materials	$2.50
Direct labor	1.00
Variable overhead	1.00
Fixed overhead	1.50 per unit

Variable overhead is applied on the basis of 100% of direct labor costs; thus $1.00 in variable overhead is incurred for each dollar of direct labor that is spent. Fixed overhead, on the other hand, is based on a budget of $15,000 annually for a production capacity of 10,000 units. These fixed overhead charges are allocated to this product because of the machinery that is used. The costs will not change for the company even if the product were not sold.

A supplier has offered to produce one of this product's major component parts. They would sell it to the AA Company for $2.00 per unit. After careful analysis, AA's cost analysts have decided that this product's current costs would be reduced by $1.00 in materials. In addition, the direct labor time would be reduced 60%. Using these data, respond to the following questions:

(a) What are the relevant costs in this problem? Briefly indicate why each is relevant to this decision.

(b) How much change in costs will result if AA decides to purchase this product from outside suppliers?

(c) If this year's production is scheduled to be 10,000 units, what will the total production costs be if the decision to buy the component is made?

(d) Should AA purchase this product? What other considerations are involved if management makes this decision?

3. Additional Processing

The BB Company manufactures leather goods for sale at retail locations. One of the most popular lines of men's wallets has been a financial success as indicated by the following income statement:

BB Company
Men's Wallets
Income Statement
for the Year Ended 19XX

Sales (24,000 units)		$192,000
Cost of sales		
Materials	$72,000	
Labor	48,000	
Overhead	30,000[a]	150,000
Gross profit		$ 42,000
Other costs		12,000
Net income		$ 30,000

[a]Manufacturing overhead costs include $6,000 in fixed costs.

The company's marketing research department has recommended that the wallet line could become even more successful if additional design features were added. The sales price could be increased by 25% if the additional processing function were added. A machine would be rented at $16,000 per year, and the labor costs would be $24,000 per year. Variable overhead is applied as a specified percentage of direct labor costs, and this rate has not changed during the time when this product has been sold.

Given these data, respond to the following questions:

(a) Identify the relevant financial data for this decision and specify the amounts involved.

(b) If additional design processing is implemented, what are the likely effects on profits? Is the additional processing a desirable alternative?

4. Discontinuing a Department

The CC Company operates a soda fountain in one of its many retail outlets. In recent years, the fountain's volume has declined significantly, so management is considering using this space for additional office space. The following income statement has been prepared as a basis for this decision:

CC Company
Income Statement
for the Year Ended XXXX

	Retail	Soda Fountain	Total
Sales	$600,000	$200,000	$800,000
Cost of sales	420,000	160,000	580,000
Gross profit	$180,000	$ 40,000	$220,000
Other operating costs	$120,000	$ 35,000	$155,000
Overhead costs	30,000	10,000	40,000
Total costs	$150,000	$ 45,000	$195,000
Net income (loss)	$ 30,000	($ 5,000)	$ 25,000

Fixed overhead costs are assigned on the basis of sales revenues (retail = 75%; soda fountain = 25%). These total costs will not change if a decision is made to discontinue the soda fountain. Using these data, respond to the following questions:

(a) Identify the relevant financial data for this decision and specify the amounts involved.

(b) What will the impact be on CC's profits if the soda fountain is discontinued? Should CC Company make this decision?

5. Special Order Pricing

The DD Company produces and sells a line of small kitchen appliances. One of its products, an electric can opener (with a knife-sharpener attachment), is sold at retail for a price of $15. Its costs are identified below:

	Per Unit
Direct materials	$ 5
Direct labor	2
Variable overhead	2
Fixed overhead	3
Total	$12

Fixed overhead costs are based on a budgeted production of 40,000 units at $120,000 annually. Present production and sales are 24,000 units.

A large department store chain has approached DD's president about the possibility of marketing this product under a different brand name. They have offered to purchase 10,000 units annually if the price will be reduced to $10 per unit. Using these data, advise the president about accepting this special sales order.

(a) What financial factors are relevant to this decision?

(b) What is the net effect on profits if the president accepts this offer? Should he take the offer?

(c) What other considerations are important to this decision?

ANSWERS

1. Matching – Terminology/Concepts

(a) 7 (frame 7, 1 pt)   (b) 10 (frame 7, 1 pt)

(c) 3 (frame 6, 1 pt)   (d) 6 (introduction, 1 pt)

(e) 2 (frame 6, 1 pt)

2. Make-or-Buy Decision

(a) Direct materials, direct labor, and variable overhead are relevant to this decision because these costs will change if the component part is bought from the outside supplier. (frame 1, 3 pts)

(b)

	Current Cost	New Cost	Savings per Unit
Direct materials	$2.50	$1.50	$1.00
Direct labor	1.00	0.40	0.60
Variable overhead	1.00	0.40	0.60
Variable costs	$4.50	$2.30	$2.20

(frame 1, 3 pts)

(c)

	Per Unit	Total Cost (10,000 units)
AA's production costs	$1.50	$15,000
Purchased part	2.00	20,000
Direct labor	0.40	4,000
Variable overhead	0.40	4,000
Fixed overhead	1.50	15,000
Total costs	$5.80	$58,000

(frame 1, 3 pts)

(d) Yes. Some other considerations are
1. Supplier's quality of workmanship.
2. Supplier's capacity to meet AA's requirements in a timely manner.
3. Effect on AA's work force.

(frame 2, 3 pts)

3. Additional Processing

(a) Relevant data

Revenues	24,000 units at $2	$48,000
Costs		
Direct labor		$24,000
Variable overhead (50% direct labor)		12,000
Fixed overhead (rent)		6,000
Total		$42,000

(frame 3, 6 pts)

(b) Profit change

The profits of this line would increase by $6,000, so the additional processing is a desirable alternative.

Increased revenues	$48,000	
Increased costs	42,000	
Profit increase	$ 6,000	(frame 3, 2 pts)

4. Discontinuing a Department

(a) Relevant data

	Soda Fountain	
Sales	$200,000	
Cost of sales	160,000	
Gross profit	$ 40,000	
Operating costs	35,000	
Contribution to overhead	$ 5,000	(frame 5, 6 pts)

(b) Profitability (if decision is made)

Sales	$600,000	
Cost of sales	420,000	
Gross profit	$180,000	
Operating costs	120,000	
Contribution to overhead	$ 60,000	
Overhead costs	40,000	
Net income	$ 20,000	(frame 5, 2 pts)

The company's overall profits will decline by $5,000. This occurs because the soda fountain's contribution to overhead ($5,000) is lost if this unit is discontinued. Thus the decision should not be made.

5. Special Order Pricing

(a) Relevant data

Revenues (10,000 units at $10)		$100,000	
Variable costs			
Direct materials ($5/unit)	$50,000		
Direct labor ($2/unit)	20,000		
Variable overhead ($2/unit)	20,000	90,000	
Contribution margin—special order		$ 10,000	(frame 7, 4 pts)

(b) Profits will increase by $10,000 if the order is accepted because there will be no increase in fixed costs. Note that the company has the capacity to produce 40,000 units per year. With the special order, the total production of 34,000 is well within DD's capacity. The additional $10,000 in contribution margin from the special order thus serves to increase profits directly. Thus the president should accept this order if profits are the only consideration. (frame 7, 4 pts)

(c) Other considerations
1. The order can be profitable only if additional capacity is not required in its production. This long-term commitment might not be in the best interest of DD Company because their volume at $15 might subsequently increase.
2. The special order should not have any direct impact on current sales. If the department store chain were a direct competitor with some of DD's current outlets, a decision to accept the offer would not be feasible. (frame 7, 4 pts)

Total possible points: 45. You should have scored at least 36.

CHAPTER 9

Long-Range Decisions: Capital Budgeting

 Can you . . .

- Explain what capital budgeting is and describe the four techniques frequently used?
- Evaluate a proposed project's profitability using the accounting rate of return?
- Determine the cost of capital? The weighted average cost of capital?
- Evaluate a proposed project's liquidity using payback period?
- Use the payback reciprocal measure properly?
- Determine the present and future value of a dollar? Determine net present value?
- Determine the internal rate of return of a project? Estimated rate? "True" rate?
- Identify the strengths and weaknesses of the major capital budgeting techniques?

After completing this chapter, you should be better prepared to make objective long-range decisions regarding commitments of financial resources.

Management accounting techniques contribute directly to short-term operating decisions. Equally important, however, is a manager's need to evaluate longer-range opportunities. Ideally, a company's financial resources will be committed to those activities that promise the most desirable results.

> **Capital budgeting** is a long-range planning tool. Its techniques are designed to facilitate selection of projects that offer the most financial potential.

Capital budgeting allows you to analyze and evaluate the long-term potential of different projects systematically and equitably. Thus all personnel who propose an alternative use of capital are assured that their ideas are treated fairly. Basically, a set of rules is developed to ensure that top management makes appropriate decisions. Before these guidelines are discussed, however, attention is directed to the setting within which relevant evaluations occur.

First, recognize that capital funds bear a cost. Even the largest corporations must sometimes borrow money. In addition, such companies must also promise their stockholders a reasonable return on invested funds. Both interest and return to stockholders are termed the "cost of capital." Managers cannot commit monetary resources to projects if the promised yield is less than costs associated with obtaining the capital. You would not invest funds costing 10% in interest into a project that offers less than a 10% return.

Since most companies have limited funds for internal investment, management generally operates on the premise that funds be allocated to only the most deserving available alternative(s). Only projects promising yields in excess of the cost of capital are even considered. Additionally, projects are often viewed as being mutually exclusive because of funds limitations. This means that of the projects being considered, only the best can be selected. Later, interrelated activities can be merged into one comprehensive project alternative if management so desires.

The final project selections require somewhat formal decisions. Four different measures are available for evaluating proposed projects. The first measure, *return on assets*, focuses on profitability, the percentage relationship between net income and the cost of assets involved. In a broad sense, assets refer to all resources that must be acquired to accomplish the desired end result. A second measure, the *payback period*, evaluates liquidity, a cash flow measure, in terms of the time (years or months) required to recover funds committed to the project. In many companies, these two measures are used as screening devices during the initial phases of project evaluations.

Two other measures, both quite technical, are also used in capital budgeting. The *net-present-value technique* measures the promised yield of a project in terms of the present value of invested funds and promised future inflows. A comparable measure, the *internal rate of return*, also offers a present-value measure of promised yields in a somewhat different form. This indicator, often termed the true rate of return, is difficult to measure without a computer. Consequently, its treatment in this book is limited.

Each of the four measures discussed are used in varying degrees as organizations make capital budgeting decisions. Both the strengths and weaknesses of these techniques must be understood if managers are to anticipate the practical problems likely to be encountered with their use.

ACCOUNTING RATE OF RETURN

Management often wants to evaluate all significant projects somewhat formally so that decision makers are assured that all important factors are properly considered. Presumably, when projects are analyzed consistently, the most desirable projects are selected.

The capital budgeting method was developed to facilitate consistent and thorough project evaluations. Since profitability is a vital concern throughout the private sector of our economy, the first measure used—the accounting rate of return—focuses on a project's profitability.

> The **accounting rate of return** assesses **profitability**, that is, the average net income after taxes generated by investing funds in a project.

Burger Kastle, Inc., a fast-food company, has an opportunity to open a shop near the local university. Since no similar operations exist in this part of the country, its management will develop a divisional organization to support these activities. This unit will operate as a self-sustaining corporation for management control and tax purposes.

The land requires an investment of $100,000, the building $30,000, and necessary equipment $20,000. After a careful analysis of similar operations in other areas, revenues are estimated to average $120,000 per year. Operating expenses should require weekly outlays of $1,500 and annual depreciation should be $6,000 ($2,000 for the building and $4,000 for equipment). Since this division will operate as a corporate unit, the 50% tax rate applies. These taxes include federal, state, and local taxes that are assessed for all organizations earning profit from sales of goods or services.

1. Expected Percentage of Return on Assets. The first step in evaluating a project's profitability is to determine expected revenues and expenses. Taken together, these data allow determination of net income after taxes. This figure can then be divided by the total investment base to obtain the return on investment. You may want to review Chapter 2, frame 1, "Return on Investment," at this point.

> **Return on assets** is the relationship of net income after taxes to investment in assets.
>
> $$\text{return on assets (\%)} = \frac{\text{net income after taxes}}{\text{investment in resources}}$$

Example. The projected net income after taxes for the proposed Burger Kastle is summarized in the following schedule:

Projected Income Analysis – Annual
Proposed Burger Kastle

Revenues		$120,000
Expenses		
Operations	$78,000	
Depreciation	6,000	84,000
Net income before taxes		$ 36,000
Income taxes (50%)		18,000
Net income after taxes		$ 18,000

This Burger Kastle is expected to generate profits (net income after taxes) of $18,000 per year. The financial investment is expected to be $150,000; therefore, the return on investment for this proposed project is 12% ($18,000 ÷ $150,000). In this case the amount of profit per year is expected to remain the same. In cases where net incomes differ from year to year, a simple average is computed as the appropriate measure. For example, if a project promised net income yields of $500, $400, and $300, respectively, the average net income of $400 would be used to determine the return percentage. ($500 + $400 + $300 = $1,200 ÷ 3 = $400.)

Exercise

Burger Kastle, Inc., is considering an investment of $250,000 in another project.

(a) How much income must then be generated to achieve the same 12% return?
_____

(b) How much income is needed for a 16% return under these changed conditions?
_____

(c) Why might an increasing rate of return target be necessitated in the business world of today? _____

— — — — — — — — — — — — — — — —

(a) $30,000 (12% X $250,000)
(b) $40,000 (16% X $250,000)
(c) As interest rates increase, a company's cost of capital also increases. Thus to ensure that returns are sufficient to cover relevant costs, the target rates of return must be increased as a part of the management planning process.

2. Decision Rules for Using Return on Assets Measures

> **When using return on assets to evaluate proposals:**
> 1. The return promised must be greater than the costs associated with the funds invested in the project.
> 2. The expected percentage of return for the project being evaluated must be better than other available investment opportunities.

Example. Assume that the funds for the Burger Kastle project were borrowed at an interest rate of 10%. Since the return from this project is expected to be 12%, the measure of profitability is greater than the cost of capital; therefore, the company should be willing to invest these funds. If, however, another proposal for funds promises a 15% return and management cannot undertake two major projects, the project with the greatest percentage of return should receive the funds.

Exercise

Consider a case where four projects are being evaluated. The company has a budget of $100,000 in available capital funds. Cost of capital is currently 10%. Data for each opportunity are as follows:

Project	Investment Required	Expected Return
A	$100,000	15%
B	125,000	18%
C	75,000	12%
D	100,000	10%

1. What project(s) should be *eliminated* from consideration? _____

   Why? _____

2. Of the remaining projects, which would you recommend funding? _____

   Why? _____

— — — — — — — — — — — — — —

1. B should be eliminated because funds are not sufficient to cover the required investment. D should be eliminated because the return promised is *not* greater than the costs associated with the funds invested in the project.
2. A should be selected because it offers a greater percentage of return than the remaining project (C).

3.   Cost of Capital.   Each of the preceding evaluations was partially based on the concept of *cost of capital.* In its simplest form, cost of capital is the interest paid when funds are borrowed. Other, more complex measurements are applied when nonborrowed funds are used. When different sources of funds are combined to finance a project, the cost of capital is determined by multiplying the percentage of each source of funds in the total investment by the percentage of payment required for each. This results in a weighted average cost of capital. The resulting figure is sometimes also called the "minimum cutoff criterion," because projects promising a return yield less than this measure are rejected.

> The **cost-of-capital** measure refers to expenses incurred when acquiring financial resources either through borrowing from creditors (interest) or obtaining investments from owners (dividends). When sources of funds having different costs are combined in a single investment, each source can be weighted to determine an *average cost of capital.* This measure also represents the **minimum cutoff criterion**.

Example. The Burger Kastle operating division is given limited authority to issue capital stock. For these purposes, the offering is restricted to officers and long-standing employees. In return for their investment, these stockholders are promised a return in dividends of no less than 8% per year. Half the money for the project is to be financed in this way. The other half is to be borrowed at a rate of 10% annually. When the two sources of funds are combined, the division's capital structure would appear as follows:

	Cost X Weighting	
Long-term debt	10% X 50%	= 5%
Capital stock	8% X 50%	= 4%
Weighted average cost of capital		9%

This cost-of-capital measure becomes the minimum cutoff criterion. Since Burger Kastle's promised return on investment is 12%, the project could be funded.

Exercise

Assume that Burger Kastle's long-term debt comprises 60% of its capital structure and carries an interest rate of 10%. Outstanding stock (equity), on the other hand, is issued with the promise that stockholders will obtain a return of 15%. What would the company's weighted average cost of capital be in this case?

- - - - - - - - - - - - - - -

	Cost X Weighting		Average Cost
Debt	10% X	60%	6.0%
Equity	15% X	40%	6.0%
Weighted average cost of capital		12.0%	

4. Risk Factors. The cost-of-capital measure can be complemented by an additional feature called the *risk factor*. This is an arbitrary percentage assigned by management to reflect the amount of risk they perceive to be involved in the investment. Investing in a totally new product would probably be assigned a higher risk factor than expanding production of an already well-accepted product.

> Cost-of-capital measures can include a **risk factor** to raise the cutoff criterion.

Example. A project to develop a new product is subjectively assigned a risk factor of 8%, while an equipment improvement project for an ongoing product line is assigned a risk factor of 3%. In these cases, the minimum cutoff criteria for all similar projects would be specified as follows:

	Cost of Capital	+ Risk	= Cutoff Criterion
Class A projects (new product line)	9%	+ 8% =	17%
Class B projects (improvements on current products)	9%	+ 3% =	12%

As projects are proposed, each is screened. If the minimum cutoff criterion is satisfied and funds are available, the project can be initiated during the appropriate planning period. Should either of these conditions be unsatisfactory, a different course of action is warranted. Management may reject the proposal or request that it be revised to meet requirements.

Exercise

Burger Kastle includes different risk factors for different kinds of projects. Class I projects require a minimum return of 13%, while class III projects require 20%. The company's cost of capital is now 10%.

(a) What is the risk associated with Class I projects? _____

(b) Class III projects? _____

(c) Can you give an example of one project in each category that will explain the reasoning involved in assigning different risks to the various project classifications?

— — — — — — — — — — — —

(a) Class I projects have a 3% risk factor.

(b) Class III projects are assigned a 10% factor.

(c) In class I projects, most of the conditions have been encountered in previous situations; thus the results are predictable with more accuracy. An example would be the replacement of equipment with a model that is closely similar in nature. Class III projects are much more uncertain as to results. When a totally new concept in equipment is attempted in an experimental program, results are difficult to determine. Thus a higher risk factor is assigned and the required return is increased accordingly.

5. Strengths and Weaknesses of the Return-on-Assets Measure. Capital budgeting measures cannot be effectively used unless both their strengths and weaknesses are understood. Although only two major strengths and two major weaknesses are discussed here, others may become apparent as practical situations are encountered.

> **Strengths of average-return-on-investment criterion:**
> — Relevant; measures profitability.
> — Understandable and easy to apply.

The two principal strengths of the average-return-on-investment criterion are its relevance and understandability. It is relevant because managers' decisions most often focus directly on a project's anticipated profitability. Since this return measure specifies the relationship of net income after tax to the investment base, attention is directed specifically to profits as the decision criterion.

The second strength of the return measure is its basic simplicity. In most cases data are readily available in a net income format. Consequently, this information need only be extracted from an ongoing system and merged with original cost estimates to provide the relevant measure. This ease of application is one of the major reasons for the popularity of the average return as a decision-making guideline.

> **Weaknesses of average-return-on-investment criterion:**
> — Does not clearly reflect expected cash flows.
> — Does not consider the timing of inflows and outflows; the possibility of reinvestment is ignored.

One major weakness of the average-return-on-investment criterion is that the net income measure does not clearly reflect the expected cash flows from a project. Profits, per se, cannot be reinvested because a significant dimension of the concept includes consideration of noncash elements: accrued revenues, depreciation, amortization of intangibles, and the like. Therefore, many contend that profitability is not totally appropriate for evaluating long-term projects that require significant capital commitments.

A second shortcoming is that the timing of inflows and outflows is not explicitly considered. By averaging a project's annual net income measures when projects extend over many years, resources flowing from early years are merged with those expected in later periods. Therefore, financial resources from each year are given equal weighting. This assumption violates the premise that dollars have value because managers are able to use these funds in other projects as they are received. Since this investment concept is quite complex, its thorough treatment is deferred to a later part of this chapter. The fact that reinvestment is ignored in the average return method makes this second limitation even more significant.

Exercise

1. What two strengths are associated with the average-return-on-investment measure?
   (a)
   (b)
2. What two weaknesses are associated with this measure?
   (a)
   (b)

- - - - - - - - - - - - - -

1. Strengths:
   (a) Relevance in that profit is an organizational objective.
   (b) Understandable because the measure is simple in design and easy to apply.
2. Weaknesses:
   (a) Profitability measures do not explicitly recognize cash as the basic criterion.
   (b) The measure of average net income fails to consider the value of using funds in early periods when they are actually received—particularly, any return that may be yielded from reinvesting these funds.

PAYBACK PERIOD

An emphasis on profitability is clearly reflected when average return on investment is used as the capital budgeting decision guideline. Many companies, however, are equally concerned with *liquidity* as a major criterion. In these situations, the need for continuous inflows of liquid resources may dominate the capital budgeting process.

> The **payback period** criterion assesses **liquidity**, viewing projects in terms of their effects on cash flows.

Projects are evaluated in terms of their relative abilities to recover cash that is initially invested. The shorter the time period in which the cash investment is recovered, the more favorable the project. Consider, for purposes of this discussion, the situation of Ace Automotive Services, Inc.

Ace's Automotive Services, Inc., has been involved in a wide range of activities during the past 25 years. Its owner recently observed still another opportunity to expand its operations. Many customers have expressed a desire to rent pickup trucks for short periods.

Ace conducted a limited marketing survey and decides to offer this service on a limited scale. The following data were developed by the company's accountant as the basis for making this decision.

The proposed project would require the purchase of 10 trucks at a total investment of $60,000. Each vehicle is expected to have a 6-year life, and for purposes of evaluation, salvage value is ignored because the amount is not considered significant. The corporation's overall tax rate is assumed to be 50%. Below are estimated revenues and expense data for the entire 6-year project.

Ace's Automotive Services, Inc.
Estimated Financial Data

Year	Cash Revenues	Cash Expenses	Straight-Line Depreciation	Net Income Before Taxes
1	$40,000	$18,000	$10,000	$12,000
2	40,000	18,000	10,000	12,000
3	42,000	24,000	10,000	8,000
4	42,000	24,000	10,000	8,000
5	44,000	30,000	10,000	4,000
6	44,000	30,000	10,000	4,000

These projections demonstrate that, in this case, expenses will tend to increase more rapidly than revenues owing to added repairs and maintenance costs during the later years of this project.

> The **payback period** measures the length of time that a project must continue before the original cash investment is recovered. Measuring a project's liquidity requires three separate steps:
> 1. Combining cash receipts and cash disbursements to obtain net cash inflows.
> 2. Incorporating the effects of depreciation to determine the after-tax cash flows.
> 3. Computing the payback period as the basis for a liquidity-oriented decision.

6. Determining Net Cash Inflows. The first step in measuring a project's liquidity is to combine all expected cash receipts and cash disbursements from operations into a net measure of annual cash flows. Then incorporate the annual depreciation measure into the income statement to provide a measure of net income after taxes. Remember that net income before tax is the basis for measuring the company's tax liability. This liability, in turn, requires an additional cash outlay.

> Prepare an income statement reflecting revenues, expenses, net inflows, depreciation, net income before taxes, taxes, and net income after taxes.

Example. The income statement for Ace Automotive Services for the first operating year would be as follows:

Revenue (cash)	$40,000
Expenses (cash)	18,000
Net inflows	$22,000
Depreciation	10,000
Net income before taxes	$12,000
Taxes (50%)	6,000
Net income after taxes	$ 6,000

Since the second year of operations is expected to have the same revenues and expenses, the income statement for the second year would be identical to that for the first year.

Exercise

Develop an income statement for the third and fifth years of operations for Ace Automotive Services:

	Year 3	Year 5

- - - - - - - - - - - - - - - -

	Year 3	Year 5
Revenues (cash)	$42,000	$44,000
Expenses (cash)	24,000	30,000
Net inflows	$18,000	$14,000
Depreciation	10,000	10,000
Net income before taxes	$ 8,000	$ 4,000
Taxes (50%)	4,000	2,000
Net income after taxes	$ 4,000	$ 2,000

The income statement for year 4 would be the same as that for year 3; that for year 6 would be the same as for year 5.

7. Determining Net After-Tax Cash Inflows. The next step is to determine the net after-tax cash inflows by using specific cash receipts, disbursements, and depreciation data.

> **To determine net after-tax cash inflows:**
> —Subtract operating expenses and taxes from revenues (eliminating depreciation).
>   *or*
> —Add depreciation to the net-income-after-taxes figure.

Example. The net after-tax cash inflows for the first operating year of Ace's Automotive Services would be as follows using the first method:

Revenues (cash)	$40,000
Operating expenses (cash)	(18,000)
Taxes	(6,000)
After-tax cash inflows	$16,000

Using the second, more simplified approach, its schedule for measuring after-tax cash inflow would be as follows:

Net income after taxes	$ 6,000
Plus depreciation	10,000
After-tax cash inflows	$16,000

Exercise

What are the after-tax inflows for year 3 of Ace's Automotive Services? _____ For year 5? _____

— — — — — — — — — — — — — —

Year 3, $14,000; year 5, $12,000.

8.   Tax Shield Effect. This measure of cash inflows after taxes is a key factor in evaluating projects in terms of the payback criterion. Depreciation is an expense that is deducted before taxes are calculated, hence the term *tax shield effect.*

> The **tax shield effect** measures the annual depreciation in dollars times the income tax rate.

Example. Ace's Automotive Services, Inc., had $10,000 the first year in depreciation. Had it *not* had this depreciation, the company's tax liability for the net inflow of $22,000 from operations would have been $11,000 (50% X $22,000). Thus taxes would have increased by $5,000 compared to the situation where depreciation was properly reflected as a tax-deductible expense. Stated precisely, their annual depreciation of $10,000 times their income tax rate of 50% resulted in a tax shield effect of $5,000.

Exercise

What is the tax shield effect for Ace Automotive Services in year 3? _____
In year 5? _____

- - - - - - - - - - - - - - - -

The tax shield effect will remain the same for each year of the project since depreciation
and tax rate remain constant.

9. Determining the Specific Payback Period. Once the after-tax cash inflow for each
year is known, it is a simple matter to combine these until the year whose cumulative
total contains the amount of the initial investment is evident. After the year in which the
investment will be paid back is known, two other considerations come into play. First,
when funds are limited and only one project can be selected, the one having the shorter
payback period should be selected. In other cases, however, management may operate on
a somewhat more rigid rule by specifying that all selected projects must return cash in less
than a specified number of years.

> The **payback period** measures the length of time a project
> must continue before the original cash investment is
> recovered. Guidelines for using the payback period as an
> evaluation criterion:
> 1. If only one project can be selected, select the one with
>   the shortest payback.
> 2. You may require that all projects must return cash in
>   less than a specified number of years.

Example. Using the data from Ace's Automotive Services, the following schedule of
after-tax cash inflows can be developed for the 6-year project (see frame 6):

Net income before taxes	$12,000	$12,000	$ 8,000	$ 8,000	$ 4,000	$ 4,000
Income taxes (50%)	6,000	6,000	4,000	4,000	2,000	2,000
Net income after taxes	$ 6,000	$ 6,000	$ 4,000	$ 4,000	$ 2,000	$ 2,000
Plus: Depreciation	10,000	10,000	10,000	10,000	10,000	10,000
After-tax cash inflow	$16,000	$16,000	$14,000	$14,000	$12,000	$12,000

Information from this schedule can then be cast into a cumulative schedule as follows:

Year	After-Tax Cash Inflow	Cumulative Total
1	$16,000	$16,000
2	16,000	32,000
3	14,000	46,000
4	14,000	60,000
5	12,000	72,000
6	12,000	84,000

As can be seen from the cumulative schedule, the original cash investment of $60,000 will be recovered at the end of the fourth year.

Exercise

1. What would the payback period be if $45,000 had been invested? _____
2. What would it be if $70,000 had been invested? _____

- - - - - - - - - - - - - - -

1. Approximately 3 years.
2. Approximately 5 years.

10.   Payback Reciprocal. The payback period measure is designed for use in making capital budgeting decisions from a liquidity perspective. Under certain conditions, however, this measure becomes much more powerful as a basis for evaluating the financial benefits promised by a particular project.

> The **payback reciprocal** measures a project's approximate true rate of return when certain conditions are satisfied. It is expressed in terms of the following relationship:
>
> $$\text{payback reciprocal} = \frac{1}{\text{payback period}}$$

Example. Ace's Automotive Services' payback period for recovering the $60,000 initial cash investment was found to be 4 years, a payback reciprocal of $1/4$, or 25%. This percentage measure is an approximation of the project's maximum rate of return.

Exercise

1. What would be the payback reciprocal for a 3-year payback? _____
2. For a 5-year payback? _____

- - - - - - - - - - - - - -

1. 33.3%.
2. 20%.

11.

> Three separate *conditions* must be present for payback
> reciprocal to be valid as a basis for decisions:
> 1. Total investment must occur at the beginning of the
>   period.
> 2. After-tax cash inflows must occur evenly throughout
>   the project.
> 3. Duration of the project must be at least twice as long as
>   the payback period.

Example. Ace's Automotive Services did make the initial investment of $60,000 at the beginning of the project; therefore, the first condition was met. Had the funds been invested over a 2-year period, the reciprocal measure would be invalid.

The inflows from Ace's truck fleet do *not* satisfy the second criterion because inflows change every 2 years. If management had anticipated after-tax cash inflows to be $15,000 annually, the reciprocal would be appropriate.

This project also fails to meet the third condition, that the number of years of after-tax cash inflows promised by the project be at least two times greater than the payback period. Ace's payback period is 4 years; the total time of the project is 6 years. It would have to be at least 8 years to meet the third condition. Therefore, the reciprocal measure would not be valid in this case.

Exercise

Consider a project that has a useful life of 8 years. The investment at the beginning of the project is $20,000, and cash inflows are $5,000 in each of the years of the project.

(a) What is the payback period in this case? _____
(b) What is the payback reciprocal measure? _____
(c) Can this measure be used as an indicator of the true rate of return? _____

    Why or why not? _____

– – – – – – – – – – – – – – –

(a) The payback period is 4 years ($20,000 ÷ $5,000 = 4).
(b) The payback reciprocal is 25% (1 ÷ 4).
(c) The reciprocal is valid in this case. The investment occurs at the beginning of the project, cash inflows occur uniformly (the same amount each year), and the project's life is at least twice as long as the payback period (8 years vs. 4 years).

12.   Strengths and Weaknesses of the Payback Period Measure. The payback period and its reciprocal are comparable to the measure of accounting rate of return in terms of strengths and weaknesses. However, unique conditions in any operating environment can significantly affect the specific strengths or weaknesses of any given measure.

> **Strengths of payback period criterion:**
> — Focuses directly on cash flows and the availability of liquid resources.
> — Considers times when inflows and outflows will occur.

The first strength of the payback measure is that it focuses directly on cash flows, ensuring management's attention to inflows of liquid funds available for reinvestment as a project progresses. A second strength is that by adding the cumulative cash inflows in a year-to-year sequence, the specific times at which resources are expected to be received are explicitly recognized. Consequently, neither the net income concept nor the averaging process have as much effect on the payback measure as when the accounting rate of return is used.

> **Weaknesses of payback period criterion:**
> — Ignores inflows after the end of the payback period.
> — Does not consider returns from reinvesting cash inflows.

One important weakness of the payback period is that it focuses only on the time periods before the invested cash is recovered. All subsequent time frames are ignored. Consequently, projects promising significant cash inflows in years beyond the payback period may be ignored when comparisons are made.

A second weakness is that this measure fails to consider any additional returns that may be generated by reinvesting funds as they are received. Therefore, the total results of all projects are *understated* in terms of their potential returns on investment. Although the payback reciprocal may offset this limitation to some extent, its conditions are so restrictive that the measure frequently cannot be used.

Payback measures, coupled with those reflecting accounting rates of return, can serve as initial screening devices in many organizations.

Exercise

1. What are two strengths of the payback period criterion?
   (a)
   (b)
2. What are two weaknesses of the payback period criterion?
   (a)
   (b)

— — — — — — — — — — — — — — —

1. Strengths
   (a) Measures focus on cash flows and thus the availability of liquid resources for future use.
   (b) The times at which inflows will occur are given explicit consideration.

2. Weaknesses
  (a) Inflows after the payback period are ignored.
  (b) Returns from reinvesting cash inflows are not considered.

REINVESTMENT

Capital budgeting techniques ensure that managerial decisions generate the highest possible return on invested funds. As the amounts invested increase, decision-making considerations become more complex. Longer investment periods may be required, and the risks involved may be more extensive. Therefore, more accurate, reliable decision measures were needed, and these have been developed.

In response to demands for in-depth financial analyses, some of the shortcomings of the average return and payback period measures were carefully evaluated. These efforts led to correction of a major problem inherent in these basic tools, the failure to consider periodic *reinvestment* of funds obtained as projects are completed. Two additional techniques, discussed later in this chapter, were developed to offset the limitation: net present value and internal rate of return.

> **Capital budgeting decisions** assume that available funds should be used to earn profits and that these funds are periodically *reinvested;* thus added returns are generated for each period that funds remain in the project.

In its simplest form, depositing funds in a savings account is an investment decision. The financial institution guarantees a return in the form of interest. Theoretically, at least, these funds are periodically reinvested, and interest is earned by the investor as long as the account remains active.

The same reinvestment concept applies to funds invested when capital budgeting decisions are made. Assume that a business manager has an opportunity to invest $10,000 in a new venture. He is promised a return of $2,000 per year for 5 years. At a minimum, this project must return an amount greater than interest paid by a savings account; otherwise, the business manager would be assuming risk with no corresponding promise of a higher return. If the project offers a potential return of 10%, one can infer that this rate applies both to the principal and any earnings that occur during the project. Generally, the earnings are presumed to remain invested in the project unless otherwise indicated. Thus investments through the capital budgeting process are similar to those where monies are invested in savings accounts. Only the return rates and amounts of involved risk are substantially different.

13.   Future Value of a Dollar.   Reinvestment assumes that the interest will be paid on both the principal and the accumulated interest earned during the preceding year. This is particularly important when multiple projects are being considered. First, earnings from projects are likely to vary. Second, the timing of earnings has a significant impact on the project's ultimate return.

> The **future value of a dollar** is determined by multiplying the interest rate times $1 of investment to determine the value at the end of year 1. The sum is then multiplied by the interest rate to determine the value at the end of year 2, and so on.

Example. $1.00 invested at 10% for 1 year is worth $1.10 at the end of the year. These funds are reinvested for one more year; the value at the end of year 2 is $1.21 [$1.10 + (10% × $1.10)]. This $1.21 is invested for another year, and at the end of year 3 the dollar originally invested is worth $1.33 [$1.21 + (10% × $1.21)].

Exercise
1. What is the future value of a dollar invested at 12% interest for 3 years? _____
2. What is the future value of a dollar invested at 15% interest for 5 years? _____

— — — — — — — — — — — — — —

1. $1.40 (End of year 1 the dollar is worth $1.12. This earns 13 cents interest, to make a total of $1.25 at the end of year 2. Reinvested, this makes 15 cents for a total of $1.40 at the end of year 3.)
2. $2.01. (End of year 1 the dollar is worth $1.15. This $1.15 earns 17 cents interest the end of the second year, for a total of $1.32, which is reinvested and earns 20 cents interest. By the end of year 3, then, the dollar is worth $1.52. This is reinvested and earns 23 cents, for a future value of $1.75 at the end of year 4. Interest on this is 26 cents, for a future dollar value of $2.01 at the end of year 5.)

14.   Timing of Earnings. The reinvestment concept has direct relevance to the timing of earnings and the impact on the project's ultimate return.

> **Decision Rule:** Projects that promise higher earnings in the early years will generate a higher total return and should be selected.

Example. A business manager is offered the opportunity to invest $20,000 in one of two alternative ways. The promised returns of cash at the end of each of the three years involved are as follows:

	Project A	Project B
Investment	$20,000	$20,000
Return (net cash inflows)		
Year 1	10,000	6,000
Year 2	8,000	8,000
Year 3	6,000	10,000

The funds are to be received at the end of each of the respective years in each project and are to be reinvested at 10%. The following table is used to measure the future value of each project at the end of 3 years:

Future of $1 at 10%

End of year 1	$1.10
End of year 2	$1.21

The *future value* promised by project A is determined by completing the following schedule:

Cash inflow (end of year 1)	$10,000
Return at 10% (during year 2)	1,000 (10% × $10,000)
Total available (beginning of year 3)	$11,000
Return at 10% (during year 3)	1,100 (10% × $11,000)
Total available (end of year 3)	$12,100

At the end of year 1, an inflow of $10,000 cash is expected. These funds can be reinvested at 10% for years 2 and 3, as indicated above. The first year's inflow of $10,000 thus generates $12,100 by the end of year 3. In addition, the $8,000 inflow at the end of year 2 can be reinvested at 10% for year 3, for a total of $8,800 additional funds available at the end of year 3. This makes a total of $20,900. Finally, the $6,000 received at the end of year 3 can be added to the total, for a final return of $26,900. The $6,000 does not generate any interest, however, because the project ends at that time.

The preceding schedule can be simplified by determining the number of years each inflow will be invested and the future value of the dollar for that number of years, as indicated below:

Future Values of Project A

Year 1	$10,000 × 1.21 = $12,100 ($10,000 invested for 2 years)
Year 2	8,000 × 1.10 = 8,800 ($8,000 invested for 1 year)
Year 3	6,000 × 1.00 = 6,000 (not reinvested)
Total future value	$26,900

Project B's future value is determined in the same way:

Year 1	$ 6,000 × 1.21 = $ 7,260
Year 2	8,000 × 1.10 = 8,800
Year 3	10,000 × 1.00 = 10,000
Total future value	$26,060

Notice that both projects required the same initial investment, the same total amount of cash inflows over the 3 years ($24,000), and the same interest rate on revenues invested, yet the future values promised by projects A and B are different. The superiority of project A stems from the fact that the timing of inflows differs between projects. When all other things are equal, the project having larger inflows in the early periods is likely to have a higher overall return on investment, a critically important concept when evaluating capital budgeting alternatives.

Exercise

Consider a situation where you have sold a piece of land. The buyer offers you $10,000 but suggests that his funds are currently committed. As a second option, the buyer suggests that he will give you a noninterest note for $16,000 to be retired at the end of 3 years. You can invest the funds for a 15% return.

(a) Would you prefer the cash today or the note? _____
   Explain your reasoning:

- - - - - - - - - - - - - -

You would select the note for $16,000, because this is greater than the future value of $10,000 invested at 15% for 3 years, $15,209.

Investment	$10,000
Interest—year 1	1,500
Balance	$11,500
Interest—year 2	1,725
Balance	$13,225
Interest—Year 3	1,984
Total	$15,209

PRESENT VALUE TECHNIQUES

Conceivably, managers could approach the evaluation of all capital budgeting decisions using future value measures. However, since projects often involve different lengths of time, the resulting measures are not easily comparable. Thus capital budgeting techniques do not convert all projects to a common future date. Instead, a measure is created of each project's returns in terms of the date on which investments are to be made. For decision making, project data are converted into measures at *period 0, the beginning of the first year* of all relevant alternatives. The measure of net present value provides a dollar index by which to evaluate the desirability of alternative investment opportunities.

> **Net present value** provides an index to compare the net
> present values of cash inflows promised by a project with
> the net present value of cash outflows. If the index is posi-
> tive (sum of the present values of the inflows is greater than
> present value of relevant outflows), the promised return is
> greater than the company's cost of capital. Between two
> projects, the one having the higher index is more desirable.
> If the index is negative, the project should be rejected.

The net-present-value technique assumes that all returns will be reinvested at the cut-off criterion—the cost of capital plus associated risk factor—for the company involved. Tables for determining appropriate measures can be obtained from any management accounting textbook. For our purposes, only sufficient data are provided to allow a general understanding of the application of the net-present-value technique.

A real estate investor has the opportunity to invest in selected rental properties. Although two alternatives are available, only one can be selected because only $60,000 in investment funds are available at this time. The promised return for each property is as follows:

	Property A	Property B
Required investment	$30,000	$40,000
Promised cash return		
Year 1	12,000	18,000
Year 2	10,000	15,000
Year 3	10,000	10,000
Year 4	8,000	7,000
Year 5	4,000	5,000

The investor's cost of capital is 10%, and the property contract expires at the end of 5 years. He must decide which alternative is superior.

15. Net Present Value. To use the net-present-value technique, consult the appropri-ate table to determine the net present value. These tables incorporate concepts identical to those previously discussed for determining future value of the dollar. The only substan-tive difference is that all future returns are *discounted* to allow evaluations to focus on period 0 (the beginning of the first project year). Referring to the present-value table below, the discount factors are as follows:

End of Year:	Present Value of $1 at 10%
1	0.9091 or 0.91
2	0.83
3	0.75
4	0.68
5	0.62

In general terms, the table measures the value of a promise to receive $1 at the end of some future period. The relevant cost of capital is 10%. Specifically, if the investor is promised a return of $10,000 at the end of year 1, that promise is worth $9,091 today ($10,000 × 0.9091). This is true because the investor could conceivably invest the $9,091 at 10%, and at the end of 1 year the value of the investment would be $10,000 (interest of $909 added to the principle of $9,091). Thus the two measures are essentially equal.

Stated in a problem context, if someone offered $9,500 today or $10,000 at the end of year 1, given a 10% cost of capital, today's amount is superior because $9,500 is greater than $10,000 × 0.9091. If the offer were only $9,000 today, however, the promise of $10,000 one year from now is superior ($9,000 is less than $10,000 × 0.9091). In a capital budgeting decision, then, if the promises of future returns are greater than the amounts invested, the decision offers a favorable yield.

> **Present value of a dollar** rests on the premise that a dollar today is worth more than the promise of receiving a dollar in the future. The key assumption is that the dollar today can be invested at some rate of interest for the time period in question; therefore, dollars to be received in the future are *discounted.*

Example. The real estate investor can use net value of the dollar to determine whether project A or B is superior. Project A requires that $30,000 be invested at period 0 to generate varying returns over a 5-year contract period. The present value of the initial investment (cash outflow) is $30,000 × 1.0, a value of $30,000. Note that this measure focuses directly on the decision date. As returns (cash inflows) are evaluated, the discount factors from the table are applied because each promised return occurs at a different date. A schedule reflects these measures:

Project A

Year	Cash Flows	Discount Factor (10%)	Computed Present Value
0	($30,000)	1.00	($30,000)
1	12,000	0.91	10,920
2	10,000	0.83	8,300
3	10,000	0.75	7,500
4	8,000	0.68	5,440
5	4,000	0.62	2,480
	Total present value (net) (indicates outflow)		$ 4,640

The computed present value of this project is positive because the project's inflows at present value exceed the comparable outflows. In fact, these results indicate that A's return rate is greater than the cost of capital. In other words, the investor would have to invest more than $30,000 in a project promising only a return of 10% to yield the same total future value. Before a final decision can be made, however, project B must be evaluated in a similar way. If its net present value exceeds that offered by project A, the second alternative would be superior.

Exercise

1. Compute the measure of net present value for project B following the same procedures as used for project A.

2. Determine which is the better project.

- - - - - - - - - - - - - - -

1. $4,190.	0	($40,000)	1.00	($40,000)
	1	18,000	0.91	16,380
	2	15,000	0.83	12,450
	3	10,000	0.75	7,500
	4	7,000	0.68	4,760
	5	5,000	0.62	3,100
		Total present value (net)		$ 4,190

2. Project A is superior because its net present value of $4,640 exceeds that of project B, which promises a net present value of $4,190.

16.   Strengths and Weaknesses of Net-Present-Value Criterion. The net-present-value technique, one of the more sophisticated approaches to capital budgeting decisions, can be effectively used only if its inherent strengths and weaknesses are understood.

> **Strengths of net-present-value criterion:**
> —Recognizes present value of the dollar and related re-
>   investment assumption.
> —Provides a workable, decision-making index.

The major strength of the net-present-value technique is that the resulting measure recognizes explicitly the present-value-of-a-dollar concept. Therefore, decision makers are made cognizant that future promises of monetary returns are not necessarily equal to the promise of one to be received immediately.

A second strength is that the net-present-value measure for each project provides a workable index for ranking available alternatives. The higher index values are associated with the more financially desirable projects.

> **Weaknesses of net-present-value criterion:**
> —Assumes that funds are reinvested at cost of capital plus
>   risk factor, if any—a conservative approach.
> —The technique is difficult to understand and apply.

The net-present-value technique is not without limitations. First is the underlying reinvestment assumption, the premise that all funds are reinvested at a return approximating the cutoff criterion, the company's cost of capital and any related risk factors. Clearly, not all future investments will necessarily generate this rate of return. Ideally, most projects will provide returns exceeding this minimum level. To the extent that this favorable condition exists, the overall promised returns are a very conservative estimate.

A second weakness is that the underlying present-value concept is not easily understood. Therefore, managers may be asked to make and/or accept capital budgeting decisions that do not appear to be wholly reasonable from their perspective. A part of this misunderstanding stems from the fact that the measure reflects little relationship to the initial investment. In the latter regard, managers sometimes find it difficult to accept a $10,000 net present value on an investment of $100,000 as being superior to a net present value of $5,000 on a $20,000 investment. This behavioral limitation can be offset by education and training.

Exercise

1. What are two strengths of the net-present-value criterion?
   (a)
   (b)

2. What are two weaknesses of this technique?
   (a)
   (b)

— — — — — — — — — — — — — —

1. Strengths
   (a) Recognizes present-value-of-a-dollar concept and the related reinvestment assumption.
   (b) Provides a workable decision-making index (in dollars).
2. Weaknesses
   (a) Assumes that funds are reinvested at cost of capital, a potentially conservative approach.
   (b) The measurement technique is not easily understood and applied.

17. **Internal Rate of Return.** The most complicated of the available capital budgeting techniques is the internal-rate-of-return measure. Although it generally requires use of a computer, a brief description of this technique is provided.

Like the net-present-value technique, the internal rate of return uses the present-value-of-a-dollar concept to develop a rate of return. The major difference between the net-present-value technique and the internal rate of return is the underlying assumption regarding reinvestment. In the internal rate technique, funds are presumed to be reinvested at a rate of return promised by the project, *not* at the cutoff criterion measure used in the net-present-value technique. Therefore, the procedures involved are much more difficult to apply.

> The **internal rate of return** provides a percentage that reflects the project's true rate of return. The use of this rate as the basis for discounting cash inflows and outflows results in a net present value of zero. The higher the percentage, the more financially favorable is the project. This technique also assumes that funds are reinvested at the same rate of return as that promised by the project.

A brief description should be sufficient to provide a comparison of the two methods: net present value and internal rate of return. The net present value provides an index in terms of dollars, whereas the internal rate of return is expressed as a percentage. In other words, under one method a favorable project reflects a positive net inflow of dollars. In the second, the resulting percentage must be greater than the cutoff criterion to be an acceptable investment alternative. Of most importance, however, is your recognition that the two approaches flow from a different basic assumption as to the reinvestment rates that will occur.

18. **Strengths and Weaknesses of Internal-Rate-of-Return Criterion.** Although the internal-rate-of-return measure is the most complex capital budgeting technique, use of a computer makes the computational tasks easier. Nevertheless, its basic complexity poses practical problems that must be acknowledged. As with the other techniques, an awareness of both the strengths and weaknesses of the internal rate of return is important.

> **Strengths of the internal-rate-of-return criterion:**
> —Clearly recognizes the time value of dollars, so that early receipts can be used more quickly to improve overall return.
> —Percentage results are more familiar to many managers.

The strengths of the internal rate stem primarily from the explicit recognition of the time value of dollars. In this sense, dollars received in the early periods are more valuable than those subsequently received. This value derives directly from the reinvestment concept discussed previously.

A second strength of the internal rate of return is its basic understandability. Managers are generally familiar with percentages as a reflection of profitability and rate of return.

> **Weaknesses of the internal-rate-of-return criterion:**
> —The complexity of measurements requires access to a computer.
> —Assumes that funds are reinvested at the return generated by the project, sometimes impossible to achieve.

Weaknesses associated with the internal-rate-of-return technique are easily discernible. First, and most obvious, are the difficulties in computing the measure. A second weakness is the underlying reinvestment assumption which presumes that the inflows will be reinvested at the same rate that the project itself generates. To the extent that the returns from reinvestments do not equal this true rate of return, the measure is somewhat inaccurate. Whether this limitation has serious implications can be determined only when its use in a practical setting is thoroughly analyzed.

Exercise

1. What are two strengths of the internal-rate-of-return criterion?
    (a)
    (b)
2. What are two weaknesses of this measure?
    (a)
    (b)

— — — — — — — — — — — — — —

1. Strengths
    (a) The time value of dollars is clearly recognized, in that early receipts can be used more quickly to improve overall returns.
    (b) Percentage results are more familiar to many managers.

2. Weaknesses
   (a) The complexity of measurement requires access to a computer in most cases.
   (b) Assumptions are made that funds are reinvested at the return generated by the project, and these results are sometimes impossible to achieve.

You may want to review the questions posed at the beginning of the chapter before completing the Self-Test that follows.

CHAPTER 9 SELF-TEST

1. Matching – Terminology/Concepts

Match the following terms to the definitions.

1. Capital budgeting	6. Payback period
2. Cost of capital	7. Payback reciprocal
3. Internal rate of return	8. Present value of a dollar
4. Liquidity	9. Profitability
5. Net present value	10. Return on assets

_____ (a) Expenses incurred when acquiring financial resources either through borrowing from creditors (interest) or obtaining investment from owners (dividends).

_____ (b) A concept based on the premise that a dollar today is worth more than the promise of receiving a dollar in the future. The key assumption is that the dollar today can be invested at some rate of interest for the time in question.

_____ (c) A technique designed to provide a measure of a project's "true" rate of return.

_____ (d) A set of techniques to facilitate management's need to commit significant amounts of resources to long-term projects and to ensure that only the most financially desirable projects are selected.

_____ (e) The relationship of net income after taxes to investment in assets. One technique used in preliminary evaluations of potential capital budgeting decisions.

_____ (f) A technique that measures the length of time a project must continue before the original cash investment is recovered.

_____ (g) The average net income after taxes generated by investing funds in a project. It is the basis for measuring return on assets.

_____ (h) A technique that views a project in terms of its effects on cash position. An alternative that promises large cash inflows in its early years is preferred when this criterion is used.

_____ (i) A technique that compares the net present values of cash inflows promised by a project with the net present value of cash outflows. A positive net present value indicates that the project's return is greater than the cost of capital involved in obtaining the resources.

_____ (j) A measure that approximates a project's true rate of return when certain conditions are satisfied. Limitations are significant and must be evaluated when this measure is used.

2. Accounting Rate of Return

The EM Company is opening a new division. Funds have been borrowed at 10%, and many new projects are being considered. This division initially evaluates its projects in terms of the accounting rate of return. Financial information for two competing projects is provided below. Only one of these two alternatives will be selected, and you are asked to advise management in this selection. The income tax rate is 40% for this division.

	Project A	Project B
Required investment	$120,000	$100,000
Annual revenues	50,000	45,000
Cash operating expenses	25,000	15,000
Depreciation	5,000	5,000

(a) Management does not want to discuss any project that fails to provide a return greater than its cost of capital. What is this division's cost of capital? _____

(b) What is the accounting rate of return on project A? _____ Project B? _____ Which project should management select? _____

(c) What are the major strengths and weaknesses of the accounting rate-of-return technique?

3. Payback Period/Payback Reciprocal

The KM Company applies the payback period and payback reciprocal techniques as potential capital budgeting alternatives are considered. The following project has been presented for consideration. Taxes are ignored at this time.

	Years 1-2-3	Years 4-5-6
Cash revenues	$80,000	$50,000
Cash expenses	50,000	40,000
Depreciation	10,000	10,000

The project requires an investment of $100,000. Using these data as a basis, respond to the following questions.

(a) What is this project's payback period? _____

(b) What are the major strengths and weaknesses of the payback period technique?

(c) What is the payback reciprocal measure for this project? _____

(d) Under what conditions can the payback reciprocal be used as a decision-making measure? Is it appropriate for this project? Why or why not?

4. Future Value/Present Value Concepts

TM Company's management is considering using some sophisticated techniques in its capital budgeting process. Their consultants provided the following table for their review.

End of Year:	Future Value of $1	Present Value of $1
1	1.10	0.91
2	1.21	0.83

(a) If $1,000 were invested today, how much would it be worth at the end of year 1? _____ Year 2? _____
(b) If you were promised $1,000 at the end of year 1, how much is the promise worth today? _____ If the funds are promised instead at the end of year 2, what is the value today? _____

5. Net Present Value

The B&L Company uses the net-present-value technique for making capital budgeting decisions. Their cost of capital is 10%, and the appropriate table is provided. Management is considering the following projects:

Required investment	
Period 0	$20,000
End of year 1	10,000
End of year 2	10,000
Cash inflows from operations	
Year 1	$20,000
Year 2	10,000
Year 3	10,000
Year 4	5,000
Present value (10%)	
Period 0	1.00
Year 1	0.91
Year 2	0.83
Year 3	0.75
Year 4	0.68

(a) What is the net present value of this project? _____

(b) How can this measure be used in making capital budgeting decisions? _____

_____

(c) What is the reinvestment assumption that serves as the foundation for the net-present-value technique? _____

_____

(d) What are the strengths and weaknesses of the net-present-value technique?

6. *Internal Rate of Return*

(a) What are the strengths and weaknesses of the internal-rate-of-return technique?

(b) What reinvestment assumption serves as the foundation for this measure? _____

_____

ANSWERS

1. Matching – Terminology/Concepts

(a) 2 (frame 3, 1 pt) (b) 8 (frame 14, 1 pt)
(c) 3 (frame 16, 1 pt) (d) 1 (introduction, 1 pt)
(e) 10 (frames 1 and 2, 1 pt) (f) 6 (frame 6, 1 pt)
(g) 9 (introduction, 1 pt) (h) 4 (frame 6, 1 pt)
(i) 5 (frame 14, 1 pt) (j) 7 (frame 10, 1 pt)

2. Accounting Rate of Return

(a) 10% (frames 1–4, 2 pts)

(b)

	Project A	Project B
Revenues	$50,000	$45,000
Cash expenses	(25,000)	(15,000)
Depreciation	(5,000)	(5,000)
Net income before taxes	$20,000	$25,000
Taxes 40%	8,000	10,000
Net income after taxes	$12,000	$15,000

Project B should be chosen.

Accounting rate of return: 12% . 15%
    Project A: $12,000 ÷ $100,000
    Project B: $15,000 ÷ $100,000   (frames 1–4, 2 pts)

(c) Strengths: 1. The measure is easily understandable.
                  2. The measure can be applied effectively because it is simple in structure and data are generally available.
     Weaknesses: 1. Net income measures do not focus directly on cash flows.
                  2. The average income measure fails to acknowledge that early inflows of resources can be used to generate added profits.
     (frame 5, 4 pts)

3. Payback Period/Payback Reciprocal

(a)

	Years 1-2-3	Years 4-5-6
Cash revenues	$80,000	$50,000
Cash expenses	50,000	10,000
Net cash inflows	$30,000	$40,000

This project's payback period is 4 years. $90,000 will be received in the first 3 years, with the remaining $10,000 in year 4. Thus the total investment will be recovered at that time. (frames 6–9, 3 pts)

(b) Strengths: 1. Focus is on cash flows.
2. Times at which resources become available for use is identified specifically.

Weaknesses: 1. Attention is directed only to the time periods prior to recovering investment; subsequent periods are ignored.
2. Returns from reinvesting early-year cash inflows are not considered.

(frame 12, 4 pts)

(c) The payback reciprocal for this project is 25%. (frame 10, 2 pts)

(d) Conditions for using the payback reciprocal:
1. Total investment of cash must occur at the beginning of the period.
2. After-tax cash flows must occur uniformly throughout the project.
3. The life of the project must be at least twice the length of the payback period.
   Payback reciprocal should not be used because two conditions are not satisfied.

(frame 11, 3 pts)

4. Future Value/Present Value Concepts

(a) Year 1: $1,000 \times 1.10 = $1,100
    Year 2: $1,000 \times 1.12 = $1,210   (frames 12 and 13, 2 pts)
(b) Year 1: $1,000 \times 0.91 = $910
    Year 2: $1,000 \times 0.83 = $830   (frames 14 and 15, 2 pts)

5. Net Present Value

(a)

Time Period	Amount	Discount Factor	Present Value
Outflows			
Period 0	($20,000)	1.0	($20,000)
End year 1	(10,000)	0.91	(9,100)
End year 2	(10,000)	0.83	(8,300)
Total			($37,400)
Inflows[a]			
Year 1	$20,000	0.91	$18,200
Year 2	10,000	0.83	8,300
Year 3	10,000	0.75	7,500
Year 4	5,000	0.68	3,400
Total			$37,400
Net present value			–0–

[a]Inflows are assumed to occur end of each operating year. (frames 12-14, 6 pts)

(b) When the net-present-value measure is positive, the project's return is greater than the cost of capital and can be accepted. A negative net present value means that the project's return is less than the relevant cost of capital. The project should then be rejected. In this case (B&L Company), the return is exactly 10% and the measure could not serve alone as the basis for the decision. Other qualitative factors would thus serve as the foundation for this decision. (frames 12-14, 2 pts)

(c) The net-present-value technique operates on the premise that cash inflows will be reinvested at the rate reflected in the present-value table used in that case. This present-value factor is often the company's cost of capital. On occasion, a subjective measure of risk will be added to the measure to ensure that uncertainties are carefully evaluated. (frames 12–14, 2 pts)

(d) Strengths: 1. Recognizes net present value of the dollar and related investment assumption.

               2. Provides a workable, decision-making index.

    Weaknesses: 1. Assumes funds are reinvested at cost of capital, a conservative approach.

               2. Technique is difficult to understand and to apply.

(frame 15, 4 pts)

6. *Internal Rate of Return*

(a) Strengths: 1. The time value of early returns of dollars is explicitly recognized in the sense that these resources can be used immediately.

               2. The measure is stated in terms of a percentage and thus can be understood easily by management.

    Weaknesses: 1. The technique is difficult to apply, and thus access to a computer is essential for this approach to be used in a practical setting.

               2. The reinvestment assumption must sometimes be violated because projects with similar returns are not available when the cash resources are generated.

(frame 17, 8 pts)

(b) The internal-rate-of-return technique operates on the assumption that funds will be reinvested at the same rate that was obtained on the original project. In many cases, however, similar projects are not available. Thus the assumption may become a severe limitation when applied in a practical setting. (frame 16, 4 pts)

Total possible points: 60. You should have scored at least 48.

SECTION FOUR

Management Accounting: An Overview

Management accounting is an indispensible aid to decision makers in both profit and nonprofit businesses and organizations. It is a powerful tool that can be used in making planning decisions, control decisions, and specialized decisions.

Section One introduced techniques for using management accounting to *plan* effectively. The most widely used techniques in a planning context are cost/volume/profit (C/V/P) analysis, profit planning, and cash budgeting. The C/V/P model is used to determine the break-even point as well as the level of activity at which a company must operate to earn a profit. After an appropriate volume level is selected, management accounting data serve as the basis for developing a profit plan. The process begins by establishing financial targets through the use of financial ratios. In manufacturing operations, a sales forecast is used as a basis for production budgets. If both are executed effectively, desired profits should be achieved. Service industries, on the other hand, use sales information to develop personnel budgets. Included in all profit plans are estimates of other expenses and all significant changes in the company's balance sheet position. With the profit plan serving as an operating guideline, attention shifts to cash receipts and disbursements budgets. In most businesses, cash receipts occur through cash sales and collections of accounts receivable. Disbursements are made for cash outlays for certain operating expenses, payments on liabilities, and other company commitments. As a final step, a projected balance sheet and income statement are prepared to summarize the profit plan.

Section Two focused on techniques for using management accounting in making *control* decisions. Basic to control decisions is effective cost accounting. Cost accounting systems provide historical cost data for management control decisions. Actual performance is compared with results expected when plans were developed. In some industries, cost data are developed using a job-order costing system that traces costs to each major project. In manufacturing industries, however, a process-costing approach is used to trace costs to departments and units produced. These data, in turn, serve as a basis for cost control decisions. In addition, standard costing, predetermining costs for products or services, provides vital information to identify variances between actual unit costs incurred and those estimated when production cost plans were developed.

Section Three demonstrated the usefulness of management accounting in making *specialized decisions.* To assure that data can be tied directly to specialized decision needs, a responsibility accounting system is established. The organization is divided into responsibility centers so that information can be communicated to managers at different levels of authority as appropriate. In this context, accounting data are used to evaluate performance and progress. Managers are held accountable for costs and other financial elements over which they have influence. One measure, the contribution margin, focuses directly on relationships between revenues and variable costs. Such data greatly assist in evaluating specific responsibility centers. Flexible budgeting offers another useful technique to facilitate management's control efforts. Management accounting is also of importance in approaching short-range operating decisions such as making or buying component parts, processing products to completion or selling them unfinished, continuing or discontinuing a department, and accepting special orders. Long-range decisions are also facilitated by management accounting, through the use of capital budgeting techniques to assess the desirability of resource commitments. Return on investment, the payback period, and measures using discounted cash flows can assure effective decision making.

Chapter 10 serves to summarize the key concepts and techniques basic to management accounting. Since these have been considered in depth in preceding sections, this final section is most useful as a means of reviewing quickly the various dimensions of management accounting and synthesizing them into a comprehensive approach to making planning decisions, control decisions, and specialized decisions.

CHAPTER 10

Review for Application

The following pages contain a summary of the most important concepts and techniques presented in this book.

FINANCIAL PLANNING

Cost/Volume/Profit Analysis

—C/V/P analysis shows the interrelationships of costs, volume, and profit. A basic concept underlying C/V/P analysis is cost variability; that is, certain costs are directly affected by changes in volume.

—Four types of costs can be identified: variable, fixed, semivariable, and semifixed.

—Break-even analysis is used to determine that point when total revenues equal total expenses. This technique revolves around the measure of contribution margin, the difference between sales revenues and variable costs.

—Profit targets can be set by determining either the required volume in units or sales dollars.

Profit Planning

—Financial goals can be set and assessed by determining return on investment, return on sales, return on assets, the current ratio, and the debt-to-equity ratio.

—Profit planning in a manufacturing company is based on a sales forecast that projects expected revenues by major business segments. Expected production costs are compared with these revenues to generate the likely profit results.

—Manufacturing costs include materials costs, labor costs, and overhead costs.

—Inventories of raw materials and finished goods are frequently part of the profit plan and must be incorporated into income statements.

—Profit planning in a service company is based on a sales forecast that identifies the number of days per month the services will be provided and multiplies that level by anticipated revenues.

—Pro-forma financial statements are used to assess the potential financial effects of management decisions. They include financial targets, projected income statements, and balance sheets.

Cash Budgeting

—Cash budgeting focuses on projecting cash inflows and cash outflows for specified future time periods. It includes cash receipts and cash disbursements.

—Historical data and projected income statements are used to estimate the amount of inflow and whether it will be cash or credit. Past collection patterns assist in predicting when credit sales will result in cash inflows. This information also allows a schedule of accounts receivable to be developed.

—Cash disbursements will include personnel expenses, selling expenses, administrative expenses, and occupancy expenses.

CONTROL DECISIONS: THE COST ACCOUNTING FRAMEWORK

—Cost accounting is the process that traces costs directly to projects, jobs, or units of product.

Cost Accounting: A Job-Order Approach

—Job-order costing traces production expenditures directly to specific projects or customer orders as a basis for management planning and control decisions. It focuses on prime costs (direct materials, direct labor) and indirect overhead costs.

—Materials requisition forms, purchase orders, and receiving slips serve as documentation for costs incurred, as do job-time tickets, personnel records, and invoices.

—Predetermined overhead rates are established based on the relationship between esti-mated overhead costs and an activity measure of expected levels of production. The difference between the overhead that is applied and that actually incurred is recorded as over- or underapplied overhead costs when the account balances are closed at the end of an accounting period.

—The T-account model is a valuable tool for tracing cost flows.

—Once flows of costs are determined, their relevance to financial statements can be readily evaluated.

Process Costing Systems

—Process costing is a system to assign production costs first to operating departments and then to units of output.

—Average costing is a specialized costing method that combines beginning inventory costs with current period production costs. Both materials and conversion costs are con-sidered. This measure is then divided by equivalent units of production, an output measure, to create a measure of average costs per unit.

—First in/first out (FIFO) costing is designed to separate prior period and current period expenses when determining measures of average cost per unit. This method is particu-larly useful when significant changes in costs occur between accounting periods, because it uses only current period costs in developing average costs per unit.

Standard Costing Systems

—Standard costs are estimated future costs that are developed as a basis for planning and control purposes. Differences between standard (expected) costs and actual costs are termed *variances* and play an important role in evaluating performance.

—Standard costs can be developed for direct materials, materials usage, direct labor, variable overhead, and fixed manufacturing overhead. Variances that show costs to be less than anticipated are considered favorable; those that show costs to be above the established standard are considered unfavorable.

—Management control reports can be used to summarize variances and their effect on gross profit. These reports serve primarily as a basis for management control activities.

SPECIALIZED DECISION MAKING

Responsibility Accounting Systems

—A responsibility accounting system separates an organization into responsibility centers so that financial data can be tailored to managers' decision-making requirements and performance can be objectively evaluated.

—Each responsibility center is evaluated by either return on investment, profits, revenues, and/or costs. Performance measures can be stated in terms of return on investment, product line income, and rate of growth in sales.

—The contribution margin can be analyzed to assess three possible sources of problems: (1) declines in contribution margin per unit, (2) quantities sold, and (3) product mix.

—Flexible budgeting focuses on revising variable cost budgets as volume changes occur. It establishes budgets for a range of possible activity levels.

—Controllability is critical in a responsibility accounting system. Control limits can be expressed in terms of dollars or percentages. When these limits are exceeded, an explanation of causes and/or problems encountered should be required.

Short-Range Operating Decisions

—Specialized decisions require that data be *relevant;* that is, the measures are likely to change in the future as the result of a current operational decision.

—Make-or-buy decisions use relevant costs, such as changes in materials, labor, variable or fixed overhead costs, and the net change, as well as nonfinancial data, such as the vendor's reputation and capacity, and the internal effect of a buy decision.

—Additional processing decisions must take into account whether anticipated volume and price are realistic and whether capacity is readily available, so that fixed overhead costs will not increase.

—Departmental continuance/discontinuance decisions focus on overall profits, not only those of the department under consideration. If a department's contribution margin is greater than necessary direct costs, its activities should probably be continued. Allocated costs must be considered separately in this decision.

—Special order decisions must consider productive capacity as a key factor in accepting or rejecting an order. If the order will require additional processing facilities, fixed costs are likely to change. If present capacity is sufficient to handle the order, no changes in fixed costs are likely.

Long-Range Decisions: Capital Budgeting

—Capital budgeting is a long-range planning tool consisting of a set of techniques to facilitate selecting projects that offer the most financial potential.

—The accounting rate of return assesses profitability, that is, the average net income after taxes generated by investing funds in a project. Cost of capital as well as risk involved are considerations.

—The payback period technique assesses liquidity, viewing projects in terms of their effects on cash position. It measures the length of time a project must continue before the original cash investment is recovered. The payback reciprocal measures a project's approximate true rate of return as a percentage, but this technique can be used only if total investment occurs at the beginning of the project, if after-tax cash inflows occur uniformly throughout the project, and if the project's life is at least twice as long as the payback period.

—Certain of the capital budgeting techniques assume that available funds are invested and reinvested in projects and that returns are generated from this overall process. Neither the accounting rate of return nor the payback period measure take this reinvestment factor into account. The two procedures that follow, although more complex, do assume that inflows are reinvested.

—Net present value provides a dollar index to compare the net present values of cash inflows promised by a project with the net present value of cash outflows. It rests on the assumption that a dollar today is worth more than the promise of receiving a dollar in the future because of the reinvestment potential. Dollars to be received in the future are discounted back to the project's initial date to facilitate comparisons of projects with varying lives.

—Internal rate of return provides a percentage that reflects the project's true rate of return, but it is a complex measure usually requiring the use of a computer.

In combination, the preceding concepts and techniques will equip you to make planning, control, and specialized decisions effectively.

Glossary

actual costs — production expenses that are incurred and assigned to production output during an accounting period.

additional processing decisions — focus on profitability of continuing manufacturing activities with respect to a product rather than selling in a semifinished condition.

administrative expenses — costs associated with compensating and supporting personnel who are involved in managing the activities of an organization or unit in addition to costs associated with discretionary decisions to obtain specialized services such as legal counseling.

allocated costs — expenses arbitrarily assigned on other than a cause/effect basis. Generally, such costs are noncontrollable and thus must be treated separately when evaluating performance in a responsibility center.

average costing — a specialized costing method that combines beginning inventory costs with current-period production costs. This measure is then divided by equivalent units of production to create a measure of average costs per unit.

average cost per unit — a measure developed by dividing manufacturing expenses of a production department by the number of equivalent units it produces during an accounting period.

balance sheet — a statement of financial position that reflects an organization's assets, liabilities, and owner's investment at a specified date.

break-even point — the level of activity in an organization that will generate revenues exactly sufficient to cover all costs, thereby yielding neither net income nor net loss.

break-even revenues — the level of sales dollars required to cover all costs during an accounting period.

break-even units — the number of units that must be produced and sold to generate revenues sufficient to exactly cover all costs during an accounting period.

capital budgeting — a set of techniques to facilitate management's need to commit significant amounts of resources to long-term projects and to ensure that only the most financially desirable projects are selected.

capital expenditures — cash outlays required to acquire long-term resources or to complete related projects.

cash budgeting — a technique designed to focus on projecting cash inflows and cash outflows for specified future periods of time.

cash disbursements — encompasses all cash payments for goods and services acquired from suppliers, employers, or any other entity. Reductions of debt and commitments of resources to long-term projects might be included.

cash receipts—all inflows of cash into a company for goods and services provided to customers as well as collections on account. Amounts obtained from investors (owners) or borrowings (creditors) are also included.

contribution margin—a financial, decision-making measure that reflects the difference between revenues and variable costs.

contribution margin effect variance—the difference between planned and actual contribution margin times the number of units actually sold.

control—the ability to influence actions or results through decisions. For example, a manager can control costs by influencing either their timing or amounts with specific decisions.

controllability—the need for managers to influence financial factors within the scope of their authority, the fundamental principle underlying a responsibility accounting system.

controls—a set of guidelines expressed in dollar amounts or percentages not to be exceeded, designed to assist management in monitoring progress and taking necessary corrective actions as plans are executed.

conversion costs—combinations of direct labor costs and those included in the manufacturing overhead classification.

cost accounting—the process that traces costs directly to projects, jobs, or units of product.

cost center—a unit within an organization in which the manager has authority to influence only costs incurred.

cost of capital—expenses incurred when acquiring financial resources either through borrowing from creditors (interest) or obtaining investment from owners (dividends).

cost/volume/profit analysis—a technique to show the interrelationships of costs, volume, and profit.

current ratio—the financial relationship between current assets and current liabilities. This ratio serves as a means of assessing an organization's ability to satisfy its short-term obligations.

debt-to-equity ratio—the financial relationship between an organization's debt to outsiders and the amount of owners' investment. This ratio serves to assess long-range financial stability.

departmental continuance/discontinuance decision—management's action to continue or cease operations in a particular operating unit. The criterion upon which this decision is based is the effect of the change on the total organizational profit.

departmental overhead—costs other than direct material and direct labor incurred within a specific operating unit and ultimately traced to units produced.

depreciation—the allocation of an asset's cost over its estimated useful life according to the method authorized by company policy.

direct labor—costs associated with personnel actively involved in the production process. These expenditures are easily traced to units of output.

direct labor costs—*see* direct labor.

direct materials—costs associated with materials used to produce goods or services. These expenditures are easily traced to output.

direct materials costs—*see* direct materials.

documentation—forms and paperwork that authorize transactions to occur. Relevant information about key events is logically recorded and retained for future use.

efficiency—producing the highest-quality goods for the most reasonable costs.

equivalent units of product—a measure of production output used to determine the average cost per unit produced. Partially completed units are converted into terms of whole units; for example, 1,000 units that are 50% completed are valued as 500 units fully completed.

financial accounting—provides financial information concerning a business's financial position and performance to external users such as owners, creditors, and government agencies.

financial ratios—measures for planning and control that focus on key interrelationships between different classifications of accounting data.

finished goods inventory—products that have been completed through the production process and are now immediately available for sale to customers.

first in/first out (FIFO) costing—procedures designed to separate prior period and current period expenses when determining measures of average cost per unit. This method is particularly useful when significant changes in costs occur between accounting periods.

fixed costs—expenditures that are nonresponsive to changes in measures of volume (e.g., units produced, hours worked). These costs remain constant in total. They decline on a per unit basis as volume increases.

fixed overhead budget variance—the difference between fixed overhead costs actually incurred and those budgeted at practical capacity.

fixed overhead idle capacity variance—difference between units at practical capacity and the planned production to satisfy the sales forecast. The financial measure is presented in terms of fixed overhead cost per unit.

fixed overhead marketing variance—difference between units in the sales forecast and those actually produced and sold. The financial measure is stated in terms of fixed overhead cost per unit.

fixed overhead volume variance—the combined effects of the planned idle capacity variance and the marketing variance.

flexible budget—a costing system that facilitates adjusting projected costs to varying levels of volume or production. Budgets for a range of permissible activity levels are established at the beginning of the planning period and then used as a basis for performance evaluations as progress occurs.

historical costs—expenses that result from past (prior period) business decisions.

historical data—financial information that results from past (prior period) business decisions and activities.

historical standards—target costs based almost wholly on past results of comparable operations.

ideal standards—target costs that can be achieved only if almost perfect production conditions are encountered. These represent perhaps the best results that could occur.

income statement—a financial statement that demonstrates an organization's progress in terms of revenues, expenses, and net income for an accounting period.

indirect overhead costs—expenditures other than direct materials and direct labor that are incurred in producing units of output.

internal rate of return—a technique designed to provide a measure of a project's "true" rate of return. The higher the measure in percentage, the more financially favorable the project.

investment center—the broadest of the responsibility centers in which managers are responsible for results achieved. The performance measures are stated in terms of return (net income) and investment (funds committed to long-term tangible assets).

job-order costing—a system designed to trace or assign production costs to major projects or programs.

labor costs—expenses incurred to acquire personnel resources to produce goods and services. This measure includes both production employees (direct labor) and those working in a support capacity, such as administration and manufacturing support.

labor efficiency variance—difference between labor hours actually used relative to hours that should have been used at standards developed. The financial measure is the standard rate per hour.

labor rate variance—difference between labor costs per hour and standard cost per hour times actual hours used during a given accounting period.

liquidity—a concept that views a project in terms of its effects on cash position. An alternative that promises large cash inflows in its early years is preferred when this criterion is used.

make-or-buy decisions—actions are based on determining whether component parts can be made for less cost than would be incurred if they were purchased from an outside vendor. Factors such as available capacity and vendor reliability are also considered.

management accounting—developing and communicating financial measures to users within the business, that is, managers, for planning and control purposes.

manufacturing costs—expenses incurred to produce goods for resale to customers. The measure includes materials, labor, and overhead (i.e., all other production costs).

marketing-mix effects variance—the portion of differences in total contribution margin for a group of products caused by combined variations between planned and actual quantities of products sold and differences between actual product contribution margin yielded and the average expected for all products in the plan.

material price variance—difference between prices actually paid for production materials and those that should have been paid at standard. The difference is applied to all materials actually purchased and is recorded at the point of purchase.

materials costs—expenses incurred to acquire the resources (e.g., major components of finished products, other parts, etc.) that are to be used in the production process.

material usage variance—difference between quantities of materials actually used and those that should have been used when standards are applied. This difference is measured in terms of the standard rate for financial purposes.

net income—the excess of revenues over costs that can be stated in terms of either before-tax or after-tax dollars.

net present value—a technique to compare the net present values of cash inflows promised by a project with the net present value of cash outflows. A positive net present value indicates that the project's return is greater than the cost of capital involved in obtaining the resources.

objectivity—a focus on factual, unbiased information as a basis for business decisions.

occupancy expenses—costs associated with providing and maintaining a facility for operations (e.g., a plant or office building). The classification includes rent, utilities, maintenance, and related expenditures.

overhead applied—costs assigned to units actually produced during a period that are based on a predetermined overhead rate (i.e., estimated overhead divided by estimated activity in terms of units, direct labor hours, machine hours, or some other variable).

overhead costs—all production expenses other than materials and labor that are specifically identifiable in the end product, primarily items such as inexpensive supplies and costs of production support activities.

overhead incurred—actual costs for all production activities not directly identifiable with units produced.

payback period—a technique to measure the length of time a project must continue before the original cash investment is recovered.

payback reciprocal—a measure that approximates a project's true rate of return when certain conditions are satisfied. The limitations are significant and must be evaluated when the measure is used.

personnel expenses—includes all costs incurred to obtain employee services (e.g., salaries, wages, commissions, social security, etc.) *other* than those specifically identified as administrative. This classification is particularly important for nonmanufacturing companies.

plans—the formalized set of actions that, if properly executed, are expected to result in achieving specified goals and objectives.

predetermined overhead rate—the relationship between estimated overhead costs and expected levels of production outputs. Rates are used for assigning overhead to units of output during an accounting period.

present value of a dollar—the premise that a dollar today is worth more than the promise of receiving a dollar in the future; thus dollars to be received in the future are discounted. The key assumption is that the dollar today can be invested at some rate of interest for the time period in question.

prime costs—the combined expenditures for direct materials and direct labor.

process costing—a system to assign production costs first to operating departments and then to units of output.

production budget—projections of the financial implications of decisions to produce sufficient quantities of products to satisfy sales forecasts and specified inventory requirements.

production department—a specialized unit in a manufacturing operation. Costs are traced initially to each department and then to goods produced by this operating unit when process costing is applied.

product line profit—the contribution margin for a defined product or group of products less costs directly assignable to the segment. Costs that are arbitrarily allocated to the products and over which no control can be asserted are *not* included in this classification.

profitability—the average net income after taxes generated by investing funds in a project. It is the basis for measuring return on assets.

profit center—a responsibility center within an organization where a manager's authority focuses on decisions relating to both revenues earned and costs incurred.

profit plan—combines financial objectives, sales forecasts, production budgets, and other financial measures into an integrated projection of future financial conditions and needs.

profit target—management's desired level of profitability measured either in dollars or in terms of a specified financial ratio.

projected data—financial information that is predicted or estimated to flow from business decisions and actions in future periods.

quantity effect variance—the portion of differences in total contribution margin for a product or group of products caused by variations between planned and actual quantities sold within the period. The financial measure used is the average planned contribution margin for all products included in the profit plan.

raw materials inventory—all products that have been purchased and are being stored for use in the company's production process.

reasonably attainable standards—target costs established at levels of performance expected to be achieved in the coming period.

relevant data—measures that are directly affected by a decision and that are likely to change in the future because of the decision made.

reliability—data that are identical in nature and could be readily developed by others as a basis for business decisions.

responsibility accounting—separates an organization into centers so that financial data can be tailored to managers' decision-making requirements. A reporting system is designed to tailor financial data to managers operating at different levels of authority in an organization.

responsibility center—units in an organization distinguishable by the scope of a manager's decision-making authority. Evaluations of performance are based on either return on investment, profits, revenues, or costs.

return on assets—performance measure (financial ratio) that relates net income after taxes to assets committed to a particular responsibility center in an organization. One technique used in preliminary evaluations of potential capital budgeting decisions.

return on investment—the relationship between net income after taxes and an organization's financial resource base in terms of the owner's investment or assets.

return on sales—financial relationship of net income after taxes to the company's net sales for the accounting period.

revenue center—unit in an organization in which a manager's responsibility is defined in terms of the ability to influence revenues through decisions.

sales forecast—projection of expected revenues by major business segment (e.g., product lines, divisions, etc.) for coming periods.

selling expenses—all costs relating to activities oriented to supporting selling efforts (e.g., incentive commission plans, advertising, promotion, and the like).

semifixed costs—expenditures, basically fixed in nature, but that can shift to higher or lower levels when specific management decisions are made.

semivariable costs—expenditures that contain both variable- and fixed-cost characteristics.

special decisions—actions taken by management in situations where the factors involved are unique and perhaps nonrecurring; consequently, all elements require a thorough analysis each time the alternatives are considered.

special order decisions—action by management to accept an offer by a customer to buy goods at less than the normal price. The underlying criterion is the overall profitability that can occur if revenues are greater than variable costs in a situation where fixed costs will not increase.

standard costing—focuses on developing estimated future product costs as a basis for planning and control decisions.

standard costs—estimated future costs developed as a basis for planning and control decisions.

traceability—assigns costs to a particular segment of the business based on a definable set of cause/effect relationships; thus traceable costs often have significant impacts on decisions.

understandability—a general criterion for evaluating the quality of decision-making information. Only when a manager is sufficiently knowledgeable about the data received to recognize their full potential and possible implications is this standard satisfied.

variability—some costs change in total in direct proportion to changes in activity level. Since these costs are generally assumed to be constant per unit of output, they often change in direct response to decisions affecting volume.

variable costs—expenditures that change in total in direct proportion to some specified measure of volume (e.g., units produced, hours worked, etc.). Variable costs are assumed to remain constant per unit as volume changes.

variable overhead efficiency variance—difference between hours used and those that should have been used at standard. The financial measure is stated in terms of the standard variable overhead rate.

variable overhead spending variance—difference between actual variable overhead costs incurred per hour and those that should have been incurred at standard. This difference in cost per hour is applied to each hour actually worked during the period.

variance — difference between costs actually incurred and those expected when relevant standards or budgets were developed.

working capital — difference beween an organization's current assets and current liabilities. This measure is an indicator of liquidity at a particular date.

work-in-process inventory — units that are partially completed in terms of materials, labor, or overhead at the beginning and end of an accounting period.

Index

NOTES

NOTES

NOTES

NOTES